Diaspora Politics

At Home Abroad

This book is intended to fill a gap in the study of modern ethno-national diasporas. Against the background of current trends – globalization, regionalization, democratization, the weakening of the nation-state, and massive trans-state migration – it examines the politics of historical, modern, and incipient ethno-national diasporas. It argues that in contrast to the widely accepted view, ethno-national diasporism and diasporas do not constitute a recent phenomenon. Rather, this is a long-standing phenomenon whose roots are in antiquity. Some of the existing diasporas were created in antiquity, some during the Middle Ages, and some in modern times. Essential aspects of this phenomenon are the unending cultural-social-economic struggles and especially the political struggles of these dispersed ethnic groups, permanently residing in host countries away from their homelands, to maintain their distinctive identities and connections with their homelands and other dispersed groups from the same nations. While describing and analyzing the diaspora phenomenon, the book sheds light on theoretical questions pertaining to current ethnic politics in general.

Gabriel Sheffer is Professor of Political Science at The Hebrew University of Jerusalem. Recipient of the Israeli Prime Minister's Prize for Political Biography, he frequently contributes to Israeli and foreign magazines and newspapers. He has published extensively on ethno-national diasporas, the Jewish diaspora, and Israeli politics and foreign policy. Among other books, he is the author of *Moshe Sharett: Biography of a Political Moderate* and editor of *Modern Diasporas in International Politics*.

To
Naomi, Hadass, Tony, and Sigal

Diaspora Politics

At Home Abroad

GABRIEL SHEFFER
The Hebrew University of Jerusalem

CAMBRIDGE
UNIVERSITY PRESS

PUBLISHED BY THE PRESS SYNDICATE OF THE UNIVERSITY OF CAMBRIDGE
The Pitt Building, Trumpington Street, Cambridge, United Kingdom

CAMBRIDGE UNIVERSITY PRESS
The Edinburgh Building, Cambridge CB2 2RU, UK
40 West 20th Street, New York, NY 10011–4211, USA
477 Williamstown Road, Port Melbourne, VIC 3207, Australia
Ruiz de Alarcón 13, 28014 Madrid, Spain
Dock House, The Waterfront, Cape Town 8001, South Africa

http://www.cambridge.org

© Gabriel Sheffer 2003

First published 2003

Printed in the United Kingdom at the University Press, Cambridge

Typeface Sabon 10/13 pt.   *System* QuarkXPress [BTS]

A catalog record for this book is available from the British Library.

Library of Congress Cataloging in Publication Data
Sheffer, Gabriel.
    Diaspora politics : at home abroad / Gabriel Sheffer.
        p.   cm.
    Includes bibliographical references and index.
    ISBN 0-521-81137-6
        1. Emigration and immigration – History.   2. Emigration and immigration –
    Political aspects.   I. Title.
    JV6021 .S54 2002
    325 – dc21

                                                                    2002024450

ISBN   0 521 81137 6 hardback

Contents

Contents

Preface and Acknowledgments

My interest in ethno-national diasporism and diasporas predates the now widely recognized cultural, social, political, and economic importance of those entities. It also predates the current increased academic interest in the nature, scope, and influence of such diasporas. Thus, whereas most observers were inclined to dismiss this phenomenon as marginal, on the wane, and uninteresting, I thought differently. Now, as I have argued throughout the past two decades, it is widely recognized that no serious discussion of current national, regional, and global politics can ignore those entities and their various roles.

Initially my attention was drawn to this phenomenon while I was researching and writing about Israeli foreign policy prior to and after the establishment of the Jewish state. This was not accidental. Because the Jewish diaspora was an important factor in the development of the Yishuv (the Jewish community in Palestine prior to 1948), in the 1948 war, and in the creation of Israel and its development, Yishuv and Israeli leaders had to take it into account when shaping their foreign policies and implementing them.

Although I had been aware of the importance of ethnic considerations in politics and in the motivations of various states, especially of Israel, when they formulate and implement their foreign policies, still I was surprised to learn of the complexity of this issue and the great ambivalence shown by Israeli politicians and officials toward the Jewish diaspora.

My acquaintance with the relationship between Israel and the Jewish diaspora became more intimate when I began regularly visiting Jewish diaspora communities and following their development. During that same period, I was working on a political biography of the first Israeli minister of foreign affairs and its second prime minister, Moshe Sharett. Though he was keenly interested in the Jewish diaspora and truly sympathetic toward that large segment of the Jewish people, still the Sharett government and successive Israeli governments had a very clear order of priorities. Already I had realized that despite repeated declarations about Israel's profound gratitude and commitment to the far-flung communities of the Jewish diaspora, actually the fulfillment of Israeli self-interests always came first. This has been known as the Israelocentric position, which in turn has substantially affected the diaspora.

My first detailed studies of homeland–diaspora relations focused on fund-raising by Jewish diaspora communities and the transfer of funds to the homeland. This has always been a very sensitive issue for all sides involved in any homeland–diaspora situation. It turns out that raising donations, transferring remittances to homelands, and making investments in homelands constitute highly intricate systems, usually involving many actors who often have divergent interests. At the core of each of these systems is a triangular relationship – among the diaspora communities, the homeland, and the host countries. More recently I have come to realize that the number of actors and interests involved is even greater and that these deserve special attention.

Those early studies led me to ponder the enormous complexity of the diaspora phenomenon and the precariousness of diaspora communities' positions in relation to their host societies, homelands, and other societal and political actors and agencies. I also began to wonder if the Jewish diaspora was indeed unique, as many had thought and wrote. It soon became clear that is was not. Looking for answers to these theoretical and practical questions only raised many further questions about this highly intricate phenomenon.

Because of my increasing interest in these issues pertaining to ethno-national diasporism, and particularly to diaspora politics, I initiated a series of meetings and a seminar with a number of outstanding scholars from Israel, Europe, and the United States that resulted in a proceedings volume published in 1986: *Modern Diasporas in International Politics*. In my Introduction to that volume I suggested that it was a first theoretical, analytical, and empirical attempt to create a new field of studies. The various contributions to that volume substantiated the overarching hypotheses that ethno-national diasporism was increasing rather than declining, that it was not a modern development but rather a long-standing historical phenomenon, that older and newer diasporas shared many features and experiences, that the Jewish diaspora was not unique, and that diasporism was an important topic for further research. However, despite the fact that the book sold well, for a long period thereafter there were only a few general and comparative publications in this field.

Though many colleagues have remained convinced that this is a marginal issue, I have continued to study and publish articles on various aspects of the Jewish diaspora experience and on more general topics concerning ethno-national diasporism and diaspora politics. Among other things, I have published articles elaborating my first definition of these diasporas, dealing with the emergence of new diasporas, and focusing on the radicalization of diasporas. I have also published articles on the security issues in host countries that involve diasporas, the impact of the new media and communications on diasporas, the distinction between trans-national and trans-state diasporas, and the continuing changes in the relationship between Israel and the Jewish diaspora.

Gradually the diaspora phenomenon has come to attract more attention. One of the indicators of that growing interest has been the greater number of international conferences and seminars that have been organized, some of which I have attended. The turning point for that increasing recognition came in the wake of the collapse of the Soviet Union and the rapid globalization processes that followed. Those trends facilitated increasing migration, permanent settlement of migrants, and the creation of new diaspora communities, and they also contributed to attitudinal changes toward migrants and diasporas. Because of various processes that will be described and analyzed later in this book, certain core groups in older and dormant diasporas became more assertive and active in the political and socioeconomic arenas. Such developments further promoted interest in the diaspora phenomenon, and the numbers of papers, articles, and books published on these topics have increased manyfold. Of great importance in furthering the development of this academic field has been Professor Khachig Tololyan's initiative and unwavering dedication to publishing the field's journal, *Diaspora*.

My decision to write this book was made only recently, because I believed that there was a lacuna that called for a general book on diaspora politics. Rather than focusing on case studies, I decided to review and use the information that could be gleaned from the vast literature on ethnicity and ethnic politics and from the numerous specific case studies of diasporas that are now available. The few more general books on the social aspects of diasporas and on the connections between migration and the appearance of diaspora communities were also helpful.

The book raises a rather long list of issues pertaining to the complex diaspora phenomenon and attempts to deal with most of them. It offers an elaborated definition of the phenomenon and sets out to analyze its various aspects. It draws some theoretical conclusions and suggests a cluster of issues that should be studied further in order to arrive at a more comprehensive theory of current diasporism.

During the years that I have been involved in the study of diasporas I have benefited considerably from cooperation with the Berlin Institute for Comparative Social Studies, and especially its director, Dr. Jochen Blaschke, and his deputy, Dr. Thomas Schwartz. Together we have made noticeable progress in initiating, conducting, and supporting research and publications in this field. Among other things, together we have organized seminars on these topics, with the participation of experienced old hands and younger scholars, and they have yielded some impressive studies on diasporism and diasporas. We would like to thank all those participants, and we look forward to continued fruitful cooperation.

I would like to thank two former students and research assistants, Dr. Michael Dahan (who co-authored one of my articles) and Mr. Shaul Shenhav, who helped with various stages of the work on this book. For their helpful comments and suggestions, thanks also go to my colleagues, Professors Abraham Ashkenazi, William Miles, Ilan Troen, Ehud Sprinzak, Robin Cohen, Jan Hjarno, Emanuel Gutmann, Ahmed Anwar, John Rex, Moshe Maoz, and Gerd Korman, as well as many others who have participated in the seminars and conferences where I have presented papers that have dealt with some of the ideas elaborated in this book. Other colleagues at The Hebrew University, especially in the Political Science Department, as well as at other Israeli and foreign universities, have also been most helpful, and I thank them all for their comments, cooperation, and suggestions.

I greatly appreciate the detailed comments made by two anonymous reviewers of the book for Cambridge University Press. Following most of their valuable suggestions, I have revised various parts of the manuscript, and I am sure that consequently this will be a better book, though for the final content of this book, I am solely responsible.

I owe special thanks to Mr. Lewis Bateman and his staff at Cambridge University Press for all that they have done to facilitate the publication of this book.

During the years that I have been engaged in diaspora studies, I have been fortunate to have received financial support from various research institutes and centers, especially at The Hebrew University. For this I thank the boards and directors of the Truman Institute and the Eshkol, Shain, and Smart centers for their generous financial support and cooperation.

Last but not least, I would like to express my most profound love, appreciation, and thanks to my beloved wife, Naomi, my two daughters, Hadass and Sigal, and my son-in-law, Tony, for their continuing understanding and encouragement while I was researching and writing this book.

I hope that this book will contribute to better understanding and sympathy for all those many millions of people worldwide who maintain special connections with their old homelands while striving to feel at home abroad.

Introduction

The highly motivated Koreans and Vietnamese toiling hard to become prosperous in bustling Los Angeles, the haggard Palestinians living in dreary refugee camps near Beirut and Amman, the beleaguered Turks dwelling in cramped apartments in Berlin, and the frustrated Russians in Estonia all have much in common. All of them, along with Indians, Chinese, Japanese, Africans, African-Americans, Jews, Palestinians, Greeks, Gypsies, Romanians, Poles, Kurds, Armenians, and numerous other groups permanently residing outside of their countries of origin, but maintaining contacts with people back in their old homelands, are members of ethno-national diasporas.

Until the late twentieth century, wherever possible, and particularly when physical appearance, basic mores, innate habits, and linguistic proficiency permitted, many members of such groups tried hard to conceal their ethno-national origins. Furthermore, they were inclined to minimize the importance of their contacts with their countries of origin (usually, and hereafter, termed *homelands*), and they did not publicize their membership in organizations serving their groups and their homelands. Such patterns of behavior were related to a desire prevalent among members of such groups to assimilate, acculturate, or at least integrate into their countries of settlement (usually, and hereafter, referred to as *host countries*).

In tandem, whether deliberately or by default, both democratic and non-democratic host societies and governments largely ignored most of these ethno-national diaspora groups. In certain cases, such societies and governments questioned the endurance capability of diasporas in general, as well as that of the diaspora groups residing in the states that those

I

societies controlled in particular. Such societies and governments tended to minimize diasporas' cultural, social, political, and economic vitality and significance. Similarly, they ignored the diasporas' various roles in host societies and their contributions to those societies. The host societies, again consciously or unintentionally, overlooked the wider domestic, regional, and global political implications of the existence of such diasporas in their midst. Yet, although various host societies and governments viewed the presence of ethno-national diasporas as a marginal and temporary phenomenon, they often regarded them as actually and potentially menacing and therefore undesirable. Consequently, host societies and governments imposed social, political, and economic strictures and pressures on immigrants who were allowed to settle permanently in those countries. The purpose of such pressures was to compel the immigrants to assimilate, to accept all prevailing social, political, and economic norms, to fully integrate into the host societies, or else to leave.

It was not only host societies and governments that held such disparaging views about diasporas' endurance and demonstrated such rancorous attitudes toward them. Contrary to some widely held notions, and despite public statements to the contrary, homeland societies and governments also demonstrated either indifferent or ambiguous attitudes toward "their" diasporas. Some homelands, such as Turkey and Greece, regarded the members of their diaspora communities as their dedicated agents in the host countries where they resided. During certain periods, some homelands, such as Ireland and Israel, viewed their diasporans as defectors or even traitors. Consequently, such societies and governments often turned a deaf ear to any pleas for help from their diaspora communities.

Usually, social and political studies focus on "real-world" developments. Hence it is not entirely surprising that until the 1970s, except for some narrowly focused studies, mainly on specific diasporas' identities, diasporas' lobbying on behalf of their homelands, and diasporans' successful or failed attempts at assimilation and integration in host countries, many academics also paid little attention to the diaspora phenomenon or to specific diasporas. In fact, like many other issues pertaining to ethnicity and to ethnic groups, ethno-national diasporism was regarded as unworthy of serious consideration and in-depth study (Armstrong 1976, p. 393). Moreover, like the politicians and their followers who espoused a variety of philosophical and ideological approaches concerning such entities – mainly ideas on nationalism and neo-nationalism, Marxism and neo-Marxism, as well as liberalism and neo-liberalism – scholars regarded those social-political formations as too anachronistic, transient, and marginal to merit serious analysis. Certain analyses of the phenomenon were predicated on normative assumptions based on those various ideologies. The result was that some observers not only predicted an unavoidable gradual disappearance of such groups but also went so far as to recommend either complete assimilation of their members or a return to their homelands. Basing their opinions on the results of purportedly sound theoretical and empirical analyses, other scholars considered the issue of ethno-national diasporism as uninteresting.

Such political positions, analyses, predictions, and recommendations notwithstanding, over the past two decades the total number of established diasporas and the numbers of their members have increased conspicuously. Moreover, individuals and families belonging to those ethno-national entities often have altered their previous assimilationist, integrationist, or acculturationist proclivities. Increasingly, Palestinians, Kurds, Turks, Moroccans, Croats, Poles, and many others who permanently reside outside their homelands do not conceal their ethno-national origins and affiliations. Moreover, because of their growing self-confidence and assertiveness, many diasporans proudly maintain their ethno-national identity, retain their homeland citizenship, openly identify as members of diaspora organizations, and are not reluctant to act publicly on behalf of their homelands and dispersed co-ethnics.

Simultaneously with recent recurring incidents of racist and xenophobic outbursts in some societies directed at foreigners and "others" in general, and at members of ethno-national diasporas in particular, there are greater numbers of host societies in which previously held negative or skeptical views are being modified or are waning. In such host countries there have emerged new, mutually reinforcing forces and processes. As a result of the reinvigoration and new assertiveness of ethnic minorities and of ethno-national diasporas, increasing numbers of host societies are altering their previous attitudes of rejection and indifference toward the others in their midst.

Again not surprisingly, in view of such developments, intellectuals, writers, journalists, and politicians also are increasingly becoming aware of the phenomenon and are acknowledging the permanence of diasporas. Some observers have even recognized diasporas' positive cultural and economic contributions to host societies. Gradually and cautiously, more host societies and their governments are accepting diaspora members' affiliations as legitimate, or at least as tolerable. In turn, these new, more favorable attitudes are further enhancing diasporans' self-confidence and assertiveness. Moreover, in some host countries, such as the United States, Canada, Britain, and Sweden, and in certain liberal circles in other Western societies, membership in such entities has even been regarded as exciting, intriguing, and advantageous. In those countries, membership and participation in diaspora activities are no longer deemed to be major obstacles on the way to integration, affluence, and influence. Again as noted, such trends notwithstanding, in the same host countries there is still racism directed at these groups.

These new dispositions and attitudes further reinforce the processes whereby wider social segments in democratic host societies are becoming more receptive to ethnic pluralism, albeit not always multiculturalism, and to diasporas. In short, increasingly diasporas are being included in the pluralist or multicultural conceptual frameworks and in the practical arrangements that are emerging in some Western democracies for the purpose of dealing with this phenomenon and its various implications. It is important to note that to some extent the diaspora members are contributing to these new trends. In fact, the very presence of such ethno-national diasporas and the cultural, social, political, and economic issues they raise are increasingly moving toward center stage in societal and political arenas. Yet, as has been noted, just as with their attitudes toward non-immigrant indigenous ethnic minorities, dominant ethnic groups still have difficulties in actually altering their basic hostile attitudes and behavior toward ethno-national diasporas. This probably is connected to the dominant groups' adamant determination to avoid losing control over what they regard as their sovereignty in their homelands and nation-states.

The newly found confidence and assertiveness among members of diasporas, on the one hand, and the greater tolerance shown by host governments and societies toward diaspora members, on the other, have generated animated discussions among politicians, academics, and laypeople. These debates usually have been conducted either in the context of general deliberations about trans-statism (in this context, meaning involvement of peoples of the same national origin, but living in various states or countries), trans-nationalism (here meaning involvement of peoples of different national origins), nationalism, and ethnicity or specifically in the context of diasporism and diasporas. Until the late 1980s, few analytical and theoretical publications had focused on the diaspora phenomenon, but since the mid-1990s the study of ethnic diasporism and diasporas has proliferated spectacularly. Furthermore, whereas previously the four notable exceptions to the dearth of theoretical publications on this issue were the influential article by Armstrong (1976), the books by Seton-Watson (1977) and Bertelsen (1980), and our edited volume, which probably was the first systematic analytical and theoretical collection on the subject (Sheffer 1986a), today books, articles, and studies on this and related issues are abundant. The numerous references to "diasporism" and "diasporas" in recent publications on ethnography, anthropology, ethnicity, sociology, political theory, comparative politics, international relations, globalization, and transnationalism, as well as the numerous seminars, conferences, study groups, and grants offered by governments, municipalities, universities, and research institutes, all attest to the fact that interest in these groups will only continue to increase.

Nevertheless, despite the current increase in attention to ethnonational diasporas, the study of these groups is still in its early stages. In this vein, as I have argued since the mid-1980s, the dramatic growth of diasporas and the intensification of their activities in the context of the current chaotic world order – which has been attributed in part to ethnic unrest and diasporas' militancy (Nye 1993; Posen 1993; Brown 1993; Gurr and Harff 1994) – warrant additional theoretical and comparative investigations in the effort to provide clarification and explanation of this increasingly important phenomenon.

The need for further in-depth studies of diasporism and diasporas is also emphasized by the recent attitudinal and practical changes toward diaspora politics, coupled with new perspectives on certain interrelated issues that substantially affect diasporas. Among other factors are the simultaneous processes of globalization and localization, regionalization, the waning of nationalism, the weakening of both the nation-state and the state, increasing international migration, migration cycles, and the roles of religion and religious fundamentalism in the survival and revival of ethnic minorities and diasporas (Smith 1999).

These new trends have resulted in a strong emphasis on study of the anthropological, cultural, social, and economic aspects of ethnicity and of ethno-national diasporas. However, as noted, there has been a noticeable lack of in-depth studies and comprehensive theoretical and comparative discussion of the political dimension of the diaspora phenomenon. Thus, the main purpose of this volume, which focuses on the general theoretical and analytical aspects of the politics of ethnonational diasporas, is to fill in that gap.

On the basis of empirical, analytical, and theoretical insights, this book proposes that despite some unique features of each diaspora, there are also profound similarities among those entities that warrant further discussion that will result in some generalizations. Therefore, it does not offer descriptions or analyses of specific cases. Various cases will be discussed briefly only as illustrations and to provide supportive evidence for the general analytical, comparative, and theoretical observations about diasporas. Similarly, this book does not offer normative or prescriptive solutions for problems created by the presence of ethno-national diasporas in host countries.

The fact that ethno-national diasporas exist and function in highly intricate environments raises multiple questions that this book will endeavor to answer. The following are very condensed formulations of the major questions and issues that will be examined in the chapters herein:

- Is the ethno-national diaspora a perennial phenomenon, or modern?
- Has the nature of ethno-national diasporas changed over the past two centuries?
- Is the identity of diaspora members of an essentialist, instrumental, or constructed nature?
- What are the roles of collectives, individuals, and environmental factors in diasporas' formation, persistence, and behavior?
- What are the main characteristics of contemporary ethno-national diasporas?
- Are all diasporas of the same type?
- Are these stable and homogeneous, or unsteady and hybrid formations?
- What are the organizational structures within diasporas, and what are the strategies and tactics they employ?
- What are the functions of these organizations and their contributions to homelands, host countries, and the emerging global society?
- Can diasporas inflict substantial damage on their hosts and homelands?
- And finally, are these groups precursors of post-modern, post-national, and trans-state social and political systems?

It is believed that the answers to this rather long list of questions will substantiate the main thesis of this book concerning these people who do their utmost to be "at home abroad." Succinctly, the main thesis of this book is that *ethno-national diasporism and diasporas do not constitute a recent, modern phenomenon. Rather, this is a perennial phenomenon. Essential aspects of this phenomenon are the endless cultural, social, economic, and especially political struggles of those dispersed ethnic groups, permanently residing in host countries away from their homelands, to maintain their distinctive identities and connections with their homelands and other dispersed groups from the same nations. These are neither "imagined" nor "invented" communities. Their identities are intricate combinations of primordial, psychological/ mythical, and instrumental elements. These identities may undergo certain adaptations to changing circumstances, yet they do not lose their core characteristics. The diasporans' struggle for survival is waged while they do their utmost to feel at home in their host countries, which in many instances demonstrate hostility toward them. And they do survive, despite the fact that their homelands, too, have inherently ambiguous attitudes toward them.*

I

Primary Questions and Hypotheses

Clarification of Terms

In view of the noticeable confusion concerning the positions of ethno-national diasporas in the current global, regional, and local cultural, economic, and political arenas, there is a need to clarify some terms, to elaborate the main questions briefly outlined in the Introduction, and to present some primary hypotheses concerning the diaspora phenomenon.

As a first step in our general analysis of the ethno-national diaspora phenomenon, a step that is intended to promote an understanding of its actual and theoretical meanings and that will put special emphasis on the nature of diaspora politics, three terms should be clarified – "diaspora," "diasporism," and "diasporic." In passing, here it should be noted that, as the editor of the field's journal, *Diaspora*, mentions in an article on the meaning and definition of the phenomenon (Tololyan 1996), the use of the plural form of "diaspora" – "diasporas" – is recent. It can be found in only a few dictionaries. In the same vein, most electronic spellers do not recognize that plural form.

Clarification of these three terms is needed especially because journalists and academics have indiscriminately applied them to a wide variety of social-political phenomena and institutions (Safran 1991; Cohen 1997). Such multiple usages of these terms have led to much confusion about their meanings. This confusion is due in part to a traditional and prevalent misunderstanding and misapplication of the term "diaspora" itself. Thus, until the late 1960s, the *Encyclopedia of the Social Sciences* did not mention the term "diaspora" at all (Tololyan 1996). Similarly, laypeople and experts alike have related, and still relate, this term only to or mainly to the Jewish exile existence in closed, frequently ghetto-like communities that have persisted outside the Holy Land. Thus, for example, as late as 1975, *Webster's New Collegiate Dictionary* defined the term "diaspora" as "the settling of scattered colonies of Jews outside Palestine after the Babylonian exile," as "the area outside Palestine settled by Jews," as "the Jews living outside Palestine or modern Israel," and as "Migration: the great black diaspora to the cities of the North and West in the 1940s and 1950s." Until its 1993 edition, the *New Shorter Oxford English Dictionary*, too, defined the term as "the dispersion of the Jews among the Gentile nations" and as "all those Jews who live outside the biblical land of Israel." Yet for the first time in its long history, in that edition the dictionary added that the term also refers to "the situation of people living outside their traditional homeland." That the term "diaspora" would be equated with the dispersed Jewish people is, of course, not entirely surprising. It is related to the Jewish diaspora's historical persistence despite extreme tribulations and to its continuous high visibility, at times even contrary to the interests and wishes of its members.

Actually, the term "diaspora" had had a wider meaning than merely the Jewish exile, a meaning that is less well known. Consider the Greek origin of the term "diaspora": *speiro* = to sow, *dia* = over. Among those who are aware of the origin of the term, it is widely believed that the term first appeared in the Greek translation of the book of Deuteronomy in the Old Testament, with reference to the situation of the Jewish people – "Thou shalt be a diaspora in all kingdoms of the earth" (Deut. 28, 25). Yet the term had also been used by Thucydides in his *History of the Peloponnesian War* (II, 27) to describe the dispersal of the Aeginetans. Thus, already at a very early period, the term had been applied to two of the oldest ethno-national diasporas – the Jewish and the Greek – that had been established outside of their homelands as a result of both voluntary and forced migrations.

Accordingly, to begin clarifying the current confusion about the term and to facilitate an in-depth discussion of the ethno-national diaspora phenomenon, at this point it is preliminarily posited that

> *an ethno-national diaspora is a social-political formation, created as a result of either voluntary or forced migration, whose members regard themselves as of the same ethno-national origin and who permanently reside as minorities in one or several host countries. Members of such entities maintain regular or occasional contacts with what they regard as their homelands and with individuals and groups*

of the same background residing in other host countries. Based on aggregate decisions to settle permanently in host countries, but to maintain a common identity, diasporans identify as such, showing solidarity with their group and their entire nation, and they organize and are active in the cultural, social, economic, and political spheres. Among their various activities, members of such diasporas establish trans-state networks that reflect complex relationships among the diasporas, their host countries, their homelands, and international actors.

As will be shown in Chapter 4, at the beginning of this millennium, many millions of Greeks, Armenians, Gypsies, Jews, African-Americans, Chinese, Japanese, and Kurds, who have more recently been joined by Koreans, Palestinians, Russians, Pakistanis, Moroccans, Vietnamese, Slovaks, Mexicans, Colombians, and numerous other groups, fit this initial characterization of ethno-national diasporas. This profile will be elaborated and explained in greater detail in Chapter 3.

Meanwhile, for a number of reasons, throughout this book the terms "diaspora," "diasporic," and "diasporism" are often prefaced by the hyphenated term "ethno-national." The first reason for this usage pertains to the intention to limit the discussion here to a relatively specific category of social and political formations. Such distinction is needed because "diaspora" has become a traveling term. Hence this hyphenated term is necessary in order to distinguish as clearly as possible ethno-national diasporas from various other groups that have been regarded as being very similar, even identical. Furthermore, this term is needed because the general public, journalists, anthropologists, sociologists, and political scientists have applied the term "diaspora" to various trans-national formations espousing what has been termed "deterritorialized identities" – that is, to groups whose hybrid identities, orientations, and loyalties are not connected to any given territory that is regarded as their exclusive homeland (Glick Schiller et al. 1992; Basch, Glick Schiller, and Szanton Blanc 1994; Kearney 1995, pp. 526–7; Guarnizo and Smith 1998).

In this vein, the term "diaspora" has been applied to a variety of formations: to members of trans-national groups adhering to the same ideology, such as communism; to members of "clashing civilizations" (Huntington 1993); to members of "pan-diasporas," like the Muslims (Yadlin 1998), the Asian-Americans, the Arab-Americans, and the Latinos worldwide who dwell outside their homelands; and to members of trans-national religious denominations and universal churches, such as the Catholic, Anglican, and Eastern Orthodox churches. Similarly, the term has been applied to large groups of people speaking the same language, such as the Francophones (Miles and Sheffer 1998) and Spanish-speakers; and the term has even been applied to the "global youth culture" (Scholte 1996, pp. 53–61). Unlike studies that have not made clear distinctions between ethno-national diasporism and all these other "cognate phenomena" (Cohen 1997, pp. 187–92; Safran 1999; Schnapper 1999), this book will focus on the former category.

A second reason for using the hyphenated term "ethno-national" is to stress that this book deals with the politics of dispersed groups whose members regard themselves as being participants in nations that have common ethnic and national traits, identities, and affinities. The most important of those traits that help in shaping the common identities of members of those entities, cementing their affinities and increasing their solidarity, is their sense of belonging to the same ethnic nation. Namely, either consciously or subconsciously, members of such groups feel and think that although certain segments of the nation (or even the entire nation, as, for example, the Gypsies) are dispersed in many host countries, nevertheless they are still affiliated with a cohesive ethno-national entity. Furthermore, in most cases, those who maintain that sense of belonging to the same ethno-national family believe that they have common ancestors, that the same blood runs in their veins, that they have a collective history closely connected to a specific homeland, that they share cultural and social mores, values, and traditions, and that they owe a degree of loyalty to their nation, and especially to that segment of the nation that resides in the homeland. In other words, the identities of those groups are based on primordial, instrumental, and mythical/psychological elements (Connor 1973, 1978, 1986, 1992, 1994; Smith 1989).

The second term, "diasporic," denotes the constitutive features and factors of those social and political formations. In this respect, special attention should be given to the common structural, organizational, and behavioral patterns that characterize all those entities. As with other ethnic formations, the boundaries that delineate the real and virtual spaces (some authors refer to these as trans-national social spaces) (Faist 2000) that those diasporas own, occupy, or control are of crucial importance during their establishment, development (Barth 1969; Brass 1991), persistence, and functioning. Boundaries and their maintenance are particularly important in the political sphere.

The most meaningful boundaries between an ethno-national diaspora and other social and political entities in a host country are not physical or geographical. That is, most significant are not the actual geographical boundaries of the neighborhoods, suburbs, towns, or regions where diaspora members permanently dwell. Rather, most important are the cultural, psychological, and social virtual boundaries. Those pertain to the spheres of influence of groups sharing the same identity and cultural traits. Those virtual boundaries, which define intra-state and trans-state social and political spaces, also determine the range of those entities' spheres of activity. Because in most cases those are not hermetically sealed borders, they do not physically isolate those groups from other groups dwelling in the same host countries, nor do they prevent cross-fertilization and mutual influences. Usually there are regular contacts, flows of information, and exchanges of resources, including cultural features, between such groups. It is true that occasionally those exchanges prompt clashes and conflicts, but on many occasions they enhance co-operation. Moreover, in certain cases, individuals and groups "cross" those boundaries, mainly through intermarriage and, wherever possible, through assimilation (Eriksen 1993, pp. 38–41; Clifford 1994, pp. 307–10). Basically, however, those borders are drawn in accordance with the scope of acceptance and maintenance of the common ethno-national identity by diasporans and in accordance with their wish to identify as such.

This observation is based on the fact that, rather than host societies and their governments, in most cases diaspora leaders and members are autonomous in determining the degree of exclusion or inclusion of "others" in their entities. Furthermore, above and beyond other common features of all diasporas, those shared identities and behavioral patterns, which are closely related to a real or imagined homeland, are at the core of the diaspora phenomenon. Those identities influence the specific characteristics of each of those entities and determine the main strategies and modes of operation vis-à-vis host countries, homelands, and other groups of the same origin permanently residing in other host countries.

Finally, use of the broad term "diasporism" is intended to emphasize that such a discernible overarching phenomenon really can be observed. When tackling this issue, the argument of this book will suggest that the various categories of ethno-national diasporas share characteristics that create distinctive structural, organizational, and behavioral similarities among them. In other words, such groups – whose historical origins are in different territories, nations, and historical periods, who reside in various host countries controlled by different nations and regimes, and who command a range of varying resources – are in fact parts of the same general social and political phenomenon.

The Problematics of Diasporism

Though the main focus of this book is on the politics of ethno-national diasporas, the fundamental questions pertaining to those groups are not discussed in isolation from other significant social, economic, and cultural factors and actors that influence their development. Moreover, the essential questions concerning the present and future political status and behavior of ethno-national diasporas are inseparable from the wider issues pertaining to ethnicity and to all other ethnic entities. These questions will be examined against the backdrop of globalization, regionalization, and the weakening of state institutions, especially of the executive branch.

In this context it is essential to note that although the entities dealt with here are of ethnic origin, not all dispersed ethnic minorities and groups constitute diasporas in the sense proposed in this book. Thus, not discussed here are native nations and other indigenous ethnic tribes and groups who, after their permanent settlement in the territory that they came to regard as their homeland, did not migrate to other territories.

Nevertheless, ethnic native nations, tribes, minorities, and ethno-national diasporas encounter similar difficulties and problems. Those are created by recent developments that have affected the positions and behaviors of those entities. Among those developments, most pertinent are the crosscutting and sometimes contradictory influences of globalization and localization, of trans-statism and localism, of the new relationships between dominant groups on the one hand and indigenous, migrant, and diasporic minorities on the other, of conflict and accommodation, and of exclusionary versus inclusionary tendencies in pluralistic states (for a similar view, see Shuval 2000). Hence, a better understanding of the ethnic phenomenon at large, and of the ongoing efforts to develop new interdisciplinary theoretical insights into the more specific issues of ethnic identity, survival, and revival in democratic and democratizing societies, should enhance our understanding of the problematic existence and intricate politics of ethno-national diasporas. As noted in the Introduction, this can and should be a two-sided, mutually enriching procedure. That is, a clearer understanding of ethnicity, gained through the availability of pertinent empirical data, analyses, and theoretical insights, will facilitate a better understanding of the origins, identities, and behavioral patterns of ethno-national diasporas. The flip side of the coin is that a more profound understanding of diasporism and diasporas will shed additional light on the wider theoretical, analytical, and comparative issues of ethnicity at large.

Furthermore, study of the politics of ethno-national diasporas should help us to better understand some of the most central social and political arrangements now emerging in the global, regional, and intra-state arenas. Within this general framework, this book is intended to contribute to a cross-pollination between studies of global, regional, and domestic political trends and studies of ethnic and ethno-national diaspora politics.

On the Historical Roots of Diasporism

The first major issue that will be addressed in this book involves the historical origins of ethno-national diasporism. As noted, this will be discussed within the context of ethnicity at large. Although we are mainly concerned with the inherent nature and political concerns of contemporary diasporas, some historical perspective on the phenomenon and on specific diasporas will be of significant interest for at least two reasons. First, examination of the historical dimension will provide further insight into a perplexing and frequently debated question regarding ethnicity and nationalism in general and diasporism and diasporas in particular – that of the ancient versus modern origins and nature of those formations. Is ethnic diasporism a recent and modern phenomenon, or does it have roots in much earlier historical periods? (For a thorough discussion of these two approaches to the study of ethnicity and nationalism, see Smith 1998.) A better understanding of this issue should contribute to clarification of further critical questions concerning the survival of some specific diasporas, such as the Jewish, Armenian, Greek, Chinese, and Gypsy, that were formed in antiquity or during the Middle Ages and that against all odds have not perished.

Such a reexamination of the temporal perspective on diasporas is also needed in view of the emphasis that political geographers, especially those who follow Jean Gottmann's teachings (Gottmann 1973, 1996; Mitchell 1997), as well as other political scientists, sociologists, and anthropologists, currently put on "spatial factors." Purportedly, these factors determine the nature and behavior of such entities. Advocates of the "spatial approach" to diasporism insist that urban, intra-state, trans-national, and global "spaces," which are determined by geographical and territorial factors, exert predominant influences on the establishment, development, and well-being of diasporas (the difference between such spaces and the aforementioned "trans-national social spaces" should be carefully noted). Those scholars further argue that as a result of the collapse of the international bipolar system that characterized the cold-war era, during the 1990s there occurred major shifts in world affairs. Such changes have made it imperative that we reconsider our basic notions about space and time as they affect all social and political entities and their affairs. According to the spatial approach, the spread of globalization, which is being intensified by large waves of trans-national migrants and their permanent settlement in host countries, by trans-state trade, finance, and production, and by the "new media," necessarily will entail a revision of our traditional view of the role of space in the development of social and political entities. Essentially those "spatialists" argue that globalization is resulting in a shift to a multidimensional global space, with unbounded, often discontinuous and interpenetrating geographical subspaces. Accordingly, that approach refocuses attention from the historical dimensions of those communities, which formerly were bounded within virtual cultural and social borders, and turns our gaze to concrete spaces in which nations, states, and ethnic groups overlap. More specifically, and more closely connected to the main issues discussed in this volume, those spatialists have challenged the notion that historical and temporal factors have been the primary forces in the emergence and development of native nations, ethnic minorities, and diasporas. Instead, they suggest that various configurations of spatial factors, such as regionalization and the rise of "global cities," are responsible for the emergence and persistence of such groups (Kearney 1995).

Here it is suggested that there is a need to provide some counterbalance for that view, which is especially popular in European academic circles dealing with these issues. Thus, whereas this book emphasizes that historical and temporal factors have significantly influenced the establishment and fate of ethno-national diasporas, it is recognized that certain arguments from the spatial approach should be integrated into the analysis of the phenomenon.

The Distinction between Migrants and Diasporans

Another important issue involved in the historical and temporal dimensions of the origins of ethno-national diasporism and of specific diasporas is the distinction that should be made between diasporas and other ethnic groups residing outside their national states or homelands. Bearing in mind certain historical and recent "migration orders and crises" (Van Hear 1998) and the ensuing actual migratory trends and their tremendous consequences, it is evident that ethnic diasporas constitute the most enduring outcomes of both voluntary and forced international migrations of ethnic groups and their permanent settlement in host countries. Nevertheless, the conceptual and definitional borderlines between individuals and groups of tourists, international immigrants, guest workers, asylum-seekers, and refugees, some of whom reside in host countries for extended periods, on the one hand, and members of permanent ethno-national diasporas, on the other, are still rather blurred. Thus second-, third-, and even fourth-generation citizens of many host countries (e.g., the United States, Australia, Germany, and Britain) are still formally and informally considered and widely referred to as "immigrants" or "migrants."

This ambiguity is due to the fact that the time periods during which transient individuals and groups are allowed to remain and choose to remain in host countries before they finally decide to settle there permanently, or migrate to a secondary or tertiary host country, or return to their homeland are highly variable, making generalizations difficult. The relative weights of the various factors that affect the durations of those transitory periods, such as the social, political, and economic situations in host countries, homelands, and alternative host countries, as well as the legal and political requirements for obtaining citizenship in host countries, also vary considerably. Therefore, what should be examined in this context is first and foremost the preliminary question to what extent the choice of permanent settlement in host countries is made by migrants before or after their arrival in host countries.

Moreover, there still is no satisfactory answer to the closely related question of why and when migrants form new diasporic entities or join existing ones. Like other sensitive issues pertaining to migration and settlement in host countries, especially where the rate of unemployment is high and anti-foreigner feelings are prevalent, this aspect involves highly charged practical ramifications, as well as controversial theoretical implications that must be clarified.

A conceptual clarification of the point in time at which immigrants formally and informally switch from one status to another will allow a better distinction between immigrants and diasporans. Among other things, it will allow us to better determine the points at which particular immigrants decide to form new diasporas or join existing ones, the points at which individuals and groups become motivated to undertake the burdens involved in diaspora existence and become active in the political arena as identified members and functionaries of diaspora organizations.

Such clarification will also have a practical angle. It will enable us to more accurately assess the numbers of people belonging to the two categories of persons residing for long periods outside their homelands, namely, members of diasporas, on the one hand, and temporary sojourners of various categories, on the other. It will also be useful for assessing the potential for the emergence and further development of new diasporas in various parts of the world. Here it is proposed that, rather than employing legalistic definitions (such as the dates of arrival and application for citizenship and its actual attainment, or the average elapsed time until migrants purchase their first homes and get suitable jobs in the host country), and rather than using social or psychological surveys and opinion polls to measure migrants' integration into host societies, the concept of "involved social actors," supplemented by individual-choice and collective-choice models (Hechter 1987, 1988; Banton 1994), should be applied to this issue, which is critical in the life cycle of each individual and each group of migrants.

These considerations are closely related to a more general need to reexamine one of the foremost issues in the study of modern ethnic diasporas: precisely why their members decide not only to maintain and nurture their ethno-national identity but also to be identified as such and to organize and act within the framework of diaspora organizations and preserve contacts with their homelands and other communities of the same origin.

In the search for a satisfactory explanation for the remarkable persistence and more recent increasing growth in ethno-national diasporism and in specific diasporas, we also must address some ongoing theoretical debates (Vertovec 1997; Anthias 1998). Among other things, those debates concern the applicability of the available theoretical interpretations for the elusive issue of ethno-genesis and the related issues of diasporas' survival and revival around the world, all in the context of the attempt to clearly distinguish between immigrants and diasporans. Because the diasporas discussed here are basically ethnic, Chapter 3 will reassess the applicability of some major overarching approaches to ethno-genesis and to ethnic identity. The first approach whose applicability must be reassessed is the "primordialist" (or "given" or "essentialist") explanation for the roots of identity that contribute to the persistence of ethnicity and ethnic diasporism. Very briefly, this approach emphasizes the roles of biological factors, physical markers such as skin color and facial contours, and cultural attributes such as common history, revered myths and legends, language, food, costumes, and folklore in creating and preserving the identities of ethnic nations and minorities, and, by implication, also the identities of ethno-national diasporas (Geertz 1963; Van den Berghe 1988; Chapman 1993; cf. Eller and Coughlan 1993).

The second is the "instrumentalist" approach. Again, the following is only a brief summary of this approach: Instrumentalists argue that affiliation into ethnic groups, including diasporas, and maintenance of that collective identity are useful for achieving practical individual and group goals (Cohen 1969). In other words, advocates of that approach argue that members of those groups maintain such identities because of practical calculations. Within that approach, the most "extreme" explanation for individual and group motivations for adhering to ethnic identities, and consequently for keeping up their ties with ethnic entities, is associated with the general argument that rational choice, which involves cost–benefit calculations, determines their decisions (Rogowski 1985).

In a sense, in between the instrumentalist and primordialist approaches are the "psychological" approach (Horowitz 1985; Connor 1993a, 1994) and the "ethno-symbolic and mythical" approach (Smith 1973, 1981, 1983, 1986, 1999; Armstrong 1982, 1995). Generally, those two similar approaches postulate that ethnic identities and ethnonational diaspora identities are not based solely on primordial factors. Those theoreticians argue that the identities of the members of such groups have their bases in subjective psychological factors or in strong attachments to symbols and myths. Moreover, those approaches hold that such groups are not necessarily part of the general modern phenomenon, but that some of them have ancient roots (Smith 1992). The applicability of that approach, especially to migrants' decisions to maintain their "original" identities, to form or to join diaspora communities, and to continue their membership in the organized entities they establish, should perhaps be reconsidered, for a priori it sounds plausible in those cases.

Finally, the applicability of the "constructionist" approach, which originally was intended to explain modern nationalism and more recently has been applied to ethnicity and ethno-national diasporas, should also be reexamined. As is well known, the advocates of that approach, who now probably constitute the majority of academics who study ethnic and national issues, assume that nations essentially are modern social constructs, artifacts created by "cultural engineers" and elites who "invent" traditions in order to organize newly enfranchised masses into new status systems and communities (Hobsbawm 1990). Among the constructionist viewpoints, that of Benedict Anderson has become widely known and highly influential. Anderson regards nations and nationalism as modern cultural artifacts that began to appear toward the end of the eighteenth century. His well-known definition of a nation as an "imagined political community" rests on the claim that members of a nation never get to know, meet, or even hear of most of their fellows, and yet all share a common image of the community and a desire to maintain it. A nation is based on its members' ability to transform "fatalities into continuity" and through print capitalism to create a coherent formation whose participants all use the same language and cultural artifacts. Also, according to Anderson, elites, rather than the rank and file, play the crucial role in kindling nationalism and forming modern nations (Anderson 1991; for critical reviews of that approach, see Newman 1991 and Aguirre and Turner 1995). Though infrequently, the constructionist approach has sometimes been applied to ethnicity in general and to the diaspora phenomenon in particular. The questionable use of that approach to the formation and persistence of ethno-national diasporas, referred to by Anderson and other scholars as "long-distance nationalism" (LDN) (Anderson 1992, 1994), emphasizes the need to reexamine its applicability to those entities, for rather than being reflective of recent construction and discontinuity, it seems that some of those entities reveal ancient origins and continuity.

Already at this stage it appears that none of these explanations alone is sufficient for disentangling the vexing riddles surrounding ethno-national diasporas' identities and their formation and growth. Furthermore, none of those approaches is capable of explaining the long endurance of those communities' structural and organizational arrangements. Therefore, the most promising avenue for studying the roots, the identity, and the formation of such groups may be a careful combination of some of those approaches, with an emphasis on personal and collective choices, albeit not pure rational choice.

Because that seems to be the case, this book will present what can be termed a synthesis approach to the questions of the genesis, identity, and history of ethno-national diasporas. It will be suggested that a synthesis can provide the key to a better understanding of the emergence of diasporism and specific diasporas, as well as their recent proliferation and growth.

Similarly, because it is presumed here that the emergence and success of diasporas depends on multiple cultural, social, and economic factors, a variety of related questions will be considered. Such a multifaceted analysis may be able to explain why, how, and to what extent ethnonational diasporas have become significant collective forces in national, trans-state, and global politics. This reassessment should be pertinent to any consequential attempt to refute certain traditional views about the evanescent nature and marginality of the phenomenon as a whole and the resultant cultural and political passivity of specific diasporas.

There is also a need to reassess the impact of the recent proliferation of diasporas and their emergence in numerous new host countries, which either accurately or inaccurately have been regarded as homogeneous nation-states, on their behavior in the domestic, trans-state, regional, and global political arenas. In this context, it will be particularly important to examine the connection between the presumed increasing political power of those communities and the simultaneously expanding power and assertiveness of other ethnic minorities, as well as the question of how the greater global, regional, and domestic dispersal of those groups affects the functioning of the institutions that host countries establish or authorize to deal with trans-state, regional, and internal political matters.

The recent substantial increases in the numbers, geographical dispersal, and organization of diaspora communities have contributed to their greater social and political visibility and influence, but also have produced mounting positive as well as negative expressions of sentiments regarding the diasporans by various non-diaspora social and political groups in the host societies. Many of those who are adamantly opposed to further growth and expansion of diasporas, resenting their greater assertiveness, draw attention to some vexing questions, such as the problem that the increasing influence of diasporas can create political and security difficulties for their hosts. More sympathetic observers seek to counter that viewpoint: To what extent are those entities really pernicious? They would argue that those entities contribute to the well-being of their host societies. Moreover, they would suggest that those diasporas can serve as bridges for cooperation between various ethnic groups, societies, and states.

Such questions lead to a further related issue: Has the emergence of more positive attitudes toward ethnicity in general and toward diasporas in particular been caused by a combination of mutually enhancing factors, or are those more positive attitudes due to just one factor, as has been suggested by various writers on diasporism and diasporas? In this context, we should reconsider how such attitudinal changes are related to the recent increases in international migration (Van Hear 1998), which almost inevitably are followed by permanent settlement of more migrants in host countries and later by negative reactions to that process on the part of the indigenous people.

Answers are needed also to questions about the sources of recent attitudinal changes in host countries and in homelands that encourage tolerance toward incipient diasporas: Are those changes due to the emergence of more favorable attitudes toward cultural and political pluralism (not only in veteran democracies but also in states that have recently been democratized, such as Spain, Portugal, and some of the former Soviet Union satellites), or are they due to an increasing recognition of the inability of host governments to hermetically seal off their borders, to stop the influx of migrants and the consequent development of new diasporas?

These issues must be discussed not only in relation to the cumulative impact of the persistence of historical diasporas (those whose origins were in antiquity or the Middle Ages) and modern diasporas (those that have become established since the seventeenth century) on significant internal and trans-state developments pertaining to immigration and residence laws and regulations, but also in relation to the awakening of previously dormant diasporas, defined as partially organized entities with substantial numbers of inactive and marginal members who had long shown little interest in mobilization and action. Among others, the Polish, Ukrainian, Slovene, and Latvian communities in the United States, Canada, and Australia can serve as examples of this group of diasporas.

These issues and questions relating to the politics of diasporas are rendered even more complex by the fact that the expanding phenomenon of ethno-national diasporas is not confined to economically developed countries and liberal democratic states. As a consequence of the new

patterns and cycles of global migration, diaspora communities are mushrooming in less well developed and non-democratic countries, such as
the Persian Gulf states, Iraq, and some former Soviet Union republics,
further illustrating that the phenomenon of ethnic diasporas is indeed
alive almost everywhere. Furthermore, the increasing need for cheap
labor because of the rapid aging of Western societies and their growing
anxiety about future labor deficits, the greater social and political openness in many regions, and the unprecedented porosity of many states'
borders all allow for the entrance and permanent settlement of foreigners in traditional heterogeneous "immigrant countries," such as the
United States, Canada, and Australia, and in hitherto relatively homogeneous states, such as Sweden, Germany, Poland, and even Japan
(Tololyan 1996; Coulmas 1999). The political implications of those
developments must be carefully watched, for they may herald the emergence of entirely new global, regional, and national political arrangements and processes.

The relative ease with which people can travel to, enter, and settle in
almost all countries worldwide also facilitates secondary and tertiary
migration. This means that when immigrants or members of established
or incipient diasporas find themselves in distress in a particular host
country, they can relatively easily move to another. The hypothesis
here is that those developments involve further ramifications regarding
the identities of diaspora groups and the politics of homelands, host
countries, and regional federations, such as the European Union and
the states participating in the North American Free Trade Agreement
(NAFTA).

These new trends have also created some diametrically opposite effects
that constitute significant political facets of the modern diaspora phenomenon and therefore should be reexamined. In some regions and states
these trends have tended to increase voluntary "ingathering" (a term
denoting voluntary movement back to the homeland, motivated by
strong ideological and emotional inclinations). Or, if one wishes to use
more neutral terms such as "return movement" (voluntary movement
back to the homeland because of practical economic or social considerations) or "repatriation" (forced return to the homeland or to another
host country), these economic and societal developments have expedited
the return of entire diasporas or significant segments thereof. In this
context, the actual role of each homeland society and government must
be reassessed, for certain governments, such as those of Greece, Armenia,
Ireland, Israel, China, and India, wishing to redress a brain drain or alle-

viate economic stagnation, have tried to "pull back" members of their diasporas. As part of such efforts, those governments have courted mainly their younger and more successful diasporans to return and reestablish themselves in the homelands.

Although the return of individuals and groups to their homelands, or to their previous host countries, has been one factor in the recent migratory trends influencing the extent and status of diasporas, nevertheless it seems that, except in certain cases, such as the Jewish and German diasporas, the net result of the migratory trends to and from host countries and homelands has not been massive disintegration of either older or newer diasporas. Rather, as noted earlier, their numbers are increasing, accompanied by greater dedication to strengthening their organizations, broadening their interests, and expanding the range of their activities. Essentially, this applies to both state-linked diasporas and stateless diasporas ("stateless" meaning that the homeland from which the diasporans originated is unknown or is governed by another nation). And it is equally the case for diasporas that were formed in antiquity or during the Middle Ages (such as the Chinese, Gypsy, Jewish, and Armenian diasporas), for diasporas that have been created since the middle of the seventeenth century (such as the Italian and Irish), and for incipient diasporas (such as the Korean, Thai, and Russian in the former Soviet republics).

Strategies Employed by Diasporas

We turn now to questions pertaining to the political orientations of diasporas that determine the grand strategies and specific tactics that diaspora communities employ in dealing with their host countries, homelands, and other actors (Iwanska 1981, Smith 1981, and Weiner 1990.)

The various survival strategies employed by ethnic groups form a spectrum, ranging from full assimilation into host societies, at one pole, to separation from dominant host societies and eventual return to homelands, at the other pole. Examination of the various strategies on this spectrum is necessary because of the delicate balance between the types of strategies that diasporas pursue in host countries and those they follow in their relations with their homelands. The operational hypothesis here is that when diaspora members are eager to assimilate or fully integrate into their host societies, which means relinquishing their ethno-national identities and either dismantling their organized communities or refraining from establishing them, they will adopt strategies intended to decrease the scope and intensity of their relations with the homeland. And vice versa, diasporas that are determined to maintain their identity will pursue strategies that will strengthen their relations with their homelands.

Another hypothesis is that the choice of full assimilation into host societies has become less popular and less common among international migrants and members of both incipient and established diasporas. If the evidence supports this hypothesis, it can be predicted that the numbers and sizes of diasporas will further increase. Such a trend will, of course, be facilitated by other related tendencies. First, there may be less pressure from host countries for assimilation of diaspora members, which seems to be the emerging trend in many host countries, including traditional assimilationist societies such as French society. In this vein, we need to examine whether or not that trend is connected to a growing realization in host countries that ethnic pluralism and even multiculturalism cannot be stamped out. On the other hand, that trend may be the result of an endemic requirement for a continuous flow of migrant workers into both developed and developing countries. A second trend that will be examined is the increasing tolerance toward politically moderate diasporas, especially in Western host societies, and the almost total separation between host societies and diasporas in non-democratic states.

Some related issues that require further exploration include whether or not there is a basic difference between the strategy choices made by stateless diasporas and those made by state-linked diasporas. On the surface, it would appear that stateless diasporas tend to select the strategy of irredentism or separation: a concerted effort to take or be given land that once was their historical homeland and ultimately establish a sovereign state in that historical homeland. In the same vein, it is necessary to ascertain to what extent state-linked diasporas refrain from pursuing a main strategy and tactics featuring radical options, such as demanding irredentism if they are living adjacent to their original homelands, or demanding considerable autonomy in their host countries. Prima facie it would seem that because of a realistic outlook and pragmatic considerations, the elites of state-linked diasporas do not consider such strategies as practical options. Thus the question is to what extent most state-linked diasporas choose as their preferred strategy either the formation and operation of multiple communal organizations or the establishment of representative organizations that are formally recognized by host governments (Weiner 1990).

Closely related is the question of the main factors preventing diaspora leaders from pursuing more radical options, such as their minority status in the host countries, their geographical dispersal within those countries, and the fact that only rarely do they feel secure enough to launch more aggressive strategies.

Hypothetically, two factors contribute to the selection of a strategy of moderation at the inception of mobilized, cohesive state-linked diasporas. First, although on certain occasions such a strategy may lead to clashes with homelands demanding commitment and action on their behalf, it is still the best option for many diasporas. Second, it appears that this is also the best way to pursue and secure diasporas' most vital interests vis-à-vis their host societies and governments. If that is indeed the case, we must consider why this strategy is perceived as less menacing to host countries. The working assumption here is that such a strategy does not pose actual or potential major threats to host societies' sovereignty and territorial integrity, which such host societies obviously regard as essential for their well-being in a changing global environment. It is also posited that when such diasporas opt for a relatively moderate and inoffensive strategy, they do so in part because they are too prudent to engage in illegal and subversive activities. Therefore, only relatively small and marginal elements of state-linked diasporas will tend to become involved in provocative activities. The majority of leaders, as well as most of those communities' members, will condemn such activities. In short, it is clear that adoption of a communalist strategy is a carefully calculated response to social and political needs. It also seems that as long as the sovereignty and security of host countries are not seriously challenged or actually jeopardized, Western host societies are now ready to tolerate and condone activism in diaspora communities. That appears to be the case even when such diaspora communities maintain close connections with their homelands and other communities of the same origin residing in other host countries. Moreover, for reasons that will be discussed in Chapter 7, it seems that most host governments are tending to condone such activism and even encourage diasporas to adopt such a strategy.

A further issue involved in diasporas' selection and revision of their strategies concerns the "contagion factor," that is, how the currently fashionable trends among other ethnic minorities worldwide affect their choices. Such contagion is especially pertinent in the current globalizing environment in which news and information travel freely and swiftly through elaborate and highly sophisticated communications networks (Dahan and Sheffer 2001). In this connection, it is hypothesized that the intricate relationships that exist among diasporas, host countries, homelands, and third and fourth actors that intervene in the affairs of those entities can have considerable impact on the organization and behavior of diasporas.

Why and How Diasporas Become Organized

It is clear that the continuing existence of diasporas hinges on their members' wishes to maintain their ethno-national identities and contacts with their homelands and with other dispersed communities of the same ethnic origin. It is less obvious why diaspora members are willing to invest substantial effort and resources in creating elaborate organizations dedicated to nurturing relationships with their host societies and governments, homelands, global and regional actors, and other groups from the same nation residing in other host countries. It is suggested here that they do so for two main reasons: first, to promote the well-being and ensure the continuity of their communities in their host countries; second, to increase their ability to extend support to beleaguered homelands and other diaspora communities of the same national origin.

As far as their patterns of operation are concerned, it seems that members of both established and incipient diasporas tend to maintain close, direct contacts with their kinfolk and friends in homelands with regard to personal and family matters. Yet once diasporas formalize their organizations and those become bureaucratized, their leaders, officials, and to some extent also the rank and file prefer to conduct most exchanges and transactions with organized counterparts in their homelands and in other diaspora communities of the same origin. In this vein, it is hypothesized that most communal contacts are mediated by bureaucratic organizations in the various diaspora communities and the homelands. Hence the extent to which organizational and bureaucratic considerations affect those relationships needs clarification.

Because individuals and diaspora organizations are frequently involved in contacts with their homelands, with other segments of their nations residing elsewhere, and with a variety of other domestic and international actors, it is important to ascertain to what extent specific diasporas are involved in establishing and expanding their developing

formal and informal domestic and trans-state networks using both con-
ventional and more sophisticated means of communication, especially
the globalized "new media." It is particularly pertinent to determine
whether this has become a general trend among most diasporas or
whether it is confined to the better-organized and richer groups, for, contrary to the long-accepted view, it now seems that not only the stronger
diasporas but also "proletarian" incipient diasporas are creating and
maintaining such networks and using the new media.

Our examination should not be confined only to these trans-state networks' structures and to the scope of the contacts conducted through
them. The content of the exchanges should also be further investigated.
In addition to general information about host countries, homelands, and
other international actors, these networks usually carry information and
resources that are elements of intricate and usually innocuous esthetic,
cultural, political, economic, and scientific trans-state exchanges, especially between homelands and their diasporas (Hall 1990, 1991). On the
other hand, it seems that as a result of the increasing self-assertiveness
and self-empowerment occurring within various diasporas, sometimes
because of their unfavorable treatment at the hands of host countries and
homelands, such trans-state networks have been known to transmit less
innocent messages and resources.

If our presumptions can be substantiated, we shall need to reexamine
some wider practical and theoretical questions pertaining to ethnic and
diaspora politics, as well as politics in general, for those trilateral networks, and sometimes also four- and five-sided networks, may prove to
be the most fertile bases for the emergence of trans-state political systems
that will exist alongside international inter-governmental organizations
(IGOs), regional trading blocs, regional defense organizations, and international non-governmental organizations (INGOs). Moreover, if these
assumptions are valid, then diaspora organizations, their modes of operation, the trans-state networks they establish and operate, and the roles
they play in domestic, regional, and international affairs should be
viewed as precursors to future developments that will significantly
change international and domestic politics.

The cultural and political exchanges between diasporas and other
actors at the various levels of politics that are carried out through those
trans-state networks are of particular significance, for they pertain not
only to the procedural and technical aspects of the operation of those
networks but also to basic issues related to diasporas' structure and
behavior. Among the more tangible and quantifiable of those exchanges

are the economic and financial resources that flow between diasporas
and homelands, including unilateral transfers of funds to homelands –
those include donations, remittances, and investments – and resources
generated by joint ventures either in homelands or elsewhere. For
obvious reasons it is difficult to obtain accurate data about donations
and investments in homelands, about joint financial ventures, about
support for diaspora organizations, and especially about cash and other
financial transfers for diasporas' clandestine activities. Yet some rough
estimates about the volume of such exchanges can be made and will be
presented in Chapter 7.

Finally, in this context, a related issue that should be explored is that
quite often the existence of such networks and the continual flows of
harmless and harmful information and resources through them generate
tension between diasporas and host governments and, on certain occasions, also with homeland governments. The tremendous progress in the
development of the globalized new media has enhanced the efficiency of
those networks, and therefore the inclination to use them, on the one
hand, and attempts to curb them, on the other. Also, this aspect will
further be examined in Chapter 7.

Diaspora–Homeland Relations

The main issue that will be explored with respect to diaspora–homeland
relations is whether or not it is indeed the case that whereas host-
country–diaspora peaceful and conflictual relationships tend to arise
from host-country reactions to diasporas' attitudes and actions, the friction and confrontations between diaspora and homeland can be attributed primarily to homelands. Thus, although it is widely held that
homelands and diasporas maintain intimate familial relations, we need
to examine other indications that actually those relationships are far
from being idyllic. The source of tension in this sphere may be the unwar-
ranted opinion held by most homeland leaders, as well as the rank and
file, that the very raison d'être of "their" diasporas is to stay in close
contact with them, express unfailing loyalty, and provide the homeland
with various resources and services.

It is also hypothesized that as long as homeland–host-country relations remain friendly, usually a reasonable modus vivendi among diasporas, homelands, and host countries can be maintained for relatively
long periods. This is true regardless of apprehension about homelands'
manipulation of their diasporas, which can lead to diaspora insurgent

activities in the host countries and illegal transfers of resources to the homelands. We need to examine the conditions under which those relationships become shattered, for a closer examination of homelands' behavior in this context may show that they tend to develop a cynical attitude toward their diasporas. Hence the issue may be one of the homelands' order of priorities. Thus the relevant questions are these: Do homeland governments consider taking actions on behalf of their diasporas only after their own interests are secured? To what extent do homeland governments try to exploit their diasporas by putting forward demands for clandestine activities that may affect the security of their diasporas' host countries? Are homelands ready to engage in open international confrontation on behalf of these diasporas? When diasporas have attempted to drag their homeland governmens into situations in which the diasporas have needed protection, have the homelands answered the call? And finally, have homelands tried to defuse situations that have threatened to escalate into serious conflict with host countries?

Who Abuses Diasporas, and Why

The last, but not least, set of fundamental questions relates to diasporas' impertinence. Here is the main question: Are diasporas indeed as subversive as they are portrayed by racists, ultranationalists, and foreigner-bashers in host countries such as Germany, France, and the United States, and even Sweden, Norway, and Denmark, which have been regarded as quite tolerant toward foreigners and migrants? The precarious existence of diasporas and the problematic patterns of loyalty that they develop seem to be potential and actual sources of friction and tension with host societies, homelands, and other international actors. Therefore, we need to examine whether or not those tensions are contributing to host societies' negative perceptions of diasporas and consequently to hostile attitudes toward these entities. And there are further questions concerning the widely held view that the clashes between diasporas and host societies are largely related to economic issues. Others would contend that the conflicts involving diasporas result primarily from deep ethnic sentiments concerning the competing identities of host societies and diasporas.

It is further hypothesized that in contradistinction to the positions of nationalist, rightist, and racist segments in host societies – segments motivated by xenophobia toward foreigners who allegedly "pollute" the host society – recently more Western host governments have been trying to minimize friction with established and incipient diasporas. To what extent, under such circumstances, are the commitments of diasporas to their respective homelands the major, root causes for the negative perceptions that breed confrontations?

Another issue to be addressed in this context involves those situations in which leaders of host countries take advantage of disputes between diasporas and their homelands and fan their discontents, sometimes even inciting diasporans to support and participate in violent operations directed against homeland governments. Such intrigues, which are feasible because diasporas have their own interests, inclinations, and agendas that do not always dovetail with those of the homeland, not only can fuel homeland–diaspora conflicts but also can trigger homeland–host-country confrontations. And we must further examine not only those cases in which diasporas in host countries generate tension and clashes but also those cases in which homelands are the instigators of disputes and conflicts with their diasporas. Because the numbers of diasporas and their members have increased of late, and their self-confidence and desire for autonomy have grown so rapidly, there are no easy ways to prevent such conflicts with their homelands. The available literature offers no clear suggestions as to how these conflicts can be prevented, nor any reliable prescriptions for managing them when they do occur. Thus the situation may be that, like most other deeply rooted social conflicts, such diaspora–homeland and diaspora–host-society confrontations may be unavoidable. Differently put, the question is to what extent these are not dysfunctional conflicts, but rather constitute an inherent part of contemporary domestic and international politics.

The ultimate question is whether, because of the difficult circumstances of their existence and by their nature, diasporas are aggressive and dangerous or whether essentially they are defensive, in which case it would be unjust to regard them as inherently harmful to their host countries. Considering Armstrong's observations about the functions that "mobilized diasporas" performed in the Hapsburg, Russian, and Ottoman empires (Armstrong 1976), and in view of their trans-state networks and connections, it is worth exploring the possibility that diasporas may serve as effective mediators between various states and regional organizations.

The statement of the problems and the preliminary discussion of the numerous issues pertaining to historical and newer ethno-national diasporas that have been presented in the Introduction and in this chapter show that diasporism is a very complex and still a highly puzzling phenomenon. In this chapter, a long, probably too long, list of definitional, theoretical, analytical, descriptive, and comparative issues, questions, and hypotheses has been presented. These matters compose the rich menu that will be addressed in the rest of this volume in an attempt to unravel the complexities of the existence of large groups of people who try to be at home abroad.

Diasporism and Diasporas in History

The Roots of Diasporism

Laypeople and experts, especially those adhering to the instrumentalist and constructionist approaches to ethnic origins, consider the advent of institutionalized and organized ethno-national diasporas to be a modern or even recent phenomenon. Thus these observers hold the view that the attributes that characterize the current diaspora phenomenon and specific diasporas can be traced back only to the middle of the nineteenth century. This is only partly true. To an extent, the development of certain ethno-national diasporas, such as the Italian and German diasporas, was decisively accelerated by the failure of the national revolutions in Europe, which caused disillusioned revolutionaries and other disgruntled persons to seek refuge in more liberal host countries. It is similarly held that additional European diasporas, such the Polish, Irish, and Russian, arose out of the subsequent worsening political and economic situations in their homelands. It has also been argued that there have been other, no less significant factors contributing to migration, to permanent settlement in host countries, and consequently to diasporas' formation since the middle of the nineteenth century: the demands for functionaries and workers in the older European empires, particularly those of Britain and Holland, and in the newer empires, such as the French and Belgian; the rapid processes of industrialization, especially in the United States; and the accelerated development of land and maritime transportation that has facilitated inter-state migration.

It is certainly true that the past 150 years or so have seen a marked increase in the entire diaspora phenomenon, including the number, size, and range of activities of various diasporas. Those waves of migrants and their early experiences in their host countries since the middle of the nineteenth century have been relatively well recorded both in official documents and in various forms of art – literature and quality journalism, paintings, photography, and cinematography. Consequently, relatively detailed accounts of the emergence of the newer diasporas are available. Thus, for example, from such records it is known that upon leaving their homelands, the migrants themselves, their families, and most of the sending societies were aware that because of the more attractive economic and political conditions in host countries, on the one hand, and because of the difficulties of transportation, on the other, any return by such migrants would be difficult, if not impossible. Moreover, most migrants and their families were aware that because of the prevailing political and economic conditions in their homelands, they would not be welcomed back. Despite the hostile new environments prevailing in many host countries, most migrants were determined to settle there permanently. Despite the difficulties that they encountered, many of those newcomers were inclined to assimilate or fully integrate into the receiving societies, and only few were inclined to organize in order to maintain their ethno-national identity and interests. Partly because of the availability of detailed descriptions of the emergence of these newer diasporas, partly because of the paucity of detailed accounts of the emergence of older diasporas, and partly because of the predominant tendency to regard nationalism as a modern phenomenon, observers have been inclined to regard the emergence of ethno-national diasporas as basically a modern phenomenon.

Yet, viewed from a much longer range and broader historical perspective, ethnic diasporism is certainly not a modern phenomenon. In fact, organized diasporas existed in antiquity, and additional diasporas arose during the Middle Ages. Moreover, though it is true that many historical diasporas died out, some have survived and are still alive and active today.

Although it is true that only scant concrete archeological evidence is available to substantiate this view about the earliest origins of ethnic diasporism, nevertheless it is clear that at a very early stage of development, human beings acquired a sense of belonging to the same "ethnie" (Smith 1986, pp. 47–68). When males began to look for mates outside their nuclear ethnic families, or work outside their homelands, and therefore when individuals and small groups began to migrate from their birthplaces (not merely demographically expanding to adjacent territories) and later permanently settled elsewhere, but continued to maintain contacts with their kinfolk still residing in their former territories, the first ethnic diasporas were formed.

This view of the earliest prehistorical origins of diasporas and thus also of the diaspora phenomenon is supported by recent ethnographic and genetic studies of the "great migrations" in ancient history. According to this approach, the term "migration" has more than one meaning. On the one hand, the term describes recurrent movements of people from one territory to another and back. On the other hand, it means expansion of groups of human beings to distant territories. The latter form of migration results in the creation of diasporas. Essentially, that was, and still is, a centrifugal process stimulated by human curiosity and urges, by demographic growth of ethnies (Cavalli-Sforza and Cavalli-Sforza 1995, p. 157), and by worsening social, economic, and political conditions in the territories of origin of such groups.

It is now widely accepted that the first "humans," who were gatherers and hunters, inhabited certain regions in eastern Africa and the Middle East. From those regions the hunter-gatherers spread out to other parts of the world, carrying with them an ability to communicate with each other, as well as common habits and certain codes of behavior. In other words, basically the dispersal of human beings – rather than of culture and cultural artifacts, including religions – was caused by an inadequate food supply, which posed grave difficulties for the hunter-gatherer economies, and by the need to find mates not belonging to the same nuclear families and small ethnic groups. That kind of human expansion did not stop after the hunter-gatherers began to live in permanent settlements. Eventually, hunter-gatherers who had settled down might again migrate from the territories they occupied and in which they and their kin had been permanently dwelling, and gradually they would begin to regard such territories as "home" and "homeland." Already at a very early stage of human development, the reality of an actual territorial homeland and the subjective and abstract concepts derived from life in such a domain were essential elements accompanying migration and diaspora formation. In fact, this remains a quintessential element of the ethnic diaspora phenomenon. It still influences the patterns of diasporas' development and collective behavior.

The domestication of animals – the horse in Asia and the camel in Arabia – and the invention of the wheel and the sail further prompted humans to migrate away from their birthplaces. Those developments also facilitated communication with those who remained in the homeland.

Combined together, the search for mates, economic needs, social rivalries and tensions, curiosity, and the technical capability necessary to reach foreign lands created recurrent waves of migrants and their eventual permanent settlement in new territories. Such waves of migrants led to defensive and offensive wars over what the indigenous populations regarded as their homelands. The purpose of the offensive wars was the occupation of new lands. The purpose of the defensive wars was to resist invasions by "others" who did not "belong." Such conflicts and wars were significant factors in the creation, persistence, and also dissolution of ethnic groups, including the earliest diasporas (Smith 1986, pp. 37–8, 86–7, 114–19). For varying emotional, cultural, security, and economic reasons, some of those migrants maintained continuous ties with their relatives who remained in their lands of origin. Such ties were based both on emotional memories of kin and home and on practical interests. Their maintenance was possible because of shared languages, and they were facilitated by gradual improvements in the available means of transportation and communication (Cavalli-Sforza and Cavalli-Sforza 1995, pp. 159–63).

In prehistoric and ancient times, such diasporas originated in "vertical-demotic ethnies." Such social and political ethnic formations were created on the basis of bonds emerging from the bottom upward, rather than from top to bottom. Those "natural" bonds entailed the delineation of group boundaries, which were protected by prohibition of religious syncretism, of cultural assimilation, and of intermarriage. Eventually, these became the parameters within which loose familial and tribal coalitions were formed and maintained. Such groups were united for battle and conquest of territories outside their homeland, on the one hand, and for defense of the homeland, on the other. In the wake of such conquests, or as a result of their acceptance by an indigenous population, such groups either coexisted with the dominant local ethnic groups or established their autonomous enclaves (Smith 1986, pp. 76, 83, 86–7). By dint of the prevailing circumstances, those groups became involved in the politics of their host countries.

In antiquity, the diaspora phenomenon was not connected solely to forced or voluntary migration out of rural areas and eventual settlement of migrants in similar surroundings. The emergence of ancient fortified settlements and villages, walled cities, and small city-states did not preclude emigration and the establishment of concentrated ethnic diasporas in foreign territories. The feeling that those were permanent settlements that migrants could return to, and the sense that such settlements and cities could provide a measure of security for the families left behind, simplified the migration decision for some of their dwellers. Such feelings also fostered their permanent settlement in foreign rural territories and urban centers, their survival there, and their contacts with relatives remaining in the homelands. Cities that served as significant commercial centers attracted nomads, migrating traders, and artisans. Some of those migrants permanently settled in the host cities and formed differentiated groups, residing in ghetto-like enclaves. In another context, mainly for economic reasons, militarily strong and economically prosperous city-states that experienced significant population growth were inclined to expand, and their citizens created colonies in both nearby and more distant territories. Later, such colonies constituted the nuclei for ancient diasporas – one of the best known, but certainly not the only one, in ancient times was the Greek diaspora. The Nabateans, whose center was in Petra (now in Jordan), and the Phoenicians, whose center was on the shores of the eastern Mediterranean (now Lebanon), were other examples of that pattern for the creation of diasporas (Avi-Yonah 1981).

Because of the proliferation of myths and legends about the historical origins of diasporism and diasporas, and because of the lack of solid archeological and other historical evidence about the earliest processes of diasporas' formation and development, rather than continuing with presentation of a general abstract analysis buttressed by random examples, the analysis here will focus on two cases. The discussion of these cases is based on long-standing traditions, on some archeological evidence, and on a variety of written records. This analysis should shed light on the formation and growth of historical diasporas, and thus on the development of the diaspora phenomenon during antiquity.

The Jewish, Greek, and Other Diasporas in Ancient Times

When one delves into the legends and myths, the sparse written records that have survived, and the more recent archeological and genetic findings related to the development of coherent ethnic groups in their homeland and their eventual diasporization, probably the most striking case is that of the ancient Hebrews/Israelites/Jews. Because of their endurance and their strong emotional attachment to their ancient homeland, which ensured the survival of such records documenting their long and turbulent history, it is not surprising that the Jews have been considered a classical or archetypal mobilized diaspora (Armstrong 1976).

Yet by no means were the Jews unique in their development during ancient times and in later eras – first as an ethnic entity (an *ethnie*), then as a "people" when their voluntary and forced migrations made them a "state-linked diaspora," still later as a "stateless diaspora" after the destruction of their ancient kingdom, and ultimately as a "state-linked diaspora" following the establishment of the state of Israel in the twentieth century. That pattern, rather than any claim that the Jewish diaspora was, and still is, the normative diaspora or the quintessential model for the behavior of all diasporas, is the sole rationale for focusing on this diaspora. (For similar views on the adequacy of this case as a paradigm for the emergence of a nation and its diaspora, see Clifford 1994, p. 303, Boyarin 1995, p. 5, and Cohen 1997, pp. 21–5.)

Against the background of these introductory remarks it should be noted that an intense debate has been raging between two schools regarding the ancient history of the Jews and particularly concerning the earliest roots of the Jewish collective identity that served as the basis for the long endurance of the Jewish diaspora. One school maintains that the parts of the Old Testament dealing with the earliest origins of the Jews are collections of myths and legends, and that solid archeological evidence to support the Bible's stories can be found only beginning with the times of the prophets and the Babylonian exile. The second school contends that there is enough archeological evidence to corroborate the Bible's description of the dawn of the Jewish nation in Mesopotamia, and that therefore those biblical texts contain more than a germ of historical truth (Ben Sasson 1969, pp. xvi–xvii; Johnson 1988, p. 7). In other words, this latter view attributes greater credence to the historical portions of the Old Testament and other related records that were produced and preserved by the Jews (Hyatt 1964; Malamat 1969, pp. 33–7; Levine and Mazar 2001).

The purpose of the discussion that follows is neither to solve this academic controversy nor to take sides with either school. The chief goal here is to illustrate the coalescence of an ethnic national identity and its development, including the emergence and persistence of a diaspora. Only for this purpose is the analysis here based on the narrative presented in the Old Testament. The approach to these issues proposed by the primordialist and psychological-symbolic schools fits the narrative of the Old Testament.

Accordingly, the origins of the ancient Hebrews were in western Mesopotamia, and there began their history. They were one of the western Semitic tribes that roamed that part of the Middle East during the Middle Bronze Age, that is, the first half of the second millennium B.C. During that period, those tribes led a nomadic life, and their caravans wandered through what are now Syria and Jordan, all the way to the eastern shores of the Mediterranean and beyond. Eventually, some of those tribes settled down and established villages and small cities in that part of the world (Malamat 1969, pp. 40–5). Here, however, it should be noted that some scholars argue that the origins of the Jews were not in Mesopotamia but rather in what is now Jordan. Other scholars maintain that the origins of the Jews were in the coastal plain of Palestine. For the reasons explained earlier, the narrative here will follow the first approach (Levine and Mazar 2001). It should cautiously be added here that recent genetic studies have shown that indeed the origins of the Jews can be traced back to Mesopotamia.

In line with the then-prevailing patterns of migration and expansion, and because of unfavorable economic and political circumstances, the early Hebrews embarked on voluntary migration out of Ur, which was one of the oldest Mesopotamian cities. Led by the tribes' elders – patriarchs like Abraham and Lot – they were heading toward the eastern littoral of the Mediterranean. Again, scholars who subscribe to the psychological-symbolic approach view legendary figures like Abraham, Lot, Isaac, and Jacob as the ancestors and founding fathers of the ethnic entity to which the origins of the Jewish people should be traced. (For more on this approach to the origins of ethnic diasporas, see Connor 1986; for specific comments about the ethnic nature of the Hebrews, see Malamat 1969, p. 44.)

Because of the existing geographical and geopolitical conditions, those tribes' migration out of Mesopotamia was a protracted voyage through the western regions of the Fertile Crescent and then south toward Canaan. According to the biblical narrative and the available historical evidence, on their way from Mesopotamia to the Mediterranean the Hebrews had to pass through territories that were densely populated by a mosaic of other Semitic tribes and tribal coalitions. Some of those tribes were sedentary, and others were still nomadic. There is archeological evidence showing that small cities and kingdoms also existed in those regions during the purported period of the initial arrival of the Hebrews in Canaan.

In any event, because the patriarchs regarded Canaan as a good place for permanent settlement, the Hebrews fought and bought their way into that part of the Middle East, cajoling local rulers to create enough space for their permanent settlement there. Because of their strong links to their families in Mesopotamia, and because of their new neighbors' hostility, initially the Hebrews maintained close contacts with their families and kin back in Ur. It appears as if, much like other migrants during that period, initially the Hebrews intended merely to form a Mesopotamian diaspora in the new land. Indeed, according to the Old Testament, the patriarchs, Abraham, Isaac, and Jacob, their servants, messengers, and other members of the Hebrew tribes traveled quite regularly to and from Mesopotamia, visiting relatives there, trading with Mesopotamia, and taking refuge there when danger loomed in Canaan. Some even went back to marry and raise children in their old country of origin. However, it was said that the desire to return to their new land, Canaan, was sufficiently strong that after short or sometimes long sojourns in Mesopotamia these Hebrews were drawn back. Thus gradually the Hebrews came to perceive Canaan as their sole homeland. Later, during their recurrent visits in Mesopotamia, or when times of famine in Canaan compelled them to migrate to look for food, they continued to feel a strong urge to return to their new homeland. At the very least they maintained connections with their kinfolk there.

Eventually the Hebrews' attachment to Canaan became so deeply rooted that they gradually began to sever their ties with Mesopotamia. That marked the point in their history of their permanent psychological acceptance of Canaan as home, which they renamed Eretz Israel ("the land of Israel"). That significant phase in their history had ethnic and religious as well as symbolic and practical meanings. It was fundamental to the formation of the "national" unit and to their persistent attachment to that territory. Since then, the bond to Eretz Israel has been one of the most essential, but not necessarily essentialist, elements in the development of their ethno-national identity. Those elements were compounded by a strong sense of superiority vis-à-vis their neighbors, that is, of being a "chosen people." Those elements of their identity enhanced their ability to survive within the basically hostile Middle Eastern ethnic and religious mosaic (Smith 1999; Grosby 1999).

Following their conquest and acquisition of parts of Canaan, the Hebrew/Israelite patriarchs made concerted efforts to shape or, if one wishes, to construct an exclusive identity, and through it to mold the various families that had constituted their original tribal coalition into a more cohesive entity. The Old Testament calls that formation a "people," or a "nation" (*Leom,* or *Am,* or *Umah,* in Hebrew). Part of that effort was dedicated to shaping the religious element in their collective identity. However, internal unity, solidarity, and cohesiveness were not easily attained. Like other ancient as well as modern nations and ethnic groups, it took the Hebrews a long time to forge a degree of communal unity. Yet even when a degree of cohesion was achieved, that ethnic group continued to face internal familial, clannish, and tribal divisions that caused disharmony, leading to continual tensions and internal strife. Despite their rivalries and confrontations, gradually the Hebrews developed a sense of solidarity that was based on their common tribal origin, historical memories, and shared attachment to the land they had conquered and acquired. In their emerging myths, which became significant elements in the collective national memory and later were included in the Bible, the initial conquest and settlement in Eretz Israel were kept closely linked to the nation's founding fathers: Abraham, Isaac, and Jacob. The strong attachment to the new homeland was extremely important, because that was the locus of both the earliest processes of nation building and the gradual development of the Jewish monotheistic creed and formal religion. It is important to remember that the peculiar Jewish religion developed gradually only after the permanent settlement in Canaan and as part of the nation-building process that necessitated setting clear cultural boundaries between themselves and their neighbors.

Eventually the national and religious elements became inextricably intertwined and suffused. In later centuries that complex served as one of the solid foundation pillars for the Jews' development as an exclusionary entity, based on strong connections to the homeland and on a primordial belief in being a chosen people who owned a promised land (Grosby 1999, p. 375; Ben Sasson 1969, pp. xvii–xviii).

Most observers regard the Israelites' exile in Babylon in the wake of the destruction of King Solomon's First Temple as the actual beginning of the historical Jewish diaspora (Cohen 1997, pp. 1–4). According to the biblical narrative, however, the Israelites experienced diasporic life out of their newly acquired homeland during much earlier periods. Thus, during the very early stages of their development as an ethnie, and later as an emerging ethnic nation, the Israelites voluntarily migrated from Canaan/Eretz Israel to various neighboring territories. As the Old Testament tells it, because of economic difficulties in Canaan, especially following protracted droughts that led to famine, and, no less important, because of political infighting concerning control over the emerging nation and its various resources, some of the patriarchs and their descendants and followers decided or were compelled to migrate to the northern and southern regions of the Near East. Many migrated to the fertile lands of Egypt.

Apparently, during the period of recurrent migrations from Eretz Israel to Egypt – probably the first quarter of the second millennium B.C. – the Egyptian kings tolerated and even welcomed the Semitic migrants, as well as other ethnic migrants. The Egyptian kings of that period, and later the Hyksos kings, who ruled Egypt from 1720 to 1570 B.C., promoted some of those migrants to senior positions in their household administrations and in the state bureaucracy. That, of course, fits the famous biblical account of the fate and life of Joseph.

Relevant to the analysis of early diasporism is the fact that the Egyptian and Hyksos kings had good reasons for showing such tolerance toward those foreigners and for their acceptance as permanent diasporas in Egypt. Like other rulers in later periods, they understood that they themselves, their households, and their kingdoms could benefit from the foreigners' acumen, talents, and innovations and from their contacts around the Middle East.

That readiness of the Egyptian and other Middle Eastern rulers to allow individuals and tribes like the Israelites to settle in the territories that they controlled, to participate in agricultural and commercial activities, and to occupy senior administrative positions facilitated the relocation of some segments of the Hebrew tribes, who by then had become firmly settled in Canaan and regarded it as their cherished homeland. Hence, it was then, in Egypt and in the northern parts of the Near East, rather than in the wake of the destruction of Solomon's temple and in Babylon, that the Israelites established their first permanent diasporic entities. Members of those diasporic entities maintained contacts with their families still living in the homeland. Later, in accordance with chain-migration patterns, Israelites continually moved from Eretz Israel to Egypt and to the northern Middle East and back. Some of them settled permanently in those host countries and formed relatively closed communities. Those Israelites joined existing diasporic entities and established new ones.

Following the formation of their diaspora in ancient Egypt, and like other foreigners there, members of the Hebrew diaspora experienced marked fluctuations in their relationships with the Egyptian rulers. It is likely that during prosperous times and the more tranquil periods of their interactions with the Egyptian rulers and society, some of those diasporans assimilated into that society. Nevertheless, throughout their sojourn in Egypt, many Hebrews did not assimilate, but held tightly to their unique ethno-religious identity. Because intermarriages were relatively rare, they also retained their original genetic pool and biological connections. Preserving such ethnic "purity" was facilitated by the fact that, again like other migrants, most of them had settled in concentrated ghetto-like enclaves. Because they were not widely dispersed in Egypt, they could more easily maintain a degree of social cohesion and a sense of solidarity. Socially and politically, the Hebrews constituted a relatively well organized group. Combined together, all those attributes were essential for the Hebrews' survival in what was basically a hostile host country, as well as for maintaining regular contacts with their kin back in their homeland. Generally, the Hebrews adjusted well to that diasporic existence. Some succeeded in the service of the Egyptian rulers, and the diaspora was reasonably integrated into the Egyptian economy. Nevertheless, some Hebrews nurtured the hope of returning to their old homeland, and some, like Joseph's legendary brothers, actually returned.

During the reign of Ramses II, one of the greatest builders in Egypt's ancient history (1304–1237 B.C.), the Hebrews' economic and political situations worsened. Ramses used them as forced laborers and even as slaves in his huge construction projects. It is no wonder that the dormant urge to return to the land of Israel gained new life among the Hebrew diasporans. It is equally unsurprising that the Egyptian rulers were averse to the idea of losing those talents and connections, as well as that cheap labor force. In view of the oppressive Egyptian policies, the Hebrews had little choice but to rebel and flee from Egypt. Some historians think that their revolt and subsequent exodus occurred during the rule of Merneptah, Ramses' successor, and that it was completed by 1225 B.C. (Malamat 1969, pp. 47–8).

Like other collective return movements caused by intolerable difficulties in a host country, the Hebrews' exodus from Egypt was not an easy operation. It required the momentous decision to launch a revolt and then actually to depart, as well as dedicated leadership and determined elites who could support the senior leaders. It also required mass mobilization, organization, elaborate preparations, and exchanges with the Egyptian authorities. Furthermore, tactical skills were needed to determine the proper timing for their exit, and clever maneuvers in actually staging the move. When all those factors converged under the leadership of two legendary figures – Moses and Aaron – the Hebrews made their dramatic exodus, a very bold political and military act.

Not all the Hebrews left; after the exodus, a sizable group remained in Egypt. Some of the returnees to Eretz Israel re-migrated to other parts of the Middle East. Their move should be regarded as a voluntary "secondary migration" of members of an established diaspora. That resulted in the establishment of yet additional diasporic centers in Syria and Asia Minor, and others joined existing diasporic entities in those lands.

The Hebrews' return to Eretz Israel marked the end of the nation's prehistorical period. According to archeological findings and written materials, the ensuing development of the Hebrews should be regarded as that people's historical phase, and thus our analysis of the later development of the Jewish people and their diaspora can be based on firmer archeological and documentary grounds (Levine and Mazar 2001). After the legendary exodus from Egypt, the Hebrews gradually conquered substantial parts of Canaan, and during the reigns of David and Solomon the Hebrews established a kingdom in those territories. Because of severe ideological and religious controversies and internal political conflicts, in 928 B.C. Solomon's kingdom was split into two separate kingdoms – the northern kingdom of Israel, and the southern kingdom of Judea.

The analysis up to this point indicates that the development of the Jewish diaspora well preceded the destruction of the northern kingdom of Israel by the Assyrian kings Tiglath-Pileser III, his son Shalmaneser V, and Sargon II, which occurred in the eighth century B.C. (the actual destruction of the capital of the kingdom, Samaria, occurred in 720 B.C.). After the Assyrian conquest of the kingdom of Israel, most of the Israelite people, especially the elites, were expelled and forcefully scattered to the peripheries of the Assyrian empire (Tadmor 1969, pp. 135–8). Because the true fate of those expellees remained unknown, shrouded in mystery, there emerged a myth that still lingers on – that of the "ten lost tribes" – and that myth is largely responsible for the occasional "discovery" of what purportedly are additional Jewish diaspora communities.

The Babylonian conquest of Judea and the destruction of Solomon's temple by the Babylonian king Nebuchadnezzar, which occurred in 586 B.C., led to an additional dispersal of Jews. Unlike the Assyrians, however, the Babylonian kings were not inclined to impose total exile and mass dispersal of conquered peoples, nor were they interested in large-scale colonization of the conquered territories. That policy applied also to the Judeans. Yet as a result of the expulsion of their political and religious elites, an important Judean cultural and religious diaspora center arose in Babylon. On the other hand, sizable groups of Judeans were not expelled, nor did they migrate to foreign city-states or kingdoms. It is quite certain that in the wake of the destruction of the Judean kingdom, both older and newer Jewish diaspora communities maintained regular contacts with their people who remained in Eretz Israel.

Thus the expulsion of the Israelites by the Assyrians and that of the Judeans by the Babylonians added new groups to the already existing Jewish diaspora communities in Egypt and in the northern parts of the Middle East that had arisen as a result of voluntary migration. Hence, long after the initial beginnings of the Jewish diaspora in Egypt and Syria during earlier periods, new Jewish diaspora centers became established in various parts of the Middle East and Asia Minor, and later in the Balkans (Ages 1973).

Partly because of a shortage of skilled labor that was needed to build the expanding center of the Babylonian empire, and partly because of their moderate religious, social, and political views, throughout the sixth century B.C. the rulers of the Babylonian empire were quite tolerant toward ethnic groups that had either migrated voluntarily or been exiled to Babylon. That combination of the need for cheap labor and the tolerance shown toward various groups of foreigners attracted more of them to Babylon, where they were allowed to prosper, and that policy also applied to the Jews (Tadmor 1969, pp. 150–3). Under those circumstances, like other ethnic expellees and voluntary migrants, Jews were able to establish autonomous communities in Babylon. At first, a Jewish community was established in the capital itself, and later other communities were established in hinterland towns and villages. That internal migration within the Babylonian empire led not only to the establishment of additional Jewish centers but also to diversification of their economic occupations. According to written sources and archeological findings, Babylonian Jews engaged in agriculture, trade, crafts, moneylending, and bureaucratic functions. Eventually the Jews established what could be regarded as international diasporic networks. Those networks served a variety of functions. The religious and political elites utilized those networks to maintain regular contacts with the people back home and in other diaspora centers, to bolster the diaspora's well-being in general, and to promote its commercial and trading enterprises in particular. Thus, in addition to material resources and mundane information, those networks transferred spiritual messages to the Jews remaining in Eretz Israel and in other countries. In short, Babylon became a center of Jewish prosperity as well as cultural and religious activity (Cohen 1997, p. 4). Similar patterns of organization and behavior characterized the Jewish diaspora in the Persian empire that succeeded the Babylonian kingdom (Tadmor 1969, p. 155). It should be added that those Jewish communities were led by very active and innovative religious and political elites. Indeed, the elites of the Jewish diaspora during the Babylonian and Persian empires succeeded in further crystallizing national cultural and religious sentiments, beliefs, and customs. They were able to establish communal religious and political organizations and to create elaborate communication networks, through which they kept in regular, meaningful contact with their people who lived in the homeland and in other parts of the Middle East and Asia Minor.

The Babylonian Jews created what can be called an "autonomous trans-state diasporic political system," in which the diaspora rather than the devastated homeland became the main national center and played the crucial role in the nation's perseverance (Tadmor 1969, pp. 156–7). In fact, the center did not shift back to the homeland even when the regional political situation changed as a result of the ascendance of the Persian empire and its new policy toward the dispersed Jews.

The Persians, under the rule of kings like Cyrus the Great, showed marked sympathy toward the Jews. Around 520 B.C., they permitted and even encouraged the Jews' second large-scale return to the Holy Land (the first having been the legendary exodus from Egypt). Eventually the Persians sanctioned the reestablishment of a Jewish autonomous entity, and later a kingdom as well as a religious center in and around Jerusalem. Subsequently the Jews reinstated their own political and religious institutions in Eretz Israel and reinvigorated an economy that had been destroyed by wars and occupation. No less important, the Jews built the Second Temple in Jerusalem. As we shall see, that would become something of a recurring pattern – a stateless diaspora rebuilding its homeland and becoming a state-linked diaspora.

During that same period, the Jewish diaspora continued to prosper in various countries outside Palestine (Johnson 1988, pp. 84–7). In sum, autonomous Jewish centers existed in Jerusalem and in a number of large cities in other countries, and the network that connected those centers allowed intensive exchanges of goods and information between the various parts of the nation.

Around 330 B.C., Alexander the Great conquered the Middle East, including Palestine. Alexander's brilliant battles and impressive conquests were followed by Greek occupation of Palestine and other territories where Jews had established diaspora centers, and that marked a turning point in Jewish history. Consequently, the Jews in Palestine and in the diaspora centers in Egypt (especially in Alexandria), Mesopotamia, and Asia Minor came under Greek political and cultural domination. On the one hand, the establishment of the Greek Empire, which controlled vast territories, facilitated communications among the various dispersed Jewish communities, but on the other hand, it also meant that the homeland had to compete more vigorously with the various diaspora centers. Simultaneously, Jewry and Judaism had to compete with the Greeks and their culture. Moreover, because there were various other ethno-national diasporas in the Hellenic world, the Jews also had to compete with the members of those diasporas. Probably the most notable of those diasporas was that of the Greeks themselves.

The initial dispersal of Greeks and the formation of diasporic entities occurred over a period of two centuries, between 800 and 600 B.C., that is, long before the time of Alexander the Great. Those diasporic entities arose mainly as a result of voluntary migration motivated by overpopulation and economic hardships in various city-states in Greece: It was a planned expansion to adjacent lands and more remote territories and their eventual colonization. Though, as noted in Chapter 1, the Greek term "diaspora" had been mentioned by Thucydides (Chaliand and Rageau 1995, p. xiii), in antiquity the Greeks themselves did not refer to their dispersal as a "diaspora" (it seems that the term was first self-applied by the dispersed Greeks in the seventeenth century, and in the context of the Hapsburg Empire). In any case, the Greek *apoieka* (namely, those who voluntarily left the homeland as colonizers and permanently resided in territories far from Greece) developed in concentric circles. The most natural zones for that expansion were, first, the Aegean islands, then Asia Minor, the eastern shores of the Mediterranean, and eventually North Africa and the western shores of the Mediterranean (Lloyd-Jones 1965; Graham 1983). In view of its voluntary nature, its strong ties with the homeland, and the existence of a common culture, it was indeed a diaspora. Moreover, in many ways the ancient Greek communities resembled the Jewish entities that had been established in the same and other territories. Yet, unlike many Jews, who regarded themselves as dwelling in permanent exile, the ancient Greeks attached no negative connotations to their dispersal. Rather, the *apoieka* was regarded as a legitimate and beneficial way to solve the economic problems of poorer citizens, to further enrich the wealthy and powerful, and consequently to strengthen the city-states back in the homeland. Later, another purpose of diasporization was to expand the political and defensive borders of the homeland, and ultimately to spread its culture. In that context, the Hellenic culture, rather than religious sentiment, served as the basis for the links between the diaspora and the homeland, as well as those among the various Greek colonies and settlements (Finley 1986). In comparison with the Jewish diaspora communities, the Greek colonies were better organized and maintained closer contacts with the homeland. In both cases, however, the ethnic entities nurtured a strong sense of superiority vis-à-vis their neighbors, and that sense of being the "chosen people" was highly functional in its contribution to their durability (Smith 1992).

Eventually the Greek diaspora centers in the Middle East, in the Mediterranean basin, and in other regions, which had proliferated and survived over several centuries, were integrated into the vast Greek Empire that had been established by Alexander the Great. However, during the reigns of his less successful heirs, the links between those Greek communities and the homeland deteriorated. While the Greek Empire was further dwindling, those colonies eventually became the bases for the Eastern Orthodox churches that would dominate parts of the Balkans and Asia Minor. What is relevant here is the fact that those churches contributed to the survival of the Greek diaspora communities in those regions.

This brief analysis of the main developmental patterns of the Jewish and Greek diasporas in antiquity, as well as some of their characteristics, illustrates an important point. It is widely believed that, except in cases of forced migration (i.e., exile), ethnic migrants have always left their homelands and established diasporic entities mainly for economic reasons. Actually, however, the details of the emergence, flowering, and deterioration of the Jewish and Greek diasporas show that they were prompted as much by domestic, regional, and international political processes as by economic concerns. Thus the historical backgrounds and developmental patterns of those diasporas were major factors contributing to their social, political, and economic organization and behavior.

Again, this somewhat detailed analysis of the Jewish and Greek cases is not intended to suggest that they should be regarded as the main diasporic paradigms. Equal attention must be given to other diasporas that were established in antiquity and still exist, such as the Armenian diaspora. And it must be remembered that although those entities had many similar characteristics, over time they took on their own divergent structural and behavioral features. Hence it would be inaccurate and inadequate to stereotype and categorize those and other diasporas according to static sociological/functional criteria so as to regard them as "labor," "middleman," "trade," or "imperial" diasporas (Cohen 1997). A different categorization will be suggested in Chapter 3.

In any case, all these diasporic entities were actively involved in contemporaneous politics in their homelands and host countries and were affected by political developments occurring there. Therefore, they were organized accordingly: They were led by established hierarchical elites, they displayed regimented features, and they developed a range of communal organizations, some of which were charged with maintaining contacts with their homelands.

Various ancient diasporas disappeared as a result of physical annihilation or as a result of voluntary or imposed gradual assimilation. Contributing to their downfall were protracted periods of merciless wars, invasions by barbarian tribes, and the emergence of hostile regimes and rulers and consequent political and economic difficulties. All those factors prompted secondary and tertiary migrations and sapped the resilience of those diasporas. Thus the Assyrian, Philistine, Phoenician, Akkadian, Elamite, Kassite, and other ethnic diasporas totally vanished. Nevertheless, there is evidence that all of those entities emerged and functioned according to the general diasporic patterns that, broadly speaking, were maintained in the Middle Ages and have been carried over to the modern period.

The Characteristics of Historical (and Modern) Diasporism

On the basis of our brief illustrative analyses of the establishment and development of the Jewish and Greek diasporas in antiquity, and on the basis of what is known about other diasporas that did not survive, it is now possible to outline the processes that led to the creation and development of most of the diasporas that were established in antiquity, as well as their principal features and their main patterns of organization and collective behavior.

As long as individuals and nuclear families were living a nomadic life and had no prolonged attachment to any particular tract of land, any practices having to do with migration from a certain territorial base, but keeping in contact with those who remained behind, were, of course, nonexistent. Hence, the first dispersions of somewhat more cohesive nomadic ethnic groups, which should be regarded as prototypes for the later, fully fledged diasporas, could occur only after the earliest differentiated ethnies and ethnic communities had been established and had acquired some durable features.

That observation is significant for understanding the entire diaspora phenomenon. It means that although throughout history some diasporas became established and lingered on without ever explicitly elaborating and expressing an ethnic identity, that element had to be present for such entities to become well developed and to flourish. That was especially important in view of the tribulations usually brought on by their inherently hostile environments. Although each historical diaspora (e.g., the Jewish, Greek, and Armenian) had its unique characteristics, they all shared certain common features. Moreover, those entities were always influenced by the main tides that swept over the members of the same ethnic groups who did not migrate but stayed put in the homeland.

One of the main characteristics of the more coherent ethnies that appeared during the late Neolithic period (a feature particularly relevant to the roots of the enduring diaspora phenomenon) was their recurrent involvement in wars and conflicts aimed at gaining control over territory. Whenever such groups succeeded in conquering or acquiring sufficient land, and in preventing foreigners from settling in their acquired territories, they could begin to nurture notions of a homeland. In addition to a shared language and a sense of group solidarity, which were elements essential for sustaining their differentiated existence, an exclusionary outlook and rejection of "strangers" had the effect that, over time, some of those groups began to take on distinguishing physical characteristics. Moreover, the nuclear and extended families that permanently settled down in what would become their homelands developed regular agrarian rites, nurtured peculiar local folkloristic habits and traditions, and eventually created animist religious beliefs and patterns of worshiping. The particular environmental conditions in the territories that such families, rural communities, and tribal coalitions occupied and permanently settled, cultivated, and defended further influenced their special physical characteristics, as well as their history, culture, and behavior patterns – the things regarded as the primordial ethnic traits (Geertz 1963; Handelman 1977; Smith 1981, 1986). Those attributes have always been important in the establishment and preservation of such diasporas.

Migrations that would result in relatively coherent social formations in foreign lands, and eventually in the establishment of organized entities, could take place only after the emergence of some shared features of an identity and the crystallization of notions about "home" and "homeland." The corollary of that observation is that some rather large ethnic groupings that coalesced during the nomadic stage of their development and then expanded to adjacent territories and settled in such territories can hardly be regarded as diasporas. That was the case in antiquity, and it still is, and it is the reason why ethnic groups such as the Tutsi, Hutu, Ibo, Yoruba, and North American Indians are not included among the diasporas discussed in this book. Only when members of such groups migrate to and settle in territories that are not immediately adjacent to their original homelands do they form incipient diasporas that can develop into established diasporas. The same applies to large tribes that "naturally" expanded over large territories that later were divided into separate states, in most cases by imperial or colonial powers. On the other hand, ethnic groups that experienced secondary or tertiary migration from one host country to another and still maintained contacts with their relatives at home are included in this category.

The myths and legends about their ancestors, the inclination to create and preserve cohesive entities, and the determination to maintain a common identity were the primary background factors that would hold such groups together after leaving their homes and migrating to distant territories. Taking into account the necessity to migrate because of chronic or temporary shortages of food and other resources, and because of internal social and political conflicts, it is not surprising that such population movements recurred and that diasporas have continually emerged since earliest times. It should be emphasized, however, that migrations occurred not only because of economic and political difficulties in the territories of origin but also because of an inherent curiosity of human beings that drove, and still drives, individuals and groups to wander and explore distant places.

In antiquity, and later during the Middle Ages, such voluntary migrations and consequent settlements in host countries were feasible primarily because of the inherent weakness of rulers and their inability to maintain effective control over the borders of their realms. During those times, most geographical borders were poorly demarcated and porous, and even at the height of the mighty Egyptian, Assyrian, Babylonian, Greek, and Roman empires their rulers could not effectively prevent adventurous groups of both free persons and slaves from migrating elsewhere, nor were they able to prevent foreign migrants from invading their peripheral territories and settling there. Such factors facilitated the establishment of some of the earliest diasporas.

Among the significant factors that led to the emergence of the relatively more cohesive ethnic diasporas, such as memories of their homelands and sentiments concerning their families and the communities that they left behind, perhaps most influential was the fact that ethnic identities were becoming more clearly defined and solidified. Initially those identities were shaped in their homelands and then adapted to the dispersed groups' needs in view of the prevailing conditions in their host countries. The ethnic identity of a diaspora was not a given. It had to be adapted in reaction to changing conditions in the cultural, social, political, and economic arenas. Hence, diasporas sometimes experienced processes of hybridization (Werbner 1997). Yet their identities were based on blood ties, similar physical characteristics, language, historical memories, shared interests, and cultural tenets, including religious beliefs and rituals, and all of those were based on strong attachments to a territory conceived of as the original homeland. Those homelands were, and still are, far more than just territories owned by an ethnic group or by a nation. Territories identified as "homelands" were accorded emotional, almost reverential, importance (Connor 1986, p. 16). Such sentiments and attributions have always been necessary for turning a group of migrants into a more cohesive diaspora whose members follow similar patterns of organization and behavior.

Prevailing notions about the historical roots of ethnic diasporas still tend to relate them to expulsion and exile, rather than to acknowledge that migration from a territory of origin was frequently caused by individuals' and groups' adventurous inclinations and by impulses to find greener pastures. That, of course, does not mean that there were no instances in which conquerors and stronger opponents did expel ethnic groups that eventually became diasporas.

The set of reasons for voluntary migration has been termed the "pull" factor. Broadly speaking, that means that when appealing political or economic conditions prevail in a potential host territory, that will attract migrants. The set of reasons for forced migration out of a homeland or a host country has been termed the "push" factor, basically meaning that migrants are driven out of their homeland or host country, usually by a superior force, or by harsh social, political, and economic circumstances. Already in antiquity diasporization had occurred from both types of causes. Most significant among the push factors were internal social, political, and religious rivalries and conflicts. Other push factors were generated by difficult economic situations in the homeland, frequently caused by severe drought and famine. On the other side, pull factors included easy access, weak regimes, and appealing political and economic conditions in host countries, as well as previous successful settlement of kinfolk in those countries that would facilitate chain-migration.

As will be argued in the following pages, all those factors still serve as important motivations and pressures for individual and group migrations that result in the establishment of diasporas.

As the cases of the ancient Jews and Greeks have shown, settling in a new host country and maintaining an ethnic identity (in certain cases buttressed by religion and by shared cultural attributes and ongoing contacts with the homeland) were not always sufficient to ensure the survival and prosperity of migrants and settlers. To defend themselves against inhospitable forces in almost all host territories, to maintain their essential unique characteristics, to ensure continuity, and to keep regular contacts with their homelands, such migrants had to organize. The Jewish and Greek diasporas are good examples of success in meeting those needs and developing elaborate hierarchical organizations. Again, this is still a major prerequisite for successful diasporic existence.

The relative abilities of such ethnic groups to maintain an ethnic identity, to organize, and to stay in contact with their homelands were not predetermined by the root causes of their migration. That is, success did not depend on whether they were voluntary or forced migrants. The fate of migrants after arriving in a host country – that is, whether they disappeared, assimilated, or retained their identity and persisted as diasporas – would depend largely on their own choices – either to blend in or take a determined stand to resist assimilation. Moreover, whether migrations had been caused by push or pull factors, the patterns of organization and political behavior for a diaspora would emerge only after the migrants' permanent settlement in host countries. These will be recurrent themes in our analysis of the behavior of twentieth-century diasporas and emerging diasporas.

Some migrants in antiquity, such as the Phoenicians and Greeks, who originally left their homelands because of orders or encouragements from the rulers of their city-states or small kingdoms, resettled in foreign territories and formed cohesive ethnic communities that maintained close contact with the homeland. In those circumstances, the migrants encountered fewer difficulties in maintaining their identity. As has been noted, some of those settlements were in fact colonies. Their establishment had been initiated and financed and also continuously supported by the homelands. In such cases, migration and the founding of diaspora communities were undertaken as a respectable mission by willing participants. Those colonists' self-perception certainly was not one of exile.

Those warriors, colonizers, and traders who conquered new territories were imbued with a sense of superiority vis-à-vis the indigenous "barbaric" peoples. That was partly a defensive tactic and partly an offensive mechanism, both facets intended to ensure their survival and persistence in hostile environments. The contempt they felt toward foreign indigenous populations increased each time the latter were defeated. In the eyes of those migrants/colonizers, the conquest of foreign territories was further proof of their own superiority and that of their ethnic group. Whenever such colonizers had decided to pursue an exclusionary strategy, contact with the indigenous population usually would be kept to a minimum, and contacts with the homeland would be diligently maintained. Yet some cultural, social, political, and economic contacts with indigenous populations were unavoidable, and the members of those diasporas had to carry on those limited contacts with their new neighbors ever mindful of prohibitions against intermarriage and against the adoption of local gods, religious beliefs, and cultural practices. Nevertheless, in certain cases those contacts paved the way to intermingling, and eventually to assimilation. Those processes led to the rise of diaspora "cores" and "peripheries," with the core members preserving the ethnic character of the diaspora, and the peripheral members eventually becoming highly hybrid groups.

In certain cases in which the ties with the homelands were neither continuous nor strong, it is difficult to regard those communities as fully fledged diasporas. They constituted border cases between colonies (which actually were extensions of the city-states of origin) and autonomous ethnic groups that maintained irregular and infrequent contacts with their homelands. Such settlements can be regarded as early prototypes of dispersed groups in the colonial empires of the modern period. When those empires deteriorated or collapsed, those colonists became detached from their homelands and either became indigenous minorities or disappeared (Cohen 1997, pp. 66–7). In any case, eventually all such ancient empires either collapsed or were defeated and dismembered. Some failed because of their inherent military weakness, and some because of their rulers' incompetence. In cases of chaotic and rapid ascendance and collapse, as, for example, in the cases of the Akkadian, Assyrian, and Persian empires, many diaspora communities were exterminated, others survived but lost contact with their homelands, and in other cases the settlers returned to their homelands. Yet, whereas all of those empires disappeared, some of the diasporas they had harbored survived.

In most instances migration from homelands did not occur as part of a deliberate effort to establish colonies. Rather, in most situations, migrations occurred because of economic considerations or because of expulsion of indigenous populations. The latter, for example, was the preferred policy of the Assyrians and Akkadians. The rulers of those empires expelled entire large ethnic groups to remote peripheral areas in their empires that were sparsely populated and frequently subject to invasion by outside "barbarian" tribes. The predominant reason for such expulsion was that the ruler regarded any concentration of minority ethnic groups at the center of the empire as a potential threat to the security of the regime and as potentially disruptive of the homogeneity of the host population. The Assyrian kings, for example, believed that such brutal expulsions would serve as a harsh warning and deterrent to other potentially rebellious ethnic groups. In fact, the Assyrians expected that such scattering would result in the total disappearance of such ethnic groups, and indeed that seems to have been the fate of the ten Israelite tribes that were expelled from Samaria in the eighth century B.C.

Despite host countries' strong rejectionist attitudes toward expelled ethnic tribes and groups in their midst, in some cases small dispersed ethnic groups became assimilated into their host societies. In other cases of expulsion, such as that of the Judeans to Babylon and later to Rome, where the ethnic diasporas were able to form concentrated communities in densely populated urban centers, they stood a much better chance of surviving. Their ability to survive was enhanced by the continuing presence of dedicated political and religious elites, by ongoing contacts with their remaining community in the homeland, and by the existence of other diaspora communities of the same origin in other host countries.

Whenever such patterns of factors obtained in a host country, expelled migrants and voluntary migrants, along with the indigenous inhabitants, formed a social, ethnic, and religious mosaic reminiscent of the mythical Tower of Babel. In antiquity there had emerged a number of such multiethnic centers – in Egypt, Babylon, Persia, Rome, and Asia Minor. In those places the rulers showed some degree of tolerance toward diaspora groups, usually because of the rulers' correct assumption that input from such groups could contribute to the well-being of their realms. Such tolerant rulers, in contrast to the Assyrian and Akkadian kings, permitted both voluntary migrants and expelled groups to settle even at the centers of their empires. They also allowed certain diasporas to return to their homelands. In those cases in which ethnic diasporas were permitted to undertake a return to their homelands, such rulers expected that out of gratitude for their leniency the thankful returnees would serve as loyal subjects or friendly neighbors, would not be rebellious, and would continue to provide resources to their benefactors. This was the case for the Jews who had been expelled by the Babylonians and who later were allowed to return to Palestine/Eretz Israel by Cyrus the Great (Tadmor 1969, pp. 159–62).

Those various patterns of treatment accorded to voluntary migrants and expellees were precursors of the patterns that later host governments would follow in dealing with such groups. Thus, from those earliest examples of the beginnings of diasporas onward there have existed two main types of host rulers/governments: those opting for forced assimilation and full integration of such groups, and those showing greater tolerance for the peculiarities of the diasporans. Those who tolerated diasporic entities anticipated both economic and political yields from the continuing existence of such organized diasporas within the boundaries of their realms.

In sum, from the time of their earliest appearance, ethnic diasporas had a number of common features. As the cases of the Jews and Greeks have shown, the most important among those factors were actual contacts (communication, trade, visits or permanent return) and virtual links (sentiment and emotional attachment, kin relationships, etc.) to their ancestral homelands. Whereas those were the most essential factors contributing to maintenance of their distinct primordial and psychological/symbolic identities, the historical narratives, legends and myths, and personal and collective memories were also needed to ensure the perseverance of diasporas. Among the members of many diaspora communities such legends and memories remained vivid for centuries. For historical diasporas that have survived since ancient times or since the Middle Ages (the Jewish, Greek, Armenian, and Chinese), their residual sentiments about their homelands and their sense of connectedness have helped them to overcome the many traumas caused by their uprooting (whether voluntary or imposed), by the difficulties of migration, by their resettlement in host countries, and by their existence in the midst of invariably hostile populations. For many members of those groups who maintained their ethnic identity, their old homelands became highly cherished places. For some, returning to their homelands would remain a distant dream that would never be realized. But for the few who constituted the cores of those diasporas, such memories were the most potent motivation for actively trying to return, or, if return was impossible, to be active on behalf of the diaspora and homeland.

The emergence and development of diasporism in antiquity consisted of a number of stages: The first diasporas were created by migrations that took place after the early nomadic tribes had begun to live in permanent settlements, had taken ownership or control over certain territories, and had begun the process of evolving an ethnic identity. Their growing attachment to their territories led to a gradual crystallization of the concepts "home" and "homeland." That facilitated the emergence of a combined primordial and psychological/symbolic identity closely connected to the homeland. Whenever wars over control of territory broke out, or when social, economic, or political conditions became intolerable, forced or voluntary migration out of homelands often occurred. Some, but not all, migrants survived the hardships created by such relocation and were able to settle permanently in host countries. Eventually, certain segments of those groups were assimilated into their host societies. In other cases, there remained core diaspora communities whose members continued to maintain their identity and cherish contacts with their homelands. Occasionally, diaspora elites succeeded in launching a return movement. But even that did not necessarily spell the end of a particular diaspora, as some members chose to remain in their host countries, and their decision to remain did not necessarily mean a loss of identity, nor did it mean assimilation or severance of links with the homeland.

An Enduring Phenomenon

As noted earlier, simultaneously with the emergence and development of the ancient Jewish and Greek diasporas, other ethnic groups were being dispersed, either voluntarily or by foreign conquerors. Thus, ethnic groups such as the Amorites in the third and second millennia B.C., and later the Arameans, Phrygians, Phoenicians, Iranians, and Nabateans, were deported to or migrated to foreign host countries where they, too, formed diaspora communities. Such groups established elaborate cultural, economic, and commercial networks that persisted for long periods and played an important role in helping to sustain those diasporas (Curtin 1984). Because of annihilation in wars, external pressures, or voluntary inclinations, some of those entities disappeared soon after their formation, but other diasporas persisted.

Those groups that were able to cope with changing situations belong to the small category of "historical diasporas" that were formed in antiquity and have survived until now. Because the only archeological and written historical evidence we have is from the Middle East and Asia, this category includes only groups whose origins were in those areas. It is likely, however, that similar diasporas emerged in other parts of the world and survived for longer periods, though we have no detailed information about them.

The political and military rulers of the post-Babylonian centralized empires that were established between the fifth century B.C. and the fifth century A.D. – the Chaldean, Persian, Greek, Roman, and Chinese empires – wanted order and stability in their empires, and they attempted to introduce universal norms and codify their laws, and that had both positive and negative effects on the historical diaspora phenomenon. On the one hand, in their attempts to forge coherent ethnic entities and to create "dynastic *mythomoteurs*" (constitutive political myths that were promoted by rulers and dynasties) (Smith 1986, pp. 58–61), the rulers of those vast empires contributed to a decrease in the political importance of their constituent local ethnic nations, of minorities, and of diasporas. In certain cases they succeeded in imposing complete assimilation, wiping out such diasporas. Nevertheless, some ethnic diasporas did not disappear, nor did their influence on political developments diminish, and those entities also belong to the category of historical diasporas. On the other hand, the prolonged periods of relative peace and security that were enforced by those empires increased the chances that ethnic diasporas could survive and perform useful cultural and economic functions for the benefit of their homelands and their host rulers. Also, those empires gave rise to some additional diasporas that persisted and prospered. An important factor contributing to that development was that the capitals and large cities of those empires became important cultural, political, and economic mega-centers that attracted traders and artisans of various ethnic origins. Whenever conditions permitted, some of those traders and "guest workers" took up permanent residence and eventually performed significant cultural and economic functions, not just trading and commercial functions. Thus, for example, Rome attracted numerous migrants who eventually settled down, established diaspora communities there, and contributed to Rome's economic power.

Ethnic groups that had been conquered or captured during the expansion of those empires, as well as groups that had been exiled from their homelands after suppression of their ethnic revolts, found their way to or were brought to these new environs. Because the rulers of the large empires appreciated the potential for those groups to contribute to their economic and administrative development, they were granted protection and some degree of cultural and religious autonomy. Again, the most pertinent example of such patterns was the Roman Empire, which permitted various diasporas not only to exist but also to prosper. Those patterns can be seen as the early precursors of the millet system that the Ottoman and Hapsburg empires introduced much later.

The gradual deterioration of the Roman Empire, and later the Byzantine Empire, was largely the result of recurrent invasions and influxes of aggressive ethnic groups that opened the door for expansion of the Arabs. On the other side, the military strength and political stability of Asian kingdoms and empires benefited the migration patterns of their people and facilitated their settlement and establishment of ethnic diasporas, especially in Europe. Some diasporas that emerged during the Middle Ages survived, and others disappeared (Dixon 1976), but all those diasporas showed striking similarities to the Jewish and Greek diasporas that had arisen in earlier periods. In any event, from the fifth century A.D. onward, the organized ethnic diasporas that emerged in Europe, the Middle East, and Asia tended to be larger than their predecessors. Among the more enduring were the Celtic, Nordic, Armenian, German, Chinese, Indian, and Japanese diasporas.

The purpose of the following discussion is to briefly describe the reasons for ethnic groups' migration and the emergence of some of the other historical diasporas. It is also intended to demonstrate the patterns of dispersal and the enduring nature of the diaspora phenomenon, to emphasize the fact that ethnic diasporas were established all over the world before the modern era, and to show the similarities among those diasporas.

The Nordic Diasporas

From the second century A.D. until well into the Middle Ages, Nordic tribes invaded many parts of western Europe and raided into territories beyond the lands that they actually conquered. They succeeded in pushing the Celtic tribes out of central Europe. Then wave after wave of the Nordic tribes that migrated from the north established diaspora communities in places such as, for example, the Danelaw, Brittany, and Russia. Some communities of Nordic mercenaries were established as far afield as Constantinople. All those entities either were annihilated by superior forces or became voluntarily assimilated, but they are mentioned here because there is no question that they left their mark and had enduring effects on most of the peoples living today in the vast areas over which they ranged.

The Armenian Diaspora

Armenia and the Armenians were first mentioned by chroniclers in the fifth century A.D. Armenia is the site of a most important Old World trading crossroads, and its strategic location and resources attracted the Persians, Greeks, Romans, and Byzantines, and later the Turks and Russians. As a result of recurrent wars, each of those empires in turn gained control of Armenia and forced Armenians to migrate. But the strategic location of Armenia also facilitated voluntary migration of Armenians to the nearby and distant territories in which they pursued their trading endeavors. There is solid evidence showing that beginning in the fifth century A.D., Armenian colonies, or diasporic entities, existed in Bulgaria and that similar Armenian diasporic entities existed in Anatolia and other Balkan countries. In the seventh century, Armenians were deported from their homeland (and some migrated of their own volition) to Byzantium, where they established successful trading communities and occupied senior positions in government. Later, those would be among the main occupations followed by members of the Armenian diaspora. Thus, in the eighth and ninth centuries Byzantium had four emperors of Armenian origin, and Armenian merchants prospered there. From the tenth century onward there has been a continuous Armenian presence in large western European cities such as Venice, Marseilles, Paris, Bruges, and London. It appears that the first large-scale Armenian migration occurred after the collapse of the Bagratid dynasty in the eleventh century, when migrants established a colony in Cilicia in southeastern Anatolia. Around the same time, Armenian communities emerged in Crimea, Hungary, Poland, and Moldavia. In the thirteenth century, Armenian communities appeared in Palestine and Egypt, and a bit later in Iraq, India, Tibet, and China. A second large wave of Armenian migration occurred in the wake of the collapse of the Armenian Cilician kingdom in the fourteenth century. As part of that wave, Armenians settled in Romania and Lithuania. In the seventeenth century they established communities in Persia, and from there they migrated and traded all the way to the Philippines (Bournoutian 1994; Hovannisian 1997). Still later, Armenian diaspora communities emerged in other parts of Europe and eventually in the New World (Bakalian 1993; Pattie 1994; Panossian 1998).

The German Diaspora

The German tribes that invaded the Roman Empire actually constituted and were recognized as a distinct ethnie. As is well known, their invasions into the empire and their settlement there contributed greatly to its downfall. During the first half of the Middle Ages, German peasants and miners settled in cohesive communities in eastern Europe, especially in Russia and in the Baltic countries, as well as in the Balkans. Consequently, German merchants were active throughout eastern Europe and the Balkans, and German mercenaries were fighting in the service of various rulers in those regions. Because of their technical and commercial talents, local rulers encouraged German immigration and permanent settlement. In various parts of eastern Europe and the Balkans they were allowed to live under "Germanic law," according to which they enjoyed certain degrees of autonomy and corporatist status. Consequently, those relatively cohesive and well-organized groups maintained what might be called their "German identity," as well as their connections to the homeland. But German migration and settlement were not confined to eastern Europe and the Balkans – their skilled craftsmen and artisans spread throughout western Europe during the fifteenth, sixteenth, and seventeenth centuries. Diaspora Germans participated in the worldwide and centuries-old process of diffusion of innovation and expertise in many areas: agricultural, commercial, military, and craftsmanship (Sowell 1996). To a great extent, German migration out of their homeland was caused by the turbulent political and security situation there, for until their unification at the end of the nineteenth century the German principalities and city-states were trapped in a web of social and political divisions and ongoing conflicts and wars. That continual political and social instability often prompted Germans to migrate and seek safer and calmer host countries. Of course, some of those German diasporic entities still exist.

The Gypsy Diaspora

Among the ethnic diasporas that arose during the Middle Ages and have survived since then, the Gypsies deserve special attention. Probably originating in northern India, which the present-day Roma regard as their homeland, Gypsies appeared in Persia in the tenth century A.D. and at about the same time in Asia Minor. In the thirteenth and fourteenth centuries some of their groups moved from Anatolia to the Balkans, and in the fifteenth century to yet other parts of eastern and central Europe. By the sixteenth century, Gypsies were living in Spain, Portugal, England, and Scandinavia (Chaliand and Rageau 1995). Initially the Gypsies were welcomed and were granted letters of protection in various central European kingdoms. But because of their nomadic life-style, as well as their "wild" and "strange" cultural and social practices, eventually attitudes toward them changed. Very few host countries would agree to admit them, and in most host countries they were shunned and persecuted. On their part, they were unwilling and unable to integrate socially and economically into host societies. Yet despite their constant wanderings and disorderly behavior, that stateless diaspora was not totally disorganized. It is true that unlike other diasporas that emerged during approximately the same period the Gypsies lacked an elaborate transstate organization, but at the level of family and tribal politics they had a certain degree of organizational cohesion and order. However, except for being subject to the laws and politics of their host countries, their participation in such matters was always minimal.

The Chinese Diaspora

As far as is known, the origins of the large overseas Han Chinese communities were in the thirteenth century A.D. After the Mongol conquest of China in 1276, sizable groups of Hans began to migrate. Again, because of political and economic difficulties at home, on the one hand, and because of inherent curiosity, on the other, Chinese migrated to and took refuge in Japan, Cambodia, and Vietnam. It was easier for the Hans to gain entrance to those territories because they had been experiencing chronic political chaos and were militarily weak. Apparently the next waves of migration out of China were initiated and encouraged by the Yuan Dynasty, which ruled China from 1260 to 1368 and whose rulers were interested in establishing trade colonies (the similarity to the Greek and probably also the Armenian expansionary pattern is clear). Consequently, by the late fourteenth century there were notable organized Chinese settlements in Cambodia, Java, Sumatra, and Singapore. In the fifteenth century the Chinese established colonies in Thailand, and a century later a Chinese colony arose in what became known as the Philippines. The seventeenth century saw Chinese refugees arriving and swelling the colony in Taiwan, which apparently had been established five centuries earlier. As will be shown in Chapter 4, since the seventeenth century Chinese diaspora communities have been established in virtually all parts of the world. Because there is an extensive literature on the Chinese diaspora communities, there is no need here to go into detail about the organizational skills, commercial talents, academic achievements, and networking capabilities of the Chinese diaspora. By the same token, there is no need here to elaborate further on its similarity to other diasporas, especially the Jewish, Armenian, and Greek diasporas.

The Japanese Diaspora

The Japanese diaspora, situated in various Southeast Asian countries, began around the fourteenth century. By the early fifteenth century Japanese colonies could be found in Korea, and 200 years later there were sizable Japanese settlements in the Philippines and neighboring countries. There are records of Japanese individuals and families who lived in the Western Hemisphere in the early seventeenth century, but it was only in the late nineteenth century that substantial numbers of Japanese migrants moved from their homeland to the New World. Hawaii was the first "Western" recipient of Japanese migrants, and for many decades it remained one of their main destinations in the West. Japanese immigration to Hawaii began in the late 1860s, before Hawaii became an American territory. A little bit later Brazil became a haven for Japanese migrants. Still later in the nineteenth century, Japanese migrated to a number of South American countries, chief among them Peru. After the U.S. takeover of the Hawaiian Islands, the road was open to Japanese secondary migration from Hawaii to the U.S. mainland. At the turn of the nineteenth century, there were about 60,000 Japanese in Hawaii and about 20,000 on the U.S. mainland. By 1920, the situation had changed substantially, with about 100,000 Japanese on the U.S. mainland and about the same number in Hawaii. Since then, the number of Japanese in the United States has continued to increase. Toward the end of the nineteenth century, Japanese began to migrate to Canada, where again they established a prosperous community (Sowell 1996).

The Indian Diaspora

The roots of the Indian diaspora were in antiquity, but diasporization can be documented only beginning in the fifth century B.C. After Gautama Buddha's death in 483 B.C., large eastward movements were undertaken by his numerous disciples, who intended to propagate his teachings. In that wave of migration the dominant motivation was neither economic nor political but rather cultural/religious. From the sixth to the eleventh century A.D., the rulers of the Indian kingdoms along India's eastern seaboard dispatched military and commercial expeditions to Southeast Asia – some with considerable success. Subsequently, those rulers developed networks that sustained the connections between the homeland and its outposts/colonies. Within that framework, for example, both Hindus from northern India, who converted to Buddhism, and Tamils from southern India migrated and settled in Sri Lanka, and those simultaneous migrations led to the long-lasting ethnic conflict in the island. The settlement of Indians in Malaya and Burma also dated to the early Middle Ages (Chaliand and Rageau 1995; Sowell 1996). Migrants' movements from western India to Africa in the Middle Ages were connected mainly to the establishment of trade outposts. In that part of Africa, the Indian migrants who became diasporans had to compete with the members of other ethnic diasporas (Persians, Armenians, and Arabs) that existed there during the same period. The Indian diaspora continued to expand throughout the Portuguese rule and particularly during the British rule over India (Helweg 1986, pp. 103–4; Sowell 1996). However, it should be noted that the Indian diaspora has never been a homogeneous ethnic entity, being composed of Hindus, Muslims, Sikhs, Tamils, and other groups that originated in various parts of that huge subcontinent. The larger cohesive groups originating in the Indian subcontinent were the indentured laborers who were brought to Africa and the West Indies, mostly within the framework of the British Empire (Cohen 1997, pp. 59–66). After World War II, the dispersal of Indian laborers and professionals became a virtually worldwide phenomenon.

In sum, the Middle Ages saw the origins of certain large diasporas, (and by no means have all of them been mentioned here) that played major roles in spreading a host of ethnic traditions, religions, and cultures, that benefited international trade as well as other economic and technical enterprises, and that greatly influenced regional and local politics. They were similar in a number of respects: Their members maintained clearly identifiable ethnic identities, and they established and operated organizations and networks to maintain regular contact with the homeland and other dispersed communities of the same origin. These examples of the historical diasporas that emerged throughout antiquity and during the Middle Ages demonstrate the enduring nature of ethno-national diasporism.

The Historical Turning Point

As noted earlier, a major turning point in the progression of organized ethno-national diasporas was reached in the middle of the nineteenth century. A new phase in the historical development of the phenomenon featured the beginnings of some new migrations, the expansion and rein-vigoration of some veteran diasporas, and especially the emergence and further development of both older and newer incipient diasporas. Gen-erally, from that period onward, both forced and voluntary migrations have greatly expanded the diaspora phenomenon and have been influ-enced by the new globalism, the economic restructuring in many regions, and the many new cultural, social, political, and ideological develop-ments of the past century. Among the latter, most influential has been the emergence of various nationalist and liberal ideologies that have affected all ethnic groups, but especially the ethno-national diasporas.

Thus ethno-national diasporism clearly is not a modern phenomenon. Like ethnicity itself, it is an enduring phenomenon. Some historical dias-poras, though relatively few, have survived since antiquity and still exist today. More of the historical diasporas that are still with us emerged during the Middle Ages. In any case, however, the nineteenth century brought a further important stage in the development of this phenome-non: the emergence of many new diasporas. On the basis of these obser-vations, the rest of this volume will focus on present-day diasporas, some of which originated in antiquity, some during the Middle Ages, and many since the nineteenth century.

3

A Collective Portrait of Contemporary Diasporas

The Non-ethnic Trans-national Formations

A comprehensive, but tightly focused, collective portrait of contemporary ethno-national diasporas, emphasizing their roles at the various levels in the political arena, is needed, for two reasons. First, as noted in Chapter 2, since the middle of the nineteenth century the ethno-national diaspora phenomenon has expanded and undergone some major transformations, as have other aspects of ethnicity and nationalism. Certainly the historical diasporas have not lost their enduring characteristics, but because of significant changes in domestic, regional, and global political and social conditions most contemporary diasporic entities have acquired new features beyond those of the diasporas that were established in antiquity and during the Middle Ages. Therefore, to accurately understand contemporary ethno-national diasporas, these new features must be clearly delineated and analyzed. The second reason that we need a comprehensive portrait is related to the existence of other types of trans-national formations that usually are lumped together with ethno-national diasporas. As noted in Chapter 1, at the least there are four categories of such entities that have been termed "diasporas." The nature of those entities and their relationships to ethno-national diasporas will be briefly reviewed here.

Global Religions
It is particularly difficult to distinguish between global religions and ethnic diasporas. The main reason is that in many instances active members of ethno-national diasporas espouse religious beliefs that are

intimately intertwined with, and partly overlap, the ethnic elements of their identities. In other words, despite the noticeable ongoing processes of secularization among many members of ethnic groups and ethno-national diasporas, it is still difficult to detach religious sentiments and beliefs from other cultural elements that constitute the primordial component of a diasporic identity (Enloe 1980; Smith 1986). For example, it is almost impossible to do so in the cases of the Pakistani, Jewish, Sikh, Palestinian, Druze, and Armenian diasporas. Moreover, in similarity to ethnic diasporas, each of the major religious churches and denominations has its recognized center with which members maintain regular contact. The Vatican serves as the spiritual center for Catholics, Athens for the Greek Orthodox, and Mecca for Muslims worldwide. Furthermore, each of those religions is organized to pursue strategies toward host societies and governments that to a great extent are similar to those pursued by ethnic diasporas. And each of those religious groups operates local and trans-national networks that also are similar to those operated by ethno-national diasporas.

Yet, as will become clearer from the profile of the ethno-national diasporas that will be presented here, spiritual/religious formations differ from ethno-national diasporas in a number of respects. First, whereas religious creeds and also the religious components of ethno-religious identities are based on total acceptance of a comprehensive dogmatic ideology whose sources are alleged to be in the transcendental realm, ethnic identities are forged by a combination of primordial cultural sentiments (including, of course, religious beliefs and feelings), practical instrumental considerations, and subjective/symbolic leanings. Second, unlike core members of ethno-national diasporas, members of religious/spiritual formations are able to deal more easily with issues of loyalty toward the religious center, on the one hand, and loyalty toward their homeland, on the other. Third, whereas members of ethnic diasporas regard certain territories as their actual historical homelands, most members of global religions, with the notable exception of Judaism, are attached to a spiritual center that is not the actual historical birthplace of the forebears of the group and that its members do not regard as such. And, theoretically more important, most spiritual/religious groups were created by the migration of a "cultural artifact" rather than by the migration of persons out of a territorial homeland (Cavalli-Sforza and Cavalli-Sforza 1995, pp. 157–9; Cohen 1997, pp. 134–6).

A recent development in this sphere is the emergence of the notion of a "Muslim diaspora" and attempts to vivify and politicize that idea. That notion has surfaced in the wake of recent large waves of Middle Eastern, North African, and Asian Muslim migrants who have permanently settled especially in western Europe and North America. Basically, the claim of the proponents of that idea is that despite the multiplicity of their countries of origin, Muslims have much in common and therefore should organize and act as cohesive social-political entities in their host countries. Because this is a relatively new development, it is too soon to estimate whether or not the idea will catch the imagination of large Muslim groups worldwide and result in the sort of very determined commitment that is required to forge effective trans-state and trans-national entities. That issue has become critical for many Muslims in the West in the wake of Osama bin Laden's al-Qaeda attack on the United States on September 11, 2001.

Political-Ideological Dispersals

The second category of non-ethnic trans-national formations, whose components may seem to resemble both ethnic diasporas and global religions, is composed of what have been referred to as political-ideological dispersals. Like religious dispersals, such groups are created as a result of the "travel" or the spread of ideas and dogmas, but not necessarily as a result of migration of individuals and groups. Therefore, in most cases, the members of such groups find it easy to square their political-ideological beliefs with their ethno-national identities. Except for adamant adherents to anti-statist and anti-nationalist ideologies, followers of most current political ideologies do not have fundamental doubts concerning their loyalty to their nation, homeland, or state. For example, that position was underscored in the aftermath of the collapse of the Soviet Union and other Communist regimes and the consequent demise of the last major universal radical ideology: communism (Fukuyama 1991, 1992). Less radical ideological movements of the same brand, such as Euro-communism, have lost much of their trans-national appeal. Consequently, such ideologies have also lost many of their adherents, as well as their potential for global unifying force and political sway. As for the parties espousing such ideologies, their rapid decline as important international political forces has been expedited by their failure to regroup, reestablish new centers, and create new networks. In that respect, and in terms of the primary source of their motivation, the remaining adherents of those ideologies differ from the members of ethno-national diasporas.

Nevertheless, ideology is still an important factor that allows for clear distinctions among various groups active in the social and political arenas, both within states and in the international sphere. Hence, two subcategories of this type of trans-national formation deserve special attention. They are mentioned here because of their partial overlap with the ethno-national diasporas that are our concern in this book. The first includes the pan-Arab, pan-Turkish, and other revived "pan-" ideologies and movements (on the pan-Turkish movement, see Landau 1995). Adopting a broad definition of "ideology," essentially not confining it to radical ideologies (Seliger 1970), the second subcategory can be delineated. In that vein, communitarianism, European-style liberalism, anti-globalism, and normative democracy, for example, can be viewed as belonging to this subcategory. Those ideologies have gained adherents in the United States, in European countries, and beyond, and various such groups have maintained some contacts and have formed some loose trans-national organizations. Thus, some liberal parties and social-democratic parties maintain trans-national networks and conduct forums for exchanging views and coordinating political activities. Despite certain similarities between these two subcategories, they differ in several important respects. Adherents of "pan-" ideologies have relatively well defined "homelands" (e.g., Turkey for the pan-Turkish movement and probably Saudi Arabia or Egypt for the pan-Arab movement), they feel an attachment to such centers and occasionally are active on their behalf, they establish organizations in countries to which their ideas have traveled, and they maintain trans-national networks. The groups in the second subcategory lack all of those characteristics, and therefore usually lack adequate mechanisms to implement their common goals. The conclusion is that although some of those movements have certain similar features, in most other respects they differ substantially from ethno-national diasporas.

Trans-national Linguistic Communities

This type of non-ethnic trans-national formation consists of people in various parts of the world who speak the same language, such as French, German, Portuguese, or Spanish. In those cases, too, usually there is a center that can be regarded as the "cultural homeland" with which the various national groups maintain some contact. Such centers cater to certain cultural needs of those who speak their languages, and they may provide some leadership and assistance toward sustaining their cultures and languages. That has increasingly been the case in view of the ongoing processes of Americanization that are contributing to the predominance of American English. In most cases, the government of the "homeland" and the other affiliated governments in those trans-national linguistic communities are the main actors in the partnerships. Those governments establish special agencies that deal with the entire range of relationships involved in maintaining a linguistic center and periphery. In France, for example, a government ministry is responsible for Francophonie in general, and for maintaining the ties between Paris and the other communities in particular. The interlocutors in those relationships are the governments of the French-speaking countries. Other linguistic "homelands," including Germany, Britain, and the United States, have established official or semiofficial agencies, such as the Goethe Institute, the British Council, and the United States Information Agency, to perform those and similar functions. In certain cases, such as Francophonie, in addition to the linguistic and cultural contacts, the French and the other governments share some political interests and occasionally also economic interests. Hence they cooperate and coordinate their activities in relevant spheres. However, political cooperation is relatively superficial, and joint activities are relatively few (Miles and Sheffer 1998). There is no need to elaborate the differences between this type of dispersion and ethno-national diasporas.

The Global Youth Culture

Though not of the same nature as the other three types of non-ethnic trans-national entities that have been mentioned, nevertheless this growing phenomenon of youth culture has sometimes been termed a "diaspora," and therefore its differences from ethno-national diasporas call for some discussion. By its nature this is a highly individualized entity, something of an illusory notion that to a great extent exists only in the eyes of the new media. Because it is simultaneously trans-national, trans-state, and highly individualized, its adherents lack a clearly definable identity. In certain respects the United States is the "homeland" for this purported diaspora, but except for influencing certain cultural trends and fashions that youngsters adopt, such as in music, hairstyle, and dress, it is far from being a globally recognized and organized entity. The networks connecting young people around the world clearly are non-formal and operate mainly through television, movies, and the Internet. Finally, there is no global or local organization that could or would wish to undertake to coordinate and foster cooperation among the many millions of young people who constitute that so-called global culture.

Finally in this context, in addition to all the previously mentioned distinctions between global non-ethnic formations, on the one hand, and ethno-national diasporas, on the other, the quintessential difference is that the former are trans-national groupings (i.e., they are composed of members of various nationalities), and the latter are trans-state diasporas (i.e., the members are of the same national origin but are dispersed in various states and countries) (Miles and Sheffer 1998).

Against the backdrop of continuing improvements in transportation and some recent striking developments in distance-shrinking technologies, simultaneously with the rapid expansion of ethnic diasporas, in terms of both size and number, also all of those non-ethnic trans-national formations have proliferated. Moreover, as a result of increasing ethnic and cultural heterogeneity and pluralism in most countries and the consequent easier access to various host governments and inter-state and regional organizations, those entities increasingly are directly and indirectly influencing domestic and international politics, both at the high level of the state houses and at the low level of the streets. Consequently, they often generate domestic, regional, and international tensions and conflicts, including conflicts with ethno-national diasporas. Occasionally, memberships in those groups overlap, sometimes to the point that it is difficult to determine which element is dominant among members of a particular coalition.

To illustrate the issue of such hybridization and overlapping loyalties that can cause cognitive and emotional dissonance and confusion for the individuals themselves, as well as for their kin and members of host societies, let us consider the following purely hypothetical case. Imagine a Japanese-born physicist who has migrated from Japan to the United States, married a non-Japanese person, and obtained American citizenship. He permanently resides in the United States, but maintains his Japanese identity as well as his interest in and ties with Japan, and on top of all that is Christian by birth, holds liberal views, and likes various aspects of the global youth culture. It is likely that such a person and his family will face difficult choices because of conflicting demands arising from the disparate sources of his hybridized identity. Host societies and governments will face similar difficulties in their relationships with individuals and groups who have such hybridized identities and overlapping loyalties. For example, overlapping and even conflicting identities and loyalties, as a result of ethnic origin and religious affiliation, often are seen among members of Muslim groups. Thus (and this is not a hypothetical case) when members of the Palestinian fundamentalist movement Hamas who permanently reside in Jordan, which is a moderately religious state, are asked "Who are you?" many will answer that they are Palestinian members of that Sunni Muslim fundamentalist movement. Yet most will hasten to add that under the prevailing circumstances in the Middle East they would be willing to stay put in Jordan and therefore owe a certain degree of loyalty to the ruler of that country. Nevertheless, whenever the issue of the future of an independent Palestinian entity is placed on the agenda, they will face great difficulties in squaring all those affinities and loyalties. Ultimately, however, involvement in host-country politics and success in influencing government policies are much greater among members of ethno-national diasporas than among members of all those trans-national groups that have sometimes been termed "diasporas."

In sum, there are two major and some secondary differences between the four non-ethnic trans-national formations, on the one hand, and ethno-national diasporas, on the other. First, in the case of the former groups, cultural traits, linguistic proficiency, ideological affinity, and popular cultural trends "migrated" and became disseminated among persons who, on the whole, stayed put in their geographical homelands. Moreover, adoption of those "traveling artifacts" did not necessarily contradict or eradicate ethnic identity. By contrast, in the case of ethnic diasporas, people migrated and resettled, and in those processes they imported with them deeply rooted traits, views, loyalties, and traditions. The second major distinction is that the former are trans-national entities, and the latter are trans-state diasporas.

Since ancient times, ethnic diasporas resulting from both voluntary and forced migrations and relocation in host countries have been integral parts of human history, but the definitional boundaries between individuals and small ethnic groups of transient international migrants, refugees, expellees, guest workers, tourists, and other types of transnational communities, on the one hand, and members of permanent ethnic diasporas, on the other, have not been satisfactorily clarified (Safran 1991). This confusion is largely due to the fact that usually the duration of residence of transient migrants and refugees in host countries is flexible. Moreover, in most cases it is not predetermined and does not depend on social, political, and economic factors in either their host countries or their homelands. Hence, there have not been clear criteria for determining the point in time when groups of tourists, migrants, guest workers, refugees, and asylum-seekers become members of diasporas (Marienstras 1989).

That confusion makes it difficult to assess the population sizes, the commitments and loyalties, and, more important in the present context, the political significance of those closely related but definitely nonidentical groups. However, because the number of different ethnic groups and the sizes of those groups residing permanently in host countries are rapidly growing, it seems that the inevitable conclusion is that sooner or later, and more often it will be sooner rather than later, most of those trans-national migrants, guest workers, refugees, and asylum-seekers will either form or join diasporic entities.

That uncertainty about the point in time at which migrants and refugees become members of diasporas has both practical and theoretical implications. The most relevant issue is to what extent the various types of transient migrants behave differently from diaspora members. Though there are certain similarities in the patterns of how the two groups interact with their host societies and governments, transient migrants and diaspora groups do in fact behave differently. Thus, in the late 1990s, it was mainly transient migrants and members of stateless diasporas who were involved in insurgency and rebellion in host countries. That forced both democratic and non-democratic host governments to view such groups as posing threats to their security and well-being. At the same time, the cleavages and disagreements between host societies and state-linked diaspora communities have, in general, become less acerbic and menacing in the eyes of the host societies and their governments. Nevertheless, despite increasing societal and governmental acceptance of ethnic diasporas, those cleavages still can cause tensions that affect international and regional politics as well as the internal politics of host countries, homelands, and other involved actors. In view of current migratory trends, it seems clear that such tensions and conflicts will continue to affect politics for the foreseeable future.

Furthermore, the prevailing state of confusion and ambiguity over the boundaries between various groups of "others" in host countries, especially between international migrants and diasporans, is partly due to the insufficient state of knowledge in this field of study. Hence the basic issues involved in those two phenomena, including a comprehensive definition of ethno-national diasporas, are in urgent need of clarification, and that will be attempted in the next two sections.

The Need for a Multifaceted Profile of Ethno-national Diasporas

Short, pithy definitions of social and political phenomena are elegant and easy to digest and remember. Occasionally, therefore, such sharply crafted definitions will be adequate and will have an enduring impact on actual developments, on entire academic disciplines, or on certain fields of study. However, when a field of study is relatively new, when the available definitions of the relevant phenomena are still partial and not fully adequate for developing useful theoretical and analytical perspectives, and when the subject matter is highly intricate, the need is not for short and elegant generalizations but for more elaborate definitions.

That is particularly true in the study of ethno-national diasporas, for the realities of the diaspora existence are far more complex than those that have been depicted and analyzed in the available theoretical and analytical publications (Marienstras 1989; Safran 1991, 1999; Tololyan 1991, 1996; Anderson 1992, 1994; Clifford 1994; Chaliand and Rageau 1995; Vertovec 1997). That is especially the case regarding the pioneering definitions that were based on examination of the roles of historical diasporas in various multiethnic empires (Armstrong 1976). That also applies to attempts to delineate "common features of diasporas" that focus on the undifferentiated reasons for migration, social features, main patterns of occupation, and desiderata of such groups (Cohen 1997, p. 26).

Classifying Diasporas

In contrast to previous categorizations and definitions, and in line with the main focus of this book, basically there are two meaningful criteria for distinguishing between the various existing ethno-national diasporas: first, the status of their respective homelands, and, second, their "age." It will be argued that these two factors substantially influence the structures, strategies, and behaviors of these entities.

Homeland Status and Diasporas

Here the distinction is between stateless diasporas and state-linked diasporas. The stateless diasporas are those dispersed segments of nations that have been unable to establish their own independent states. The state-linked diasporas are those groups that are in host countries but are connected to societies of their own ethnic origin that constitute a majority in established states.

Of the two, the stateless diasporas form the smaller category, currently including ethnic groups or "nations" such as the Palestinians, Kurds, Tibetans, and Sikhs. Those diasporas strive to establish or reestablish independent national states. This category also includes the following groups, though their cases are even more complex: the Gypsies, the black diaspora in Europe, South America, and Latin America, and, in a sense, also the African-American community. These are borderline cases, because it is difficult for the majority of each of these diasporas to unequivocally define where their homeland is. Similarly, under the current circumstances, these entities have neither the wish nor the power and resources to achieve the goal of establishing a national state. In any case, this has been a shrinking category. In the past it included the Jewish and Armenian diasporas and various other diaspora groups that previously had been segments of ethnic nations that persisted under the yoke of the Soviet Union – the Ukrainians, Estonians, Latvians, Lithuanians, and so forth – for it should be remembered that under Soviet rule none of those societies controlled sovereign states.

The larger category, that of the state-linked diasporas, includes all other existing ethno-national diasporas, regardless of their age, their organization, or the nature of their relationships with homeland and host country.

There is no direct correlation between a diaspora's link to an established national state (nor a diaspora's statelessness) and the social and economic status and organization of most members of that diaspora. Members of both stateless diasporas and state-linked diasporas can be "proletarian" (i.e., from poorer segments of their homeland societies, such as the Pakistanis, Indians, and Moroccans in the United Kingdom, most Palestinians in the United States and Kuwait, both Christian and Muslim Lebanese who have recently migrated to the United States, and the Latin Americans in the United States) or "capitalists" (middle-class migrants and richer migrants, such as the recent emigrants from Hong Kong to Canada and the United States, white South Africans who have migrated primarily to other Anglo-Saxon countries such as Australia, and Israeli Jews who permanently reside in various host countries). In the same vein, some of those groups are unorganized (as is the case for the white South Africans), some are loosely organized (such as the Palestinians in the United States and Canada), and some are well organized (such as the Colombians in the United States and Israel).

The Age Factor

Here distinctions must be made among historical (or classical) diasporas, modern (or recent) diasporas, and incipient diasporas (i.e., diasporas in the making, groups of migrants who are in the initial stages of forming organized diasporas). This latter category includes the Pakistanis, Chinese, and South Koreans in the Persian Gulf area (Weiner 1986; Glick Schiller et al. 1992; Sheffer 1993a; Van Hear 1998) and other groups that for various reasons are in only the initial stages of organization, such as the Palestinians in Europe and North America and Russians in the Baltic republics. As a result of some recent migrations that have occurred against the backdrop of the political transformations that followed the collapse of the Soviet Union, and also as a result of the growing economic gap between poor and rich countries, some new state-linked diasporas have emerged.

Though the nature and status of the stateless diasporas and incipient diasporas will be discussed, the main focus of this book is on two contemporary types of ethno-national diasporas. Those of the first type are the "historical state-linked diasporas," such as the Jewish, Greek, Chinese, and Armenian. As discussed in Chapter 2, those diasporas emerged in antiquity or during the Middle Ages, and now they have become linked to nation-states that were created in much later periods. The second type is that of fully fledged "modern state-linked diasporas," namely, those that were established after the seventeenth century, such as the black, African-American, Italian, Polish, and Irish diasporas.

During certain periods in their history, some historical diasporas, as well as some modern diasporas, became dormant, which means that most of the diaspora members were deemed to be assimilated or fully integrated into their host societies. In such cases, those groups lost many of their ethno-national traits and substantially severed their connections with their old homelands. Recently, some of those diasporas have experienced revival. They have reorganized and become active in their host countries and in their homelands. Examples include notable segments of the Polish, Croatian, Slovenian, and German diasporas and some Scandinavian groups in the United States and Australia.

The need to distinguish three different categories of such diasporic entities is a further indication that these are among the more intricate social and political formations currently in existence, and they must therefore be characterized appropriately. Furthermore, in order to bypass the many previous predictions and prescriptions about their future, they should be defined in a manner that will avoid the normative disparaging definitions and characterizations that were influenced by the traditional Marxist, liberal, and assimilationist approaches to ethnicity in general and to ethno-national diasporas in particular. Their new portrayal should also jettison the earlier assumptions that those groups constituted a temporary phenomenon, that their members were bound to assimilate and lose their unique identity, that they were in exile, and that they were artificial or purely imagined social and political entities.

Hence the following profile of ethno-national diasporas is intended to capture the full scope, diversity, and complexity of those groups. It is also intended to capture the range of their multifaceted activities using various levels of analysis. In fact, this is an elaboration and refinement of the "operational definition of ethnic diasporas" that I proposed in the mid-1980s (Sheffer 1986b, pp. 8–11), which, as far as I can ascertain, was the first attempt to offer such a comprehensive characterization of those diasporas. It is proposed that this elaborate profile will fit most, if not all, existing ethno-national diasporas. It is based on the common attributes and organizational and behavioral patterns of historical, modern, and incipient diasporas. The enduring elements of diasporism and of specific diasporas discussed in Chapter 1, the new factors pertaining to contemporary diasporas that have developed because of globalization and liberalization, and the issue of their continuity will be elaborated in connection with this profile. Most important, in line with the main thrust of this book, the profile highlights the political aspects of the diaspora phenomenon.

A General Profile of Contemporary Diasporas

As discussed in Chapters 1 and 2, ethno-national diasporas arise as a result of both voluntary migration and imposed migration to one or more host countries.

Contrary to a widely held view, except for serving as a basis for assessment of whether or not first-generation migrants would return to their countries of origin, and for assessing the nature of their initial contacts with their kinfolk back in the homeland, identifying the reasons for migration from homelands is not crucial for an understanding of the nature of diasporas, their organization, and their behavior in host countries. This is especially true regarding the economic backgrounds of such migrants. That is, understanding diasporas and their behavior does not depend on whether at the time of migration from their homelands migrants were rich or poor, for upon arrival in their host countries both rich and poor migrants have to deal with similar problems and face similar dilemmas.

Most migrants make the critical decision whether or not to settle permanently in a host country and join an existing diaspora, or help to establish one, only after arriving in the host country, and in view of the prevailing political and economic conditions there. Surveys and polls have shown that upon their arrival in host countries, very few migrants are emotionally or cognitively in a position to make a firm decision whether or not they intend to live away from their homelands permanently, and whether or not they wish to maintain their connections with the homelands (Barghouti 1988; Magnifico 1988; Krau 1991; Gold and Phillips 1996; Gold 1997; Sheffer 1998; Van Hear 1998). Furthermore, relatively few migrants or refugees who voluntarily decide to leave their homelands because of ideological and political reasons are driven by prior intentions to settle and integrate or assimilate into their host societies, on the one hand, or to join or organize diasporic entities, on the other.

The fourth feature of the profile concerns the permanent settlement of ethnic migrants in host countries. Thus, migrants sometimes will leave their homeland to go to a host country but will stay there only temporarily because they encounter local restrictions on their permanent settlement or because of economic, political, or social difficulties there, after which they will move on to a second host country. In some cases they may even move to third or fourth host countries.

Only when migrants reach welcoming host countries where they intend to reside permanently do they begin to consider assimilation, integration, or joining or establishing diasporic entities. As noted earlier, pinpointing that juncture in the personal history and collective history of migrants is critical not only for a proper understanding of the development of particular diasporas but also for distinguishing among the various types of transient migrants and diasporans. Such distinctions can be useful, because those who from the outset do not intend to settle in their first host country, those who later consider it unfriendly and therefore migrate to another host country, and those who are determined to return to their homelands will not be interested in joining or establishing diaspora communities. Those migrants will not face the dilemma of assimilation versus creating or joining diaspora communities.

Large groups of migrants who in their host countries established new societies that eventually gained independence are not included in the category of ethno-national diasporas. That is the case notwithstanding the fact that members of such groups may still have felt affinity for their old homeland and may have maintained cultural ties with it. The main reason for excluding such groups from the discussion here is that they either forged or adopted new identities in their new places of residence, and consequently their strongest loyalty was to the new societies and states that they had formed. In fact, those individuals and groups had come to regard their newly founded countries and states as their exclusive homelands.

Hence, ethno-national diasporas are those groups that remain minorities in their host countries and thus potentially may face the possibility of expulsion, as well as social, political, and economic hardships and rejection.

The readiness and capability of migrants to maintain their ethno-national identities in their host countries and to openly nurture their communities and support their homelands are two additional crucial features of our comprehensive profile of the ethno-national diasporas. Whereas most observers have stressed how the structural, social, and political environments can affect migrants' abilities to maintain their identities in their host countries (Gold 1992, pp. 4–14), here the emphasis will be on migrants' capabilities and readiness to make tough decisions that will affect their situations and their options in host countries. Hence, the critical formative stage in the development of diasporas is reached only after migrants have overcome the initial shocks involved in leaving their homelands. Only afterward can they begin to cope with the difficult problems involved in settling in host countries: interacting with the culture prevailing there, confronting the daunting tasks of finding jobs and renting or buying suitable housing, establishing social relationships, and finding sympathetic and effective support systems.

When migrants consummate their initial adjustments and solve the immediate problems involved in settling down in host countries, they face the main dilemma in their new lives: whether to opt for eventual assimilation or maintain one's ethno-national identity. In addition to the need to resolve that crucial strategic dilemma, this phase requires many tactical decisions, especially in regard to the migrants' expectations concerning better economic and political opportunities, and the extent to which those expectations are met will impact their decisions regarding assimilation or full integration. Such dilemmas and questions can become further complicated if migrants opt for mixed marriages, or if the receiving societies offer tempting incentives and rewards to migrants who are willing to give up their old identities and undertake the problematic process of intensive integration that eventually may lead to assimilation. At that stage, another issue usually arises: How will host societies and governments react to the migrants' inclination to assimilate and integrate?

In some host countries, especially non-democratic states that have tight restrictions on entry and allow only brief residence for migrants and guest workers, all the previously mentioned dilemmas and issues are irrelevant. In certain host countries, the social and political environments can be so hostile that even when there are no formal constraints, migrants may be unwilling even to entertain the idea of assimilation and integration into the host societies, or of establishing organized diasporas (Brand 1988, pp. 107–48; Van Hear 1993, 1998, pp. 199–202; Lesch 1994). In any event, the decisions that migrants make on reaching that stage of their introduction into their host countries will have far-reaching consequences for them, for their kin in their countries of origin, and for the host societies and governments.

Migrants base their decisions about their future in their host countries on a complex mix of emotional and rational considerations. This has to do with the observation that their primordial and psycho-logical/symbolic identities, compounded by practical instrumental con-siderations, strongly influence most of their decisions in their host countries. Individual and collective decisions to maintain ethno-national identities are not sufficient for the establishment, revival, or maintenance of diasporas. They must be followed by equally critical decisions to take up membership in diaspora organizations or, when those do not exist, to assist in establishing and then operating them. Intensive efforts in this sphere are essential. Without such organizations, diasporas cannot thrive or even exist in what are basically hostile environments.

Organization probably is the most important factor that allows us to distinguish between the various types of transient migrants who stay for relatively long periods in host countries, on the one hand, and the members of incipient and established diasporas, on the other. Yet, usually only the core members of ethno-national migrant groups actually join ethnic organizations or become involved in their operation. Because of increasing attitudes of relative tolerance toward migrants, mainly in Western democratic host countries, in certain cases assimilation and sub-stantial integration may eventually occur, causing severe membership losses to incipient diasporas as well as established diasporas.

During the initial period after migrants arrive in host countries, most decisions concerning their future strategy and patterns of behavior are made by individuals or by small groups – nuclear families, extended families, fraternities, and associations – which means that these migrants and their families and associations should be regarded as functioning social actors.

As soon as communal organizations are formed, or as soon as migrants join existing diaspora organizations, they face the need to make additional collective choices. At that juncture, they must decide on the main strategy that they will pursue vis-à-vis their host societies and governments, their homelands, other dispersed segments of the same nations, and international organizations.

The menu of available strategies is large, beginning with assimilation, ranging through various modes of accommodation, and ending with separation, and, in the case of stateless diasporas, including support for secession in an attempt to seize land from dominant societies and create their own nation-states in their homelands. More specifically, this spectrum includes the following strategies: assimilation, integration, acculturation, communalism, corporatism, isolation, autonomism, secession, separation, and irredentism (Iwanska 1981; Smith 1981, 1986; Weiner 1991; Sheffer 1994).

Memories of the uprooting from their homelands, initial hardships in their new host countries, the need to make critical decisions about settling there, the compelling necessity to decide whether or not to resist total assimilation, and the efforts migrants invest in establishing and running communal organizations all tend to promote solidarity among members of such groups. In other words, diaspora solidarity is not based solely on ties to homelands, but rather only fully develops in host countries and reflects the diasporans' situations and needs there.

On the basis of such solidarity, a degree of cohesion emerges within those groups. Again, solidarity and group cohesion are founded on the primordial, cultural, and instrumental elements in their collective identities. To ensure the survival, continuity, and prosperity of diasporas, their common sentiments and sense of unity must overcome generational, educational, social, and ideological differences and gaps that always exist within diaspora groups. Otherwise such diasporas will disintegrate and ultimately disappear. Without a significant degree of solidarity, any domestic and trans-state activities will be almost impossible. Furthermore, solidarity and a sense of identity provide the motive force for promoting and maintaining ongoing contacts among a diaspora's elites and its grassroots activists. Those relationships are of major social, political, economic, and cultural significance for the diasporas, their host countries, their homelands, and other interested actors.

The traits just discussed constitute also the foundation on which diasporas organize and from which they later implement their strategies and carry out their collective activities. A major purpose of those activities is to increase the ability and readiness of diaspora members to maintain their interest in their homelands and in cultural, economic, and political exchanges with those homelands.

The establishment of diaspora organizations and participation in those organizations can create the potential for dual authority, and consequently also for dual or divided loyalties or ambiguous loyalty vis-à-vis host countries. Development of such fragmented loyalties often results in conflicts between diasporas and their host societies and governments.

To avoid undesirable conflicts between diasporas' norms and the norms and laws set by host governments or by dominant groups in those host countries, most state-linked diasporas accept the basic rules of the game prevailing in their host countries. At certain periods in diasporas' development, however, actual or alleged dual or divided loyalties, generated by dual authority patterns, can create tensions and conflicts between social and political groups in host countries and diasporas. Under certain circumstances, such tensions can lead to homelands' intervention in host countries on behalf of their diasporas, or to homelands' direct intervention in the affairs of their diasporas.

Communal cohesion and solidarity, recurrent problems facing diasporic entities in their host countries, diaspora members' wishes to support their homelands, pressures originating in homelands to provide such support, and the sheer bureaucratic momentum of diaspora organizations all prompt diasporas to become engaged in a wide range of cultural, social, political, and economic activities. Diasporas' activities are intended to meet certain basic needs that no other social or political organization can meet or would wish to meet. Yet, because most members of organized diasporas are citizens of their host countries and enjoy certain rights there, in many cases their organizations do no more than complement the services provided by host governments.

Consequently, diaspora organizations function on a number of levels – that of the local diaspora communities, host countries' societies and

governments and trans-state activities. In this context, of particular practical importance, and therefore also of considerable theoretical and
analytical interest, are diasporas' exchanges with their homelands. Diasporas exist as trans-state formations, and in addition to their activities
aimed at sustaining the diaspora communities themselves, their exchanges
with homelands and the help that they extend to homelands constitute
an essential element in diaspora communities' functions.

The conduct of such exchanges is facilitated by the existence of elaborate, sometimes labyrinthine, intra-state and trans-state networks.
Those networks expedite the transfer of significant resources to homelands, to other segments of the same diaspora, and to other interested
and involved states and organizations outside the host countries. The
creation and regular operation of such networks are critical for sustaining all diasporas.

Because of their importance and wide range of goals and functions,
those trans-state networks can become sources of trouble for diasporas.
The activities of such networks can lead to clashes with various elements
in host societies, including other diasporas, and may deeply disturb host
governments, for those activities may be regarded as the most blatant
expressions of diasporas' dual, ambiguous, or divided loyalties. In
extreme cases, the existence of such networks may be perceived as an
indication that such ethnic communities are acting as fifth columns in
host countries.

Some of the trans-state networks, in addition to serving the legitimate
and peaceful interests of diasporas and their homelands, have played
more sinister roles. In some cases they have transferred sensitive information and illegal materials. It is therefore understandable that host governments may become suspicious of such networks and their operators,
for they can indeed serve as conduits of resources for illegal activities
such as international terrorism, for the supply of weapons, and for
money transfers to combative ethnic groups. The existence of such networks can also rouse the suspicions of international organizations such
as the United Nations and Interpol.

As a result of the combination of the foregoing characteristics, diasporas are predisposed to come into conflict with their homelands, host
countries, and other international actors. The likelihood of such conflicts
is closely related not only to economic competition with other groups in
host countries but also to absolute and relative degrees of economic and
political deprivation (Gurr 1993). Such conflicts are sometimes caused
by cultural subjective factors related to diaspora members' identity and

identification, as well as the complex patterns of divided and dual authority and loyalty.

The tensions and clashes involving diasporas and other domestic and international actors get attention in the news media and in political circles and therefore may cause damage and grief to all sides. Basically, however, most state-linked ethno-national diasporas are interested in cooperating with host societies and governments.

In this vein, diasporas are capable of significant contributions to host societies' culture and economic well-being. They can serve as bridges between friendly segments in their host societies, on the one hand, and their homelands and international actors, on the other. In short, exchanges through those networks can provide significant cultural, economic, scientific, and political benefits to all parties involved (Shain 1999).

The Applicability of the Profile

As noted earlier, certain features of contemporary diasporism are similar to those that typify diasporas that were established in earlier periods. The most significant common characteristics of historical diasporas and modern diasporas can be summarized as follows:

- All diasporas have been created as a result of voluntary or imposed migration.
- In most cases, decisions to join or establish diasporic entities have been made only after migrants have settled in their host countries.
- Diasporans generally have been determined to maintain their ethnic identities and have been capable of doing so. Those identities have been important bases for promoting solidarity within diasporic entities.
- Most diasporas have established intricate support organizations in their host countries.
- They have been involved not only in economic activities in their host countries but also in significant cultural and political exchanges with their homelands and other diasporic entities of the same national origin.
- They have maintained contacts with their homelands and other dispersed segments of the same nation.
- In some cases, blatant hostility and discrimination have forced individuals and groups to join or establish ethno-national diaspora organizations.

However, because of changed social and political conditions prevailing today in almost all corners of the globe, both established and incipient diasporas are acquiring additional new features that are enriching their traditional character and adding to the great complexity of the diaspora phenomenon.

The increases in complexity (La Porte 1975) are particularly reflected in some changed patterns within the traditional triangular relationships involving diasporas, homelands, and host countries. Those changes include, for example, more diversified migration patterns, adding further complexity to the background factors involved in the establishment of new diasporas and sometimes the revival of older dormant ones. The new ways in which homelands are getting involved in migrants' exit and return (i.e., in trafficking) also figure in this new equation. Additional changes have occurred in other spheres: in homeland governments' agency roles, in the timing of migrants' departure from homelands, in their destinations, in the arrangements made for their arrival in host countries, in the terms of migrants' settlement in host countries, and in the formation of diaspora organizations. Changes have also occurred in diasporas' multiple connections with their homelands through sophisticated trans-state networks, in the multiplicity of exchanges they conduct with other diaspora communities, in the balance of power between diasporas and homelands, in the patterns of authority and loyalty, and in the possibilities of return to homelands.

It should be reiterated that when strictly applied, such a multifaceted characterization/profile of the main attributes of contemporary ethno-national diasporas excludes a relatively large number of ethnic groups that bear certain similarities to diasporas, such as the Anglo-Saxon predominant groups in the United States, Australia, New Zealand, and Canada. The same applies to the Spanish and Portuguese in Latin America and South America, as well as to the French segment in Canada and the Walloons in Belgium.

However, migrants who are leaving rich countries, who permanently reside in foreign states but retain their original citizenship, and who are inclined to establish communal organizations and keep meaningful contacts with their homelands should also be considered as potential members of ethno-national diasporas. This is a departure from the widely held view of those particular groups. Usually they have been regarded as tourists or temporary residents. Thus, if actually formed, their communities should be classified as incipient or established diasporas. Thus, for example, according to recent estimates, in the mid-

1990s more than seven million Europeans lived for extended periods outside their homelands in host countries within the European Union. Because of the hope that eventually there will be complete cultural, social, and political integration of the member states of the European Union, until now these groups have attracted little scholarly attention. Yet in view of the slow pace of that integration and the increases in their numbers, those groups merit special attention and additional study. Likewise, scant attention has been paid to the fact that proto-diaspora communities of Americans exist in host countries around the globe: Since the late nineteenth century, a sizable American colony has existed in France, especially in Paris; similar American communities exist in Germany, Britain, Japan, and the Philippines. Increasing numbers of elderly people from Scandinavia, Britain, and Germany have established diaspora communities in various southern European countries, such as Spain and Italy. Though until recently those entities have not been included in the discussions about diasporas, they should be. The inclusion of those overseas Americans in this category raises some interesting theoretical questions: Can the Americans, who themselves are of diverse ethnic origins and are citizens of a civic state rather than an ethnic state, be regarded as belonging in the category of ethno-national diasporas, or do they constitute yet another borderline case?

Occasionally such groups will play significant roles in their host countries' internal politics, as well as in regional and international political and economic affairs. In that respect they resemble other ethno-national diasporas. Aside from any overt or clandestine activities that they might undertake, their mere existence in host countries is a factor influencing both international relations and host countries' internal politics. Such was the case for several small American proto-diasporas: that in Libya on the eve of Muammar al-Qadaffi's revolution in 1969; that in Lebanon during the 1982 war and in its wake when Americans were caught in the cross fire between the Israelis and the Palestinians, Syrians, and Lebanese; and that in the Persian Gulf region during Desert Storm. Those Americans found themselves in the middle of local and international hostilities that required their homeland's active assistance and intervention. British and French citizens residing in conflict-prone zones have found themselves in similar situations. The need to protect and even rescue such groups has led to American, British, French, and German political and military intervention in the internal affairs of some smaller states hosting those proto-diasporas. In some cases the interventions led to marked exacerbation of international tensions.

From a definitional point of view, the case of African-Americans and blacks in other countries in the Western Hemisphere, especially in the West Indies and the Caribbean islands, as well as in Britain, is somewhat similar to that of the Gypsies. Yet by any account, their cases are far more complex. Whereas some African-American and black leaders, intellectuals, and rank and file tenaciously claim that those groups constitute fully fledged diasporas that are imbued with an explicit yearning for close contact with Africa, which they view as their homeland (Edmondson 1986; Shepperson 1993), others in the Caribbean islands, Latin America, and the United States do not regard themselves as such. Following the publication of the best-seller *Roots* and a general reawakening in the African-American and black communities in the 1960s and 1970s, many members of those groups began searching for their ethnic roots in Africa and became active in the movement that viewed the African-Americans and blacks as a cohesive African ethno-national diaspora. It seems, however, that by the 1980s and 1990s many African-Americans who previously had been inclined toward the diaspora argument had lost interest in that pursuit. Moreover, although such matters are hardly quantifiable, now it appears that most of them show little interest in their purported homeland, which in any case would be either the enormous African continent or vast regions within it, with which it would be difficult to maintain meaningful political and economic contacts. Thus, despite ardent efforts by generations of African-American leaders, politicians, and scholars – Marcus Garvey, W. E. B. Du Bois, Malcolm X, and, to a degree, Jesse Jackson, to mention only a few outstanding persons who have been active in this field since the late nineteenth century – to promote pan-Africanism and the interlinked idea of a cohesive African diaspora, relatively small segments of that community actually identify and define themselves as members of a diaspora in the sense discussed here (Harris 1982; cf. Shain 1999, pp. 135–7).

In sharp contradistinction to this skeptical view of the African transnational community, there is a substantial group of observers and scholars who have begun to see the African-Americans and blacks in the Western Hemisphere and in the United Kingdom and western Europe (known as the "Black Atlantic") as a "cultural diaspora." Proponents of that notion of cultural diasporism apply it especially to African-Americans and blacks, and in doing so they diminish the significance of the historical roots of those groups and their connections with their perceived homeland. Instead, they emphasize the construction and reconstruction of identity. Consequently they regard those identities as globalized, cosmopolitan, creolized, and hybridized (Hall 1990; Gilroy 1994; Cohen 1997, pp. 33–41, 129–54). As part of that approach, those observers strongly emphasize literature, music, and other cultural aspects as quintessentially necessary unifying factors and as sound bases for declaring those entities to be diasporas. Some of those scholars rightly point to the close connections between the cultural aspects and the social and political aspects in the existence of those groups.

Yet the inclination of some African-Americans and "Atlantic blacks" to perceive themselves as a fully fledged ethno-national African diaspora lingers on, along with their intention to maintain actual political and economic connections with Africa (especially Liberia). In the mid-1990s, for example, a number of congresses were held in the United States and in Africa that were intended to promote those ideas, including the possibility of large groups returning to Africa. In these instances, African governments, especially, because of internal and international considerations, voiced skepticism and tacit opposition to such a return.

The case of the African-Americans and blacks in South America and Latin America, as well as in western Europe, sharpens our focus on some of the difficult definitional and theoretical issues pertaining to the inclusion/exclusion of various groups in the category of diasporas discussed here. Although there is no doubt that members of the black Atlantic group can be seen as constituting a diaspora, the question that remains open is the location of their homeland. Is it the whole of Africa, or the different countries that their ancestors left, such as those in the West Indies? The more specific case of African-Americans and the blacks in Latin America and South America is even more complex and ambiguous. Their inclusion in the category of ethno-national diasporas must depend exclusively on whether or not the rank and file and their leaders regard themselves as diasporans and their groups as diasporas. As in the case of other diasporas such as the Jewish and the Armenian, the question of their inclusion in that category is a matter of their identification, their explicit connections with their homelands, and their organization for diaspora activities.

In the final analysis, despite the many ambiguities regarding the identities, orientations, and loyalties of those groups, it seems that, as in the cases of various other diasporas, the core elements of the Black Atlantic, the black, and the African-American communities should be regarded as parts of the ethno-national diaspora phenomenon analyzed here, and indeed we shall pursue that line.

On the other hand, reviewing the situation of diasporas in developing countries, especially in Africa, it seems that some large groups that still maintain tribal forms of organization, and whose descendants reside in more than one state, should not be considered ethno-national diasporas as defined here; see the discussion of "borderland cultures" by Cohen (1997, pp. 189–90). Such is the case, for example, with the Fulani, Yoruba, and Hausa in sub-Saharan Africa, the Berbers in North Africa, most of the native tribes or "first nations" in the Americas, the Bengalis in the Indian subcontinent, and the Bedouin in the Middle East. The main reason for their exclusion from the discussion here is that most of them became dispersed not as a result of intended or forced migration out of their homelands but as a result of what can be regarded as "natural" gradual expansion. That expansion should be attributed to their population growth, their need for more pasture and arable lands, and their inherent inclination to wander during the nomadic stage of their historical development. During much later periods, disregarding the ethnic compositions of the populations in those vast areas, colonial and imperial powers such as the British, French, and Portuguese in Africa and to some extent the Spanish and Portuguese in Latin America and South America imposed artificial boundaries on those people and on their territories. Those boundaries often split ethnies, as well as smaller units such as ethnic extended families and tribes, ultimately leaving them politically divided and living in different states. Those factors produced situations such that those groups seem to resemble diasporas. Therefore, those large "ethnic categories" (Smith 1981, 1986) constitute potential and actual non-diasporic irredentist groups (Chazan 1991; Smith 1992). As noted, the same applies to the first nations in North America. For such aggregate reasons, those groups are not included in the ethno-national diaspora category. Only if large groups migrated out of the homeland and settled in distant countries should they be regarded as diasporas.

In order to clarify the status of groups that constitute borderline cases, the positions of the Kurds and the Palestinians (on the Kurds, see Whalbeck 1998) and various ethnic groups in the central Asian republics of the former Soviet Union, such as the Uzbeks, Turkomans, Baluchi, and Azerbaijani, who resemble classic irredentist groups, should be studied in greater detail. All those groups fall into the category of ethno-national diasporas discussed in this book. One reason for their inclusion is that in addition to the segments that reside along the "artificial borders" of existing states (such as the Kurds in Turkey, Iraq, Iran, and

Syria and the Palestinians in Israel, Palestine, Lebanon, Syria, and Jordan), those groups have branched out far beyond their historical homelands and adjacent states, forming diaspora communities in host countries that do not share geographical borders with their homelands. More important is that some of those groups, especially Turkic groups in the former Soviet republics, have reestablished connections with their cultural homeland, Turkey, and thus they belong to the revived pan-Turkish movement and behave like other state-linked diasporas.

Although it would be difficult to determine the numbers of their communities and their sizes and current locations, the multitude of displaced persons and refugees in the Balkans, Africa, and Asia should be included in the category of ethnic diasporas. Those groups were forced to migrate out of their homelands because of frequent wars and long periods of hostilities, and given the currently existing non-democratic regimes and political arrangements in those regions, many of those people cannot return to their countries of origin. Because many have permanently settled in new host countries, it is not proper to regard them as refugees. Furthermore, despite the intense hostility toward them from the indigenous populations, they have acquired all or most of the characteristics of incipient ethnic diasporas. Some, such as the Tutsi and Hutu, who voluntarily moved out of Rwanda to Zaire and back, or were expelled from Rwanda, should be classified as incipient diasporas (Prunier 1995, 1997).

Other borderline cases that fit the composite profile of ethno-national diasporas include the Hispanic groups, particularly the Mexicans who have migrated and continue to migrate to the United States. That is because many of them have become dispersed all over their new host country, often settling far from the American–Mexican border, even as far as Canada. Because of the vastness of the United States and the fact that some do settle far from the Mexican border, they cannot be regarded as typical borderland-culture groups or non-migrant irredentist groups. Thus the Hispanic groups should be regarded as state-linked diasporas, because many of them resolutely assert their ethno-national identities, they do not apply for U.S. or Canadian citizenship, they establish communal organizations, and they maintain contact with their families and communities back in their homelands (for a similar view of the Mexicans in the United States, see Shain 1999, pp. 165–95). It is obvious that implementation of the North American Free Trade Agreement (NAFTA) will further increase the migration and permanent settlement of Mexicans and other Hispanics in North America. Their larger numbers will encourage their eventual organization as diasporas. An emerging issue that should be further studied is the trend toward creation of a pan-Latino diaspora in the United States. However, because it is a recent development, there are few data on it, the analyses are still very sketchy, and therefore any theorizing about it would be premature.

Qualitative Factors Influencing the Diaspora Phenomenon

In implementing the profile of ethno-national diasporas proposed earlier in this chapter to include some entities in this category and exclude others, we perceive a need to make distinctions between quantitative and qualitative factors, both of which affect the status of those groups and entities and hence the validity of the definition/profile and its evaluation. The quantitative factors are, for example, the dates of migration, the timing of migrants' decisions to settle permanently in a host country, host countries' naturalization and citizenship laws, formal membership in diaspora organizations, financial contributions to communal organizations, well-defined political activities on behalf of homelands, and the frequency of visits to and communications with the homelands. Here it should be emphasized that the qualitative factors are not less important. First and foremost, these are the psychological desire and considered determination of migrants to maintain their ethno-national identities in their host countries, and to openly identify as such. In other words, in the current world climate, belonging to a diaspora depends primarily on one's self-definition rather than on the way that host societies and governments define or perceive those formations. Thus ethnic migrants who opt to assimilate, who do not have continuing interest in their homelands, who are reticent to publicly identify themselves as members of a specific diaspora, who do not express a certain degree of loyalty toward their homelands, and who do not establish or maintain tangible ties with those homelands will not become diasporans.

Likewise the "awakening dormant diasporas" (Sheffer 1986b, p. 4, 1994) cannot be measured and assessed only on the basis of quantitative factors. Rather, the most meaningful manifestations of such revivals are through "soft" qualitative factors. Most notable among those groups are communities that in the wake of recent dramatic upheavals in international politics, especially the collapse of the Soviet Union and the liberalization in China, have begun to show renewed interest in their homelands. Not surprisingly, this revivalist trend is especially prominent among groups whose origins were in central and eastern Europe, the

Baltic states, and the Balkans. Such trends can be detected among Polish-Americans (Pienkos 1991) and among Hungarians, Slovenians, Croats, Ukrainians, Latvians, and Estonians in the United States, Canada, and Australia.

Scandinavians in the United States, especially in the Midwest, constitute another interesting case that is influenced by factors that can be measured only qualitatively. Though it is neither a widespread tendency nor the beginning of a reemergence of dormant diaspora communities, there are certain indications (such as renewed interest in the history and current situation in old homelands, more frequent visits to those homelands, and interest in economic ties with those countries) that some of the assimilated groups have become interested in renewing their contacts with Norway, Denmark, and Sweden. And that trend is not confined to Americans of Scandinavian origin. Some Americans of Dutch and German origin are showing similar renewed interest in their ethnic roots. Yet, for the time being, those and other groups that in fact are only potentialities hardly fit in here, for the vast majority of the members of such prospecitve groupings have been assimilated into their host countries, and the chances that they would adopt diaspora patterns of behavior are small.

In this context it is relevant to note how Americans report their ancestry. According to the 1990 federal census, 58 million Americans claimed German ancestry, 39 million claimed Irish ancestry, 33 million English, 24 million African-American, 15 million Mexican, 10 million French, 9 million Polish, 6 million Dutch, 6 million Scottish, and 5.5 million Jewish. Such data can be of help in assessing which are the reawakening groups, the scope of their revival, and the possibility of the reestablishment of dormant diasporas by people who regard themselves, and who have been regarded, as totally assimilated into the host-country society.

The most relevant qualitative factors that determine membership in diasporas are choice, identity, and identification. Because it would be difficult to measure the impact of these three factors on the inclination to establish or join diaspora communities, they raise the most perplexing dilemmas that individuals and groups of migrants actually encounter. Similarly, these factors intrigue and perplex students of the diaspora phenomenon. The issue is that hardly any host society or government tries to compel individuals or groups of migrants to establish organized diasporas, join them, and remain members of such entities. Quite the contrary: Though to a great extent imposed assimilation (which in certain cases had been disguised as the melting-pot concept) has ceased to be a primary strategy for dealing with migrants, and, as noted, more host societies are showing greater tolerance toward those migrants, those societies and governments are still reluctant to permit or encourage the formation of organized diasporas or grant them official recognition. In any case, the need to make critical choices concerning identity and identification as diaspora members entails the necessity to deal with some of these complex non-quantifiable issues. Despite that growing inclination to discreetly but implicitly tolerate the activities of organized diasporas, host societies and governments are not likely to help those groups resolve their dilemmas. Rather, as noted earlier, host societies and their governments face serious problems of their own because of the emergence of ethnic diasporas in their midst. Although some governments may try to frustrate attempts by incipient and established diasporas to organize and act in the political and economic spheres, they can hardly influence individual and small-group decisions to preserve their ethno-national identities and organize. To illustrate this point, let us turn to some concrete cases. Russian Jews and Pontic Greeks in the Soviet Union, Palestinians in Kuwait prior to the Persian Gulf crisis, and Gypsies in central and eastern Europe throughout their beleaguered history have all maintained their identities, associations, and external connections despite severe limitations imposed by those host governments. The members of those diasporas held on to their ethnic identities, and some identified as such. Those diasporans continued to create and maintain both clandestine and legal organizations and channels of communication with their homelands, as well as with their fellow ethnics elsewhere.

Democratic societies and governments such as those of the United States and France have tried to influence the integration and assimilation processes of migrants and diasporas through various governmental assimilatory and integrationist policies and by extolling the melting-pot ideal. In the long run, however, they and other hosts have found it difficult to alter in any meaningful way the inherent inclinations of ethnic migrants who are determined to maintain their identity, and thus such government efforts have failed to halt the development of diasporic entities (Glazer and Moynihan 1975). That should be kept in mind by anyone attempting to assess the potential for endurance and growth of both historical and modern diasporas.

These observations also pertain to the behavior of incipient diasporas. When such groupings find themselves simultaneously pressured by host governments to assimilate or integrate and pressed by homelands to maintain their identities, it is often the case that the ethnic identity prevails. Essentially, the personal decisions that migrants make regarding these dilemmas will determine the pace and intensity of the evolution of incipient diasporas into organized diasporas, as well as the tempo for the awakening and expansion of dormant diasporas.

Members of dormant diasporas face similar dilemmas during periods of dramatic change in their homelands and times of extreme hardship in their host societies. During periods of change in their homeland those individuals and groups tend to revive their identification with the diaspora and consequently also with the homeland. That can result in intensive contacts with homelands and explicit readiness to extend assistance to them. Irish-Americans faced such choices after the rise of the Irish Republican Army (IRA) and during periods of escalation in the conflict in Northern Ireland. Because of the devastating warfare in the former Yugoslavia, Serbs, Croats, Albanians, and Slovenians in the United States, Canada, and Australia have found themselves in a similar situation. Such choices confronted Ukrainians and Lithuanians in the United States and Canada during the upheaval in the Soviet Union in the late 1980s (Rubchack 1992). During the protracted civil war in Lebanon, Lebanese communities in Latin America and the United States had to make such decisions. And Palestinian-Americans had to make up their minds about the two *Intifadas* in the Israeli-occupied territories in the early and middle 1980s and in 2000.

Then there are the decisions that members of both historical and modern diasporas, like the Jews, Chinese, Armenians, and Indians and other Asians, must make regarding their membership in diaspora organizations in basically hostile host societies, for even the relative tolerance shown toward diaspora communities in various Western states, such as the United States, Canada, Britain, Holland, and Sweden, has not relieved the diasporas of the burden of facing those dilemmas. Rather, the new lenient atmosphere probably has made decisions more complex: It is more difficult to withstand assimilationist opportunities when host societies are more tolerant. Despite growing inclinations among some ethnic groups in Western countries to be rid of some of the burdens that are created by their identity and escape into the welcoming arms of their host societies, today the majority of the members of those ethnic groups prefer to maintain their distinct "original" ethno-national identities and, depending on circumstances, create, join, or revive ethnic diasporas.

There is a certain degree of implicit congruence between the attitudes of host governments that show greater tolerance toward the presence and regular activities of diasporas and the attitudes of the members of those groups themselves, especially those who basically wish to maintain their identities and contacts with their homelands. On the other side, non-democratic receiving governments, such as those of Saudi Arabia and other small Persian Gulf states, still have little enthusiasm for integration of foreigners, whether from Arab or non-Arab countries (Owen 1985; Weiner 1986; Brand 1988; Amjad 1989). Rather, those governments have pursued explicit exclusionary, segregationist, and discriminatory policies toward ethnic migrants, especially those who have shown an inclination to organize into diasporas. Moreover, some of those governments have expelled individuals and groups of migrants who have shown a wish to settle for periods longer than those governments originally anticipated. Nevertheless, the growing demand for workers for both menial and skilled tasks forces most Western governments and other governments to allow migrants to remain for extended periods. But almost invariably those governmental policies are coupled with various degrees of restriction on migrants' immediate integration into local societies. In the final analysis, by permitting the entry of such guest workers, those governments are unintentionally preparing the ground for the almost unavoidable eventual emergence of permanent diasporas.

The main outcome of all these contradictory trends is that ethnic groups, including ethno-national diasporas, have gained relative freedom to pursue informal cultural autonomy, that is, to maintain most of their traditions and mores in their host countries. Occasionally that freedom has been further enhanced by a reluctant inclination, especially on the part of democratic host governments, to accept cultural diversity as a fait accompli. There have, of course, been some unintended consequences of all these perplexing processes and difficult decisions. Thus, despite societal and governmental opposition, in some poorer non-democratic host countries the existence of ethnic diasporas may help to pave the way toward legitimized pluralism, and the existence of ethnic diasporas in modern rich societies contributes to the emergence of multiculturalism.

In most cases, such trends are reflected in the attitudes of both receiving governments and diasporas toward language. Today, more host governments and societies are tolerating the use of foreign languages in both the public and private domains. For example, many governments and private employers do not require that guest workers, travelers, and members of diasporas applying for certain kinds of jobs be proficient in the local language. In view of the economic difficulties facing most Western governments and their increasing reluctance to spend on welfare and education, few host governments are willing to invest substantial resources in intensive language instruction for migrants, though some host countries, like the United States, Canada, Australia, and most European Union member states, provide schooling for migrants' children in their native languages.

Also, there has been a subtle change of heart among migrants and diasporans concerning the learning of host-country languages that in turn affects the relationships between host governments and those groups. For example, many Hispanics and Asians in the United States and many Turks in Germany, particularly those who settle in enclaves populated almost exclusively by their kin, do not see any immediate need to learn the languages of their host countries. Like most new developments among diasporans, this is a growing phenomenon. For example, according to a survey done in 1990, among migrants who entered the United States between 1965 and 1969, 6% did not speak English; among those who entered between 1970 and 1974, 7% did not speak English; among those who entered between 1975 and 1979, 7.5% did not speak English; among those who entered between 1980 and 1984, 9% did not speak English; and among those who entered between 1985 and 1990, 17% did not speak English (*Economist* 2000). It is plausible that the current percentages are even higher. What that means is that language is losing its former critical significance as a factor that either impeded or facilitated acculturation and integration: In some host countries, language no longer poses impenetrable cultural and social barriers between diasporas and their host societies. In certain cases, knowledge of the new lingua franca, English, is a sufficient qualification for full or partial entry and integration into the host society.

On the other hand, and contrary to a widely accepted view, the ability to speak and read one's homeland language is not an essential requirement for joining and belonging to a diaspora community, nor for communicating with the people back in the homeland. Moreover, no longer is knowledge of the homeland language an absolutely necessary sign of allegiance to the diaspora and the homeland. The reawakenings of the Polish, Ukrainian, Croatian, Lithuanian, and Slovenian diasporas in the United States and Canada show that such revivals are possible despite a marked decline in the use of those homeland languages. In the same vein, the fact that second, third, or fourth generations of diasporans do not speak the old native language does not mean that they cannot be committed to their communities and cannot reinvigorate their sense of belonging to their diasporas (cf. Landau 1986, pp. 98–100, 2001).

Rather than a requirement of profound knowledge of the homeland languages, even scant acquaintance with those languages, acceptance of national values and cultural traditions, and membership in diaspora communities and regular participation in the activities of their various organizations are the important, almost essential, factors determining allegiance to those diasporas and to their homelands. That observation is supported, for example, by comprehensive polls conducted in the American Jewish community (Kosmin et al. 1991).

Such recent developments, including the increasing but non-quantifiable respect for ethnic culture that is reflected in, among other things, the popularity of ethnic food (e.g., Indian food in Britain and Thai food in the United States), fashion (e.g., Japanese fashion in Europe), music (e.g., North African music in France, and black music in the black-Atlantic areas), and literature (e.g., best-selling novels by Japanese, Chinese, and Indian diasporans living and writing in the United States and England), make it easier for diasporans to both earn respect and maintain their identities (Gilroy 1987, 1993; Clifford 1994). By the same token, and regardless of proficiency in their native languages, diasporans can learn the history and culture of their nations and participate not only in innocuous cultural activities but also in more sinister political activities being pursued by leaders of their organizations. The greater freedom diaspora members now enjoy in preserving their identities, in publicly showing their ethno-national identification, and in joining social and political associations also increases their ability to develop and maintain regular ties with their homelands.

Whereas the greater tolerance accorded the various forms of ethnic existence is a primary reason for the current flourishing of diaspora communities and their increasing contacts with their homelands, the availability of rapid international transportation and the great variety of new means for global communication also facilitate the maintenance of trans-state contacts with homelands and other dispersed segments of the same nations. Furthermore, such technological advances make it more difficult for repressive governments to intercept and frustrate contacts with homelands and other diaspora communities. Because regular communication between members of diaspora communities and officials in the homelands has been so enhanced, the ability of diasporas to exert some influence over developments in their homelands has also increased. Because international travel has become much easier, except during periods of turmoil in their homelands or in host countries, the numbers of visits to homelands by diaspora members have increased dramatically.

Also, the fact that the world is rapidly "shrinking" makes it easier for homeland leaders to visit their "subjects" in their diasporas. Though again it would be difficult to measure impacts, during such visits the leaders can encourage diaspora members to maintain contact with the homelands, they can recruit financial support for homelands, and they can help to resolve controversies between homelands and diasporas and disputes among various factions in the diasporas. Some of those have been quite memorable visits. That was the case with the galvanizing visit to the United States of Israel's first prime minister, David Ben-Gurion, after the establishment of the Jewish state in 1948, as well as the visit of the Polish president, Lech Walesa, in the late 1980s, and the visit of the Palestinian leader Yasir Arafat in the 1990s. To the annoyance of some host societies and governments, those and other visits by homeland leaders have served as rallying events for regroupings and reorganizations of their diasporas. Visits by lesser politicians and officials are no less significant for fostering better relationships between homelands and their diasporas. Because heads of state and national leaders usually are reluctant to offend host governments, they most often leave the task of promoting homeland–diaspora relations to their subordinates.

Though again it would be difficult to measure their impact, other modes of communication between diasporas and their homelands may be of even greater significance. For example, real-time television coverage of dramatic events, such as the many instances of ethnic unrest and uprisings in the post-cold-war era, can trigger all sorts of contradictory emotions and reactions among diasporans. Occasionally such intensive coverage may fuel spontaneous revivals of dormant diasporas and prompt decisions to organize and launch massive political and fund-raising campaigns on behalf of either their homelands or their co-nationals in other host countries. Recent examples abound: During periods of intense discord and armed conflict in their respective homelands, or as a response to persecution of their fellow ethnics in other diaspora communities, American Jews, Palestinians, Armenians, Kurds, Croatians, Slovenians, Serbs, and Albanians all have mounted campaigns of protest ranging from orderly lobbying to violent confrontation, and most have gained considerable coverage in the news media and in the relevant academic literature.

Improvements in transportation and communication, together with the globalization of electronic banking, facilitate transfers of goods and information, as well as remittances and other financial transactions, not to mention more sinister exchanges with homelands. The most important aspect of such developments is that communications through all those channels and networks are almost unstoppable. Neither host countries nor homelands can stop diasporans from creating and operating such networks to strengthen their multifaceted relations with homelands and other diaspora communities. It is clear that the scope and intensity of diaspora–homeland contacts no longer depend on close proximity to the homelands, nor on the goodwill of host governments, but solely on the intentions and strategies pursued by diasporas and, to a lesser degree, by their homelands.

All these considerations about the inclusion of ethno-national groups in the diaspora category, and the various quantitative and qualitative factors influencing their existence, provide the basis for the discussion in Chapter 4, which examines data on diasporas around the world.

4

Diasporas in Numbers

A numerical estimate of the scope of contemporary diasporas is essential for any further analysis of the phenomenon. However, as in the case of the data pertaining to other aspects of contemporary ethnicity, it is extremely difficult to obtain anything approaching precise figures on the actual sizes, compositions, and dispersals of ethno-national diasporas. The lack of accurate data and the ambiguity in the available statistics are connected to what can be called the "data politics" of the diaspora phenomenon. Moreover, that illustrates the great social and political sensitivity of this issue for all parties involved – homelands, host governments, other ethnic groups residing in host countries, and the diasporic entities themselves. In other words, to some extent the unavailability and inaccuracy of such data are neither accidental nor the result of "objective" difficulties in data collection and processing. In most cases the problem stems from deliberate policies of homelands and host governments intended to suppress or falsify information about modern diasporism, that is, to conceal its actual impressive magnitude, rapid growth, and emerging significance.

The European Union provides a good illustration of such data politics. It is true that information about place of birth and citizenship is available from most European Union member states. Some European Union countries, however, prohibit the registration of ethnic origins, culture, race, religion, and political affiliation of migrants. That is a new development. Before and during World War II such registration was the norm in most of the European states. Unfortunately, the Nazi regime used such information in its abominable efforts to exterminate Jews, Gypsies, and communists. To prevent the recurrence of such a situation, western European countries introduced restrictive laws and regulations to guard the privacy of such information.

In any case, the incomplete and confusing demographic data are closely related to the inadequacies of the prior definitions of ethno-national diasporas, the confusion over the definitions of migrants and diasporans, and the failure to distinguish between (a) "immigrants" and various types of transient sojourners in host countries and (b) persons who have made a firm decision to settle permanently in host states and create or join diaspora communities there. Drawing clearer lines of definition between these two categories, as in the profile suggested in Chapter 3, should help to clarify the issue of which groups should be included in the category of ethno-national diasporas, and consequently the scope of the phenomenon and the numbers of diasporans.

The inadequacies of the available data are further compounded by inherent conceptual difficulties in identifying various categories of people in migrant ethnic groups who have experienced varying degrees of acculturation, integration, and assimilation in their host countries. That is, we have yet to make clear distinctions among "core members," "members by choice," "marginal members," and "dormant members" of ethno-national diasporas. To clarify that issue, we shall suggest such distinctions.

"Core members" are those persons who are born into the ethnic nation, who avidly maintain their identity, who openly identify as members of their diasporic entity, who are ready to act on behalf of their community and homeland, and who are recognized as such by the community itself and by its hosts. "Members by choice" are descendants of mixed families, converts, and so forth, who fully participate in the life of the diaspora. "Marginal members" are those persons who maintain their ethnic communal identity but do not identify as such or purposely distance themselves from the community. "Dormant members" are those persons who have assimilated or fully integrated, but know or feel that their roots are in the diaspora group; under certain circumstances those persons will identify with the diaspora and can be mobilized by its leaders and organizations (for similar distinctions regarding the Jewish community in America, see DellaPergola 1992).

A further reason for the imprecise data on diasporas is that authoritarian and intolerant nationalistic host governments tend to suppress information about such groups. That is because of their acknowledged reluctance to encourage additional international migrants who might end up as members of permanent diasporas in their states. Also, that tendency to suppress information concerning diasporas is connected to host governments' fears of civil disorder and conflict that might be initiated by xenophobic groups within the host societies. Recently such xenophobic and hostile attitudes have surfaced in various countries in reaction to the proliferation of migrants and diasporic entities, as, for example, in most Persian Gulf states. In an effort to avoid any adverse consequences, the governments in that region have been careful not to disclose accurate, up-to-date information about the Palestinians and other permanent settlers within their borders (Van Hear 1998, pp. 80–6). Similarly, the available data on Moroccans in Spain and France remain partial and outdated, as do the data on Turks in Germany, where there have been disorderly protests against migrants and guest workers and even violent confrontations.

A fourth reason for the lack of adequate data on diasporas is that some host governments, especially in authoritarian regimes such as Saudi Arabia, Egypt, and Iraq, are unwilling to admit that within their borders there are large groups of migrants and members of diasporas and that consequently the populations they control are becoming heterogeneous. Combined religious, cultural, and economic considerations motivate those governments to either minimize or totally conceal their numbers of migrants and members of permanent diasporas. Moreover, the mushrooming global interest in ethnicity and ethnic groups, the claims that those groups are putting forward, and the potential threat that they pose to their hosts are motivating those governments to try to gain better control over legal and illegal immigration and, as far as possible, to suppress information that might encourage the entry of migrants and their subsequent permanent settlement.

More specifically, those governments are worried that if the ethnonational diaspora groups should become aware of their actual numbers and hence their potential political power, they might demand greater cultural and political autonomy, or increased social and economic rights and benefits. Thus internal social tensions and security concerns are responsible for much of the secrecy and ambiguity surrounding the numbers of migrants and diasporans.

Finally, in some cases, especially in developing African and Asian countries, there is the additional problem that the demographic data in general, and particularly the statistics about specific segments, are simply inadequate or inaccurate.

For parallel political reasons, diaspora leaders and activists may be reluctant or unable to provide accurate figures about the numbers of members in their communities and organizations, their geographical distributions in their host countries, the trends of their natural growth and intermarriages, and their rates of integration and assimilation. To some extent that reluctance to gather and release such data stems from fear of expulsion from host countries where xenophobia is on the rise (such as Germany vis-à-vis its Turkish workers, France and its North Africans, and Israel and guest workers from Romania, Turkey, and Ghana who have become members of permanent diaspora communities there). Diaspora leaders have also had to avoid further fueling the antagonism of ultranationalist and ultraconservative groups (as in Austria and Australia, where there have been considerable increases in anti-foreigner sentiment). Diaspora leaders may also be reluctant to provide demographic data because they do not want members of their communities and homelands to know how many of their number are being lost to assimilation and integration.

Except for falsification of data, suppression of data, and accidental failure to provide full and accurate data about ethno-national diasporas, the most difficult data problems arise from definitional ambiguities in countries where data about social and economic factors are plentiful. To illustrate this point, the data sets to describe ethnic groups that are published by the agencies of Western states or by interested organizations such as the United Nations can be arranged in a wide variety of ways: "composition by race," "composition by nationality," "national origin," "place of birth," and "ethnic origin." Furthermore, except in most European Union states, data have been arranged according to categories such as "ethnic composition," "linguistic composition," and "ethno-linguistic composition." To further complicate and confuse matters, sometimes data on ethnic groups, such as Jews, Palestinians, Lebanese, Moroccans, and so forth, can be found under the heading "religion."

Still another difficulty in obtaining reliable data derives from the accelerating rapidity of developments in the migration sphere. Most notable is that since the late 1980s there have been tremendous influxes of migrants into western Europe (for migration trends in that region, see Parfit 1998), the Persian Gulf, and Scandinavian countries as well as into the traditional receiving countries such as the United States, Canada, and Australia. Most of those have been chain-migrants – that is, they have moved to host countries where they have family and compatriots in established diaspora communities of different historical ages and at varying stages of development and organization. Thus, over the past decade the numbers of migrants who have joined existing ethnic diasporas or have settled and formed incipient diasporas have considerably increased, and still there is no accurate, up-to-date information about those rapid developments.

The recent influxes of migrants into receiving countries whose governments try to curb the migration trend, such as Germany, France, Italy, Austria, Denmark, Canada, Australia, and the United States, have also raised the question of information concerning illegal newcomers who stay for long periods, or even permanently, thus swelling the ranks of established and incipient ethnic diasporas without ever being accounted for in the demographic data. For example, since the early 1990s it is estimated that 750,000 Moroccans have crossed through Spain and settled in France, Holland, Belgium, and elsewhere in Europe. There is no doubt that those migrants have joined the incipient Moroccan diaspora in western Europe, but that has not been reflected in the official data on minorities and diasporas published by those countries. Similar developments followed the disintegration of Yugoslavia. Legal and illegal migrants from the states that had composed Yugoslavia, as well as from Albania, now reside in western Europe, but their numbers are not reflected in the published statistics. The same applies to illegal immigrants in the United States and Canada, and also in Israel. Even in those three cases, where ample data are available on almost all other social and economic aspects, there are only rough estimates of the numbers of such migrants and their locations, their regional concentrations, and other demographic details.

Yet another aspect of this problem concerns data on the movements and fate of many thousands of refugees from the Balkans, again especially from the former Yugoslavia, and more particularly from Bosnia and Kossovo. Similarly, there are only very crude estimates of the numbers of refugees in Africa and Asia who have remained in their host countries for long periods and are eventually forming and joining incipient diasporas. These include Muslims who were driven out of Burma, Christians driven out of southern Sudan, and Ghanans driven out of Nigeria (Van Hear 1998).

To more closely reflect recent developments in diasporism and diasporas, as well as to offset definitional difficulties and data shortcomings, the available figures on incipient and established diasporas – official and semiofficial – probably should be adjusted upward. That should allow for a more realistic assessment of the dimensions of this worldwide phenomenon. Such a judicious upward adjustment has been attempted in regard to the figures presented next.

TABLE 4.1. *The Main Historical Diasporas: Diasporas Established in Antiquity or during the Middle Ages (Estimated Numbers in Main Host Countries)*

Diaspora	Numbers	Main Host Countries and Areas
Armenian	5,500,000	Iran, Turkey, Lebanon, Syria, Germany, France, U.S., Canada, Australia, Georgia, Russia, Ukraine, Azerbaijan, central Asian states
Chinese	35,000,000	Burma, Vietnam, Kampuchea, Malaysia, Korea, Singapore, Philippines, Indonesia, Taiwan, Japan, Thailand, U.S., Canada, Australia, Peru, South America, Europe
Druze	1,000,000	Syria, Lebanon, Israel
German	2,500,000	U.S., Australia, Latin America, central and eastern Europe
Greek	4,000,000	Albania, Cyprus, Turkey, U.S., Australia, Canada, South Africa, Ethiopia, Germany, western Europe, Middle East
Gypsy	8,000,000	U.S., Canada, former Soviet Union republics, the Balkans, eastern, central, and western Europe
Indian	9,000,000	Fiji, Guyana, Jamaica, Kenya, Kuwait, Malaysia, Mauritius, Nepal, Burma, Oman, Pakistan, Saudi Arabia, Thailand, South Africa, Singapore, Sri Lanka, Trinidad, Tobago, United Arab Emirates, U.K., U.S., Yemen
Jewish	8,000,000	U.S., Canada, South Africa, U.K., France, Australia, former Soviet republics, Latin America, eastern Europe

Sources: Moneni (1984); *UN Demographic Yearbook*, 1985, 1986; Horak (1985); Kettani (1986); Gerholm and Yngve (1988); Segal (1993); Chaliand and Rageau (1995); Sowell (1996); *Encyclopaedia Britannica* (1998, 1999).

In accordance with the foregoing observations, especially in view of the definitional and statistical shortcomings, Tables 4.1, 4.2, and 4.3 offer what we believe to be a reasonable first attempt to estimate the real numbers of the main historical, modern, and incipient diasporas, as well as an outline of their main current concentrations and host countries.

Even a cursory examination of these three tables provides some interesting insights into the ethno-national diaspora phenomenon. The data show that in terms of simply numbers, diasporism today is indeed a substantial phenomenon. These data indicate that more than 300 million

TABLE 4.2. *Modern Diasporas (Estimated Numbers in Main Host Countries)*

Diaspora	Numbers	Main Host Countries and Areas
African-American	25,000,000	U.S.
Black Atlantic	1,500,000	U.S., Canada, U.K.
Hungarian	4,500,000	Czechoslovakia, Romania, U.S., Canada, former Yugoslavia, former Soviet republics
Iranian	3,500,000	Iraq, Lebanon, Syria, Turkey, United Arab Emirates, U.K., Germany, U.S., Canada, Australia, Central America, South America, western Europe
Irish	10,000,000	U.S., U.K.
Italian	8,000,000	Britain, Argentina, Brazil, Germany, U.S., France, Australia, western Europe
Japanese	3,000,000	U.S., Hawaii, Brazil, Peru, Canada
Kurdish	14,000,000	Iraq, Iran, Syria, Turkey, Germany, France, other western European countries
Lebanese (Christian)	2,500,000	Egypt, Syria, Persian Gulf states, Argentina, Brazil, Mexico, U.S., Australia, Canada, France, western Africa
Polish	4,500,000	U.S., Canada, western Europe, former Soviet republics
Turkish	3,500,000	Germany, Bulgaria, Holland, Cyprus, Greece, Denmark, Sweden, Norway, U.S., Austria

Sources: See Table 4.1.

persons permanently live outside their homelands and can be regarded as members of ethno-national diasporas that fit the general profile presented in Chapter 3.

The data show that virtually all attempts by governments (such as those of Germany, France, Canada, Japan, Australia, the United States, Kuwait, and Israel) to curb further legal and illegal migration to most countries – and, consequently, to prevent the emergence of new diasporas and the growth of existing ones in those countries – have thus far failed. Rather, diasporas appear and continue to grow in all those countries, entailing political implications of the first order.

In addition, the data show that in only a relatively few instances does a single ethno-national group tend to migrate to a single country. Most

TABLE 4.3. *Incipient Diasporas (Estimated Numbers and Main Host Countries)*

Diaspora	Numbers	Main Host Countries and Areas
Albanian	1,000,000	Greece, Germany, Denmark, Sweden, Norway, Holland, Italy, U.S., former Yugoslavia
Algerian	1,500,000	France, Germany, Tunisia, Morocco
Bulgarian	500,000	U.S., various states in western Europe, former Soviet republics
Colombian	250,000	U.S., Israel
Croatian	350,000	U.S., Canada, Australia
Cuban	750,000	U.S.
Czech	2,500,000	U.S., various western European states
Egyptian	1,000,000	Iraq, Saudi Arabia, Libya, U.S., Canada, Persian Gulf states, western European states
Filipino	2,000,000	U.S., Canada, Persian Gulf states, western European states
Israeli	750,000	U.S., Canada, South Africa, Australia
Haitian	750,000	U.S., Canada, Bahamas
Jamaican	300,000	U.S.
Korean	3,500,000	China, Japan, U.S., Australia, former Soviet republics
Latvian	120,000	U.S., Canada, Australia
Lithuanian	850,000	U.S., Canada, Australia
Malayan	5,000,000	India, Thailand, Singapore
Mexican	20,000,000	U.S., Canada
Moroccan	1,500,000	France, Germany, Holland, Spain, Belgium, Denmark
Pakistani	750,000	United Kingdom, Holland, Denmark, Norway, Persian Gulf states
Portuguese	2,000,000	France, Canada, U.S., U.K.
Puerto Rican	600,000	U.S.
Russian	25,000,000	U.S., Australia, western Europe, former Soviet republics
Serbian	130,000	U.S., Canada, Australia
Slovak	1,500,000	Hungary, U.S., Canada, former Yugoslavia
Slovenian	200,000	U.S., Canada
Spanish	1,000,000	France, Germany, Switzerland, U.S., U.K., Canada
Syrian	750,000	Argentina, Brazil, U.S.
Tamil	3,200,000	Sri Lanka, U.S., Canada, Australia, western Europe
Ukrainian	1,800,000	Poland, Estonia, U.S., Canada, Australia
Vietnamese	1,000,000	Kampuchea, Japan, U.S., Canada

Sources: See Table 4.1.

move in many different directions and end up as diasporic entities in a number of host countries. That pattern has at least three major political implications.

First, and probably most important, their dispersal over a number of host countries leads to the development of trans-state networks among the diasporas' various branches. Thus, with the proliferation of diasporas and their greater geographic dispersal, those networks become further extended to include new incipient entities that migrants establish as a result of initial, secondary, and tertiary migrations (legal and illegal) to various host countries. Consequently, those networks, which in most cases today take full advantage of the new media, are becoming increasingly elaborate and complex and are carrying substantial quantities of various resources – money, information, intelligence, and political and diplomatic support (Dahan and Sheffer 2001).

The accelerating processes of globalization and the spread and elaboration of diaspora networks boost diasporas' political involvement in and influence on events at the global, regional, and state levels. Those expansionary processes have been evident, for example, in the development of the Palestinian and Kurdish stateless diasporas and their increasing political significance. With every wave of Palestinians and Kurds who were driven out of their homelands or who left voluntarily for political, social, and economic reasons and settled in various host countries, their international trans-state networks became more extensive. Through those networks, the Palestinians, the "overseas Kurds," and dispersed Albanians have intensified their contacts with similar communities in other host countries and have marshaled more intangible and material resources. Eventually those resources either have been transferred to their homelands or have been used in host countries to promote their causes.

Second, extension of those networks not only solidifies their connections with their homelands but also strengthens the ties among the various diaspora communities of the same origin. The Jewish diaspora is renowned for the intensive political exchanges that its various communities conduct through such networks. The Armenians, Greeks, Poles, and recently even the Gypsies are making use of their networks for the protection and promotion of the interests of their people.

The third implication of the proliferation and expansion of such networks is that from the various viewpoints of the diasporic entities, the host countries, the homelands, and the fourth and fifth actors involved in all those relationships, the "exchange game" is becoming far more complex, and sometimes it yields unpleasant surprises for all parties involved, though in more instances the results are beneficial for all those involved.

More generally, the tentative data presented here confirm that actually there are very few remaining homogeneous nation-states. Quite the contrary: Most states are ethnically pluralistic, albeit not necessarily multicultural as far as the laws and governmental policies are concerned. Moreover, these data confirm the lesser-known fact that there are very few countries that do not host diasporas. It has been said that Poland, Portugal, Japan, Taiwan, and North Korea, which have "exported" some of their own citizens, are still homogeneous countries. But because of the increasing reach and volume of migration patterns, even in those hold-outs and other similar countries sizable incipient diasporas are beginning to appear. Thus, when ethnic pluralism develops and ethnic mosaics exist, they are tending to be composed not only of indigenous minorities but also of ethno-national diasporas.

A further conclusion is that in addition to the establishment of new diasporas and the expansion of existing ones in traditional democratic receiving countries, such as the United States, Canada, and Australia, at the beginning of the twenty-first century ethno-national diasporas are beginning to emerge in countries that previously had not been regarded as likely targets for permanent settlement of ethnic migrants, such as the small Persian Gulf states, Sweden, and Japan. Thus there will be additional societies and regimes that will have to begin considering the political ramifications and adjusting their political systems to those new developments.

A few points that were made in Chapter 3 should be restated here to emphasize their political importance. Up to this point, the discussion has focused on those entities whose data were included in Tables 4.1–4.3. However, we have excluded some ethnic groups that bear certain similarities to the diasporas we have been discussing. Thus, Anglo-Saxons, French, and other closely related groups of European origin, such as Finns, Danes, Norwegians, and Swedes, in the United States, Australia, New Zealand, and Canada have not been included. The main reason for their exclusion has to do with identity and identification: Most members of those groups do not regard themselves as diasporans and do not maintain contact with their ancestors' countries of origin. Also, the Anglo-Saxons and Francophones constitute the majority, or essential parts of the majority, or the dominant group in the countries and regions of their settlement, which have come to be considered their sole homelands. It should nevertheless be noted that despite complete or almost complete assimilation and integration of the Scandinavian groups into their new homeland societies, in certain cases memories of their old countries of origin have not totally faded. Consequently, such groups have established communal organizations and are behaving like fully fledged diasporas. Since the 1960s, for example, there have been active, diaspora-like Danish organizations in Australia and New Zealand. Among those diasporans there have been prosperous Danish businessmen who were forced to leave Denmark because they had collaborated with the Nazis during World War II, and there have been workers from the agriculture and dairy industries who were displaced by increasing mechanization in those industries in Denmark. All of those have maintained their identity and contacts with their old homeland. As noted, here we refer to them as clear borderline cases.

The main political implication of the developments discussed in this section seems to be that when dramatic changes take place in their ancestral homelands or their host countries, such groups tend to perk up and become active on behalf of their old homelands. It will be theoretically interesting and politically significant to see in the near future how those groups will conceptualize and actually deal with their identities and how they will relate to their old homelands and to other diaspora communities of the same and different origins. Because the best way to think of these groups is as proto-diasporas, some of them may play, either publicly or behind the scenes, cultural, political, and economic roles in shaping their host countries' foreign affairs. Their presence in host countries, especially in hostile ones, can have further political implications: When political situations become unstable, or during actual civil crises in host countries, they may try to drag their homelands into the situation to intervene diplomatically or militarily.

As noted in Chapter 3, most observers do not regard as diasporas a number of large tribes, or what have been termed "traditional ethnies" (Smith 1981), and their descendants. Among others, this category includes the Azeris in Iran and in other former Soviet republics, the Turkmen in Iraq, Iran, and Afghanistan, the Tatars in central Asia, and the Bengalis in the Indian subcontinent. Politically, those groups have been and will remain major sources of conflict and instability in their homelands and in host countries.

Moreover, because of new political developments, it seems that in the future the ethno-national diaspora category will include the groups of displaced persons and refugees of longest standing in Europe, Africa, and Asia. For either security or economic reasons, those groups were forced to migrate during and following wars and conflicts in their homelands, and it is likely that many of those displaced persons will not be allowed to return to their homelands. Other groups that during long periods of tension in their regions and homelands migrated voluntarily, but hoped to return to their homelands, may decide to stay put in their new host countries even after the tensions in their homelands subside. Eventually all those groups may settle in their host countries, relinquish the status of refugees, and regardless of the hostility of host populations and difficult social and economic conditions, assume all or most of the characteristics of diasporas. Then the social and political boundaries and contours of whole regions may change, and in those regions and countries new ethnic mosaics may emerge.

On the other hand, although, strictly speaking, groups like the Kurds and Palestinians have greater similarities to other irredentist minorities than to diasporas, nevertheless for all practical purposes they constitute diasporas and are discussed as such here. Those groups have become significant political actors not only in regional host countries but also far beyond. The violent reaction of the Kurdish diaspora in western Europe to the kidnapping and arrest of Abdullah Öcalan, leader of the PKK (Kurdistan Workers party), is a powerful illustration of that point.

On the basis of these data and comments, we can now proceed to examine the intricate processes involved in the making of diasporic entities, their development, and their undoing.

5

The Making, Development, and
Unmaking of Diasporas

Following the sudden, unpredicted collapse of the Soviet Union and consequently the end of the cold-war era, politicians and academics began to focus on what they regarded as the most significant structural and behavioral issues pertaining to the new global politics. Within that context, neo-realists, neo-liberals, and neo-culturalists were considering subjects such as the contemporaneous disarray in the international system and its impact on patterns of foreign relations, the "clash of civilizations," the implications of the purported global hegemony of the United States, the chances of further major and "small" wars, nuclear proliferation, democratization and peace, multilateralism versus bilateralism, the roles of international institutions, the international political economy, and other such matters. Focusing on those concerns, politicians and analysts, especially in the United States, were paying little attention to some equally important matters, such as the reemergence of ethnicity as a central issue in domestic and international politics. More specifically, they did not attach sufficient importance to the ongoing establishment of new ethno-national diasporas, the reawakening of dormant ones, the regrouping of established diasporas and the processes of their development and their unmaking, and the impacts of all those processes on global, regional, and domestic politics.

Such neglect not only has been characteristic of academic deliberations in the sphere of international relations, which have focused on the aforementioned list of developments, but also has been typical of scholars in the field of ethnic studies in general and in the specialty of ethno-national diasporas in particular. As noted in the Introduction and in Chapter 1, only in the 1990s did certain changes occur in that respect

(Hammar 1990; Glick Schiller et al. 1992, 1995; Tololyan 1996; Van Hear 1998; Demetriou 1999).

In view of the demise and disappearance of some ethno-national diasporas and the increasing numbers of incipient diasporas, and in view of the fact that those entities are becoming significant actors at various political levels, there is a need to further explore the political aspects of the making and unmaking of diasporas. This is especially needed to supplement the partial explanations for those phases in the life cycle of diasporas that have been offered by scholars who have focused on international migratory trends and "migration orders" (Van Hear 1998).

Migrants' Difficulties in Crossing the Rubicon

Whereas the earlier studies focused on global and regional systemic changes that purportedly influence migratory trends, the emphasis here is on the calculations and decisions of individuals and small groups. These must be examined against the backdrop of the economic, social, and political factors that affect the emergence and demise of such entities. In other words, our focus should be on migrants' and diaspora members' motivations, their organization, and their relationships with their families, peer groups, host countries, and homelands, as well as on the chances for continued survival of the entities they create.

Some of the difficulties confronting potential members of ethno-national diasporas are generated by the fact that numerous actors are involved in their emergence, existence, and demise. Hence, as far as possible, for both practical and theoretical reasons, the attitudes and policies of all actors involved must be considered. That is, the development of diasporas must be analyzed from the perspectives of the migrants, but also from the perspectives of host countries, homelands, and various other relevant actors.

Above and beyond the constraints imposed by the economic, social, and political environment, the most critical issue confronting migrants after they settle in host countries still is whether they should acculturate, integrate and assimilate, or remain apart and nurture their ethno-national identities, maintain contacts with their homelands, and join diaspora organizations. The second set of emotional, cognitive, and practical questions facing migrants at that initial stage of residence in host countries includes their attitudes toward an array of social and political forces in their host societies, and especially toward host governments, for although some politicians and members of receiving societies may welcome or condone migrants' integration, most politicians and government bureaucrats in receiving countries are still ambivalent about those trends, as well as about the formation of diasporas. In other words, in most host countries, especially in non-democratic ones, there are legal and bureaucratic obstacles that migrants have to overcome before they can form or join diaspora organizations. Simultaneously, migrants must deal with formal and informal pressures emanating from domestic, regional, and global organizations and associations militating against the permanent settlement of migrants. A third kind of emotional and practical pressure on migrants arises from kin, social groups, and governments in their homelands. Almost invariably those groups have mixed, ambiguous attitudes toward "their" incipient and permanent diasporas.

The Proliferation of Incipient Diasporas

Despite such crosscutting and overlapping pressures on migrants, it is evident that the number of incipient diasporas continues to increase. Among the many diasporas in the making, most notable are the Turks and Turkish Kurds in Germany, Sweden, and other western European states who have been migrating from their homeland since the 1960s. In some host countries, including Germany, the Turks are on the verge of becoming a permanent, well-organized diasporic entity. Similarly, Moroccans in France, Spain, Denmark, Holland, and Germany are forming incipient diasporas. The same is true for many other groups: the South Koreans in the United States, Canada, the Middle East, Australia, and Japan; the Filipinos in the United States, Japan, Australia, and various Asian and Middle Eastern countries; the Pakistanis in Britain, Denmark, and other European and Persian Gulf states; the Gypsies, who have begun to organize; and the 20–25 million Russians in the former Soviet republics, who currently are becoming the largest incipient diaspora. Those and many other diasporas in the making will be joining the historical and modern diasporas.

The new ethno-national groups that either are on the verge of becoming fully established, permanent diasporas or are still in the early stages of development exhibit most and sometimes all of the features of the diaspora profile presented in Chapter 3. Among other things, most recent incipient and newly established diasporas have grown out of voluntary rather than imposed migration, and therefore they definitely do not regard themselves and should not be regarded as exiles. As with other contemporary diasporas, members of those groups are holding fast to their ethno-national identities, and they have created communal organizations, or are on the way to doing so. And they are activists in trying to protect their social and political rights. They are equally determined to maintain explicit and implicit contacts with their homelands, and they develop trans-state networks, even if in only rudimentary form, first connecting them with their homelands and later with their co-ethnics in other host countries. They frequently face serious dilemmas concerning loyalties to their homelands and to their host countries.

The new consensual view that diasporas are made and unmade as a result of both voluntary and forced migration (Sheffer 1986a, p. 9; Cohen 1997, pp. 25–9; Van Hear 1998, pp. 40–7) is a departure from the traditional view that diasporas had always been "exilic communities." That long-established view was based primarily on the history of the Jewish people since the Babylonian period, and, as discussed in Chapter 2, it did not take into account that a Jewish diaspora probably existed long before that. Because the Jewish diaspora was regarded as *the* archetypal diaspora, the notion that all diasporas were exilic communities was erroneously applied to most other diasporas. A departure from that explanatory model is important not only for understanding the making of diasporas but also for advancing our understanding of the assimilation and integration of those groups and their return, that is, the unmaking of diasporas. Although today this more comprehensive approach is becoming accepted, there is no such agreement about other underlying factors affecting those two crucial phases in the development of diasporic entities.

Because similar forces influence the entire life cycle for all types of diasporas, the creation of incipient diasporas and the demise of established diasporas show many similar characteristics. In other words, migrants and diasporans confront similar emotional and cognitive difficulties, as well as systemic political and economic restrictions. That is true not only on their arrival in new host countries and their settlement there but also when they voluntarily return or are forcefully repatriated to their homelands. To those difficulties one must add the pressures emanating from other actors, such as competing groups within a diaspora and other diasporas and indigenous ethnic minorities in the same host country. Moreover, increasingly, regional bodies (especially the European Union) and global organizations (especially the United Nations and its specialized agencies, such as the International Labor Organization) have become interested and involved actors.

As has already been noted, the various earlier explanations offered for the proliferation of ethno-national diasporas and for their undoing shared one basic weakness. They presumed that the causes for migration were also the reasons for becoming members of diasporas, on the one hand, or for returning to the homeland, on the other. Although migration and the rise of ethno-national diasporas are indirectly related, actually those are separate phenomena and should be examined as such. As noted in Chapter 1, the traditional explanations suggested for the making and unmaking of diasporas can be divided into two groups: The first stresses the "push" factors, and the second emphasizes the "pull" causes. Those twin forces provided the main theoretical basis for numerous analyses of the emergence of the Jewish and Irish diasporas and for the return of certain segments of those diasporas to their homelands. Besides the fact that the explanations were too abstract and generalized, their main weakness was their focus on systemic and environmental conditions in host countries, as well as in homelands, and their failure to focus on the migrants themselves and on the roles of other actors. The second weakness of those approaches was that when they were trying to explain various aspects of diaspora establishment and demise, the emotional and rational considerations in the social, political, and economic realms usually got lumped together. Hence there is a need for more differentiated explanations.

Indeed, some recently proposed explanations offer more differentiated and sophisticated interpretations. They can be divided into four categories. Those in the first category emphasize the impact of the new and more favorable global conditions, especially the increasing ability of international migrants to move more freely and easily from one country to another, as well as the porosity of state borders. Additionally, those explanations emphasize a global contagion, that is, a strong urge that "infects" people in almost all countries, causing them to move out of their homelands to seek greener and more promising pastures away from their countries of origin. Those in the second category of recently proposed explanations feature the "open-system perspective" on migration. That school postulates that a migration system is a network of countries linked by migration flows and by the prior and consequent relationships among those countries (Bilsborrow and Zlotnik 1995). Those in the third category deal with change, transition, and crises in "migration orders." That approach emphasizes the impact of an admixture of rational economic and political "push" factors on migrants' motivations to leave their homes and go to host countries where they can establish diasporic entities and prosper; according to the same logic, diasporans sometimes return to their homelands. Those in the fourth category stress that changes in the social atmosphere and attitudes in host countries can have the greatest impact on such decisions. Each of the four approaches merits an additional brief discussion.

The Impact of Globalization

Besides the new ease of transportation and better communication, proponents of this explanation cite multiple factors that encourage the diaspora phenomenon. The first factor is the current situation in the global economy, especially the emerging liberal trade arrangements and capital-flow policies implemented by host countries. Purportedly, these new conditions and policies allow host countries to take advantage of the special attributes of diasporas – their wide reach, cosmopolitan attitudes, trans-state networks, and ongoing contacts with homelands and other communities in other host countries – to promote the interests of the host countries (Cohen 1997, pp. 158–62). The second factor is the attraction of large cities. According to that theory, such "mega-cities," or "world cities," or "global cities" attract migrants who, because of their links to global cultural, economic, and trade networks, can easily prosper there (Sassen-Koob 1990; Prevalakis 1998). The third factor is the emergence of what have been termed "deterritorialized social identities." Essentially the argument of the proponents of that approach is that in the wake of economic and cultural globalization, "horizontal groups" (coherent social groups whose areas of settlement cross the borders of nation-states and who have multiple affiliations and associations) have emerged and eventually have gained acceptance and legitimacy (Caesarani and Fulbrook 1996; Faist 2000). Allegedly, each of those factors encourages massive migration, eventually leading to the emergence and prosperity of diasporas. Similar arguments have been applied to the demise of diasporas and to diasporans' return movements to homelands.

Proponents of that approach suggest that despite the many political, economic, and emotional obstacles that migrants face as they leave their homelands, reach desirable and hospitable host countries, and permanently settle there, or decide to return to their homelands, the new international environment offers favorable conditions that help remove, or at least lower, such hurdles. The global system has generated, so it is argued, greater tolerance, openness, and readiness to accommodate migrants to host countries, on the one hand, and returnees to their homelands, on the other. It is also suggested that these recent trends offer migrants a wider range of countries in which to reside, at least temporarily. Furthermore, although some Western countries, such as the United States, United Kingdom, France, and Germany, periodically reconsider their policies toward illegal migrants, guest workers, and political refugees seeking asylum and try to restrict their entry, fundamentally they are both unwilling and unable to totally seal off their borders and prevent migration and the subsequent permanent settlement of foreigners. And finally, because of almost total elimination of the borders between European Union states and the impossibility of implementing the idea of "Fortress Europe," the option to stop migration from other continents, regions, and non-member states, and thus to prevent the establishment of diasporas, is practically nonexistent. Similar interpretations have been suggested regarding the effect of NAFTA on the migration of Mexicans and other Latinos and the eventual emergence of their diasporic entities in the United States and Canada.

Migration Systems
Scholars who adopt the migration-systems approach base it on a number of premises: First, migration flows create trans-national systems composed of sending countries and receiving countries. Like other social, political, and economic systems, over time those systems change, mainly through the feedback mechanism. The constituent states, which are thought of as subsystems, play a crucial role in such changes through both direct and indirect inputs. Direct inputs are in the form of explicit policies and actions, and indirect influences are in the form of cooperation with political and social associations in the receiving states and with international non-governmental organizations. Systemic networks are among the mechanisms that transform macro-level factors into inputs that influence groups' and individuals' decisions to migrate. Essentially, that approach offers a functionalist model in which migrations are caused primarily by economic factors and serve economic interests. Thus, that attempt at explanation does not deal with the entire spectrum of reasons for migration, and for the rise and fall of diasporas (Van Hear 1998, pp. 17–18).

Migration Orders and Crises
Basically, the migration-orders approach regards business cycles and long-term economic restructuring as the most important factors in determining the patterns of migration and subsequent permanent settlement

in host countries. According to that approach, gradual "low-intensity changes" in those factors produce long-term "transitions" or increases in migration during a given cycle. In turn, so it is argued, "moderate systemic changes" lead to "cumulative transitions," and "acute systemic changes" cause "migration crises." To those factors that approach would add the impact of the noticeable weakening of the nation-state in the post-cold-war era and the disintegration of what has been regarded as the "Second World." Proponents of that view argue that such trends are further exacerbated by the irreversible permeability of most international borders – the cases of the United States, Canada, France, and Germany are often cited as illustrations that there is almost no way to stop the inflow of legal and illegal migrants. It is further argued that the new political freedoms being experienced in nations and societies that previously were firmly controlled, coupled with the current appalling economic conditions and unstable political conditions in former Second World countries, have created a tremendous outflow of migrants that will only continue to grow. Thus, the contention is that perhaps 450 million people in the former Eastern bloc have been brought into the global pool of potential migrants. That pool may expand even further if China relaxes its emigration controls (Van Hear 1998, p. 3). Such predictions have thus far been only partially vindicated. The possibility, or rather the threat, that all those hundreds of millions of Russians and other ethno-nationals in the former Soviet Union would hurry to pack their suitcases and migrate out of their homelands has not been realized yet. Migration from China to Russia, however, is on the rise and is causing substantial problems in various parts of Siberia. Furthermore, current migratory trends are being accelerated by political crises, especially in Third World countries, where severe persecutions, ethnic cleansing, and political upheavals have pushed millions out of their homelands in search of refuge and safe havens. Those factors motivate numerous migrants to gravitate from poorer to more affluent countries, but not necessarily to the most prosperous countries. Moreover, contrary to the accepted wisdom and expectations, those poorer migrants are moving not only to geographically and culturally proximate host countries but also to more distant ones. For example, poor Iraqis and Albanians invest enormous effort and make great sacrifices to leave their homelands and reach hospitable host countries far from home, such as the United States, Britain, and even Australia. Coupled to the notion of "gravitation," the same set of factors has also been applied to returnees to homelands.

In sum, that approach suggests that the combination of those factors creates transitory and sometimes crisis conditions that influence the patterns of migration and eventual permanent settlement in host countries, as well as the return of diasporans to their homelands. Some scholars who espouse that explanation agree with the "globalists" who claim that migration is being facilitated chiefly by the greater ease of transportation and communication. According to that view, globalization is allowing legal migrants to reach remote countries and illegal migrants to penetrate the borders of both democratic and non-democratic countries, to settle in those countries, and to maintain contacts with their homelands.

A somewhat different aspect of that explanation concerns the notion of "global contagion" and its influence on the inclination of ethnic groups to migrate, organize, and eventually mobilize for action in the host countries (Gurr 1993, pp. 132–35). The gist of the argument of that variant is that in addition to the many consequences of the communications revolution, which facilitates the instantaneous spread of news, fashions, social and political ideologies, and patterns of cooperative and conflictive behavior, people are becoming less parochial in regard to many aspects of life, including migration and settlement in host countries. Thus, the ready availability of information about migration trends and specific conditions in different host countries and homelands further influences migration. Again, this also applies to the return to homelands. A critical review of this aspect, however, indicates that the increasing contagion does not necessarily mean that when migrants actually leave their homelands they fully intend to settle permanently in host countries and sever their connections with their countries of origin.

That approach regards individual and household decisions to move out of homelands or to move again out of host countries as having only secondary importance in explaining the recent large waves of migration and the increases in diaspora communities. Along with the minor influence that approach attaches to individuals' and households' motivations to migrate, it emphasizes structural and systemic economic reasons for migration to host countries and back to homelands. In that vein, it focuses on the disparities between the countries and regions of origin, on the one hand, and target countries, on the other, and equally on migrants' networks, on "migration regimes," and on the "macro-political economy" at large. Those factors influence migration directly, and they indirectly influence the formation of diasporas and diasporans' return to homelands (Van Hear 1998, pp. 14–17).

The Impact of Conditions in Host Countries and Homelands: The "Dual-Market Theory"

Although not entirely unrelated to the foregoing suggested explanations, this one centers on migrants' perceptions of the situations in host countries and homelands. Its proponents argue that the main reasons for migration and consequently for the rise of incipient diasporas and their transformation into permanent ones are recent changes in economic conditions, especially in Western host countries that are the most attractive and desirable destinations for immigration and settlement. That explanation would suggest that regardless of cyclical economic shifts between growth and recession in those countries, and despite relatively high rates of permanent unemployment, such as in Germany, Italy, France, and Britain, there are increasing demands for cheap labor, especially menial and unskilled workers, in a wide range of industries and service sectors. Accordingly, potential migrants tend to rely on optimistic information about the availability of jobs and other commercial and economic opportunities, and they assume that no great risk is involved in moving to those host countries and settling there.

The second component of that proposed explanation is that, with the exception of some authoritarian regimes – such as Saudi Arabia, Kuwait, and Iraq, which during the Gulf War expelled the Yemenite, Palestinian, and Egyptian incipient diasporas that had begun to emerge in those host countries – the chances that there will be massive expulsions of migrants and incipient diasporas have been reduced considerably. Consequently, when thinking about their future, potential migrants must consider whether or not the chances for permanent settlement and establishment of a diasporic entity in various host countries are good, and those already abroad must consider whether or not returning to the homeland will improve their condition. Thus the optimistic outlook among potential migrants should be attributed, so those analysts postulate, partly to the new liberal international atmosphere and partly to the extensive media coverage of any major population movement.

The third element stems from the view that in developed countries, including those that have only recently joined that club – such as some Asian countries, especially those that were known as "the tigers" – there are slow but clearly discernible processes that are advancing racial and ethnic tolerance. The implication is that such developments will increase the inclination and ability of ethnic groups to enter such countries, establish themselves there, and create permanent diaspora communities. Japan is regarded as one of those previously homogeneous countries that gradually is becoming more tolerant of migrants' arrival and prolonged residence.

The four explanations are not totally wrong. Yet the new migration orders, transitions, and crises, the more agreeable global economic environment, the more favorable social and political conditions in an increasing number of desirable host countries, and the contagion created by globalization all are factors that contribute only indirectly (i.e., intervening variables) to the processes that are producing increasing numbers of incipient diasporas and bringing about the demise and disappearance of some established diasporas. The root causes for the rise of additional ethno-national diasporas and the disappearance of some others must be sought in a different set of factors.

Host Countries' and Homelands' Attitudes

Before discussing an alternative explanation for the simultaneous proliferation of new diasporas and the demise and disappearance of established diasporas, in this section we shall consider the attitudes of host countries and homelands toward those two opposing trends.

Here it should be emphasized that there is no symmetry in the way homeland societies and host societies, on the one hand, and their governments, on the other, treat these phenomena. The Irish, Greek, and Israeli societies, for example, frowned on those members who voluntarily migrated to the more economically developed, richer, and freer host countries and have not returned. The primary reasons for that disparaging attitude were patriotic and nationalistic. Those societies experienced considerable consternation out of deep concern about "brain drain," the loss of human capital, and the consequent weakening of national morale, honor, and cohesion. More recently, against the backdrop of the marked decline in patriotic and nationalistic fervor in most sending countries and the successful structural changes in their economies, the social pressures intended to discourage emigration have diminished. That is the mood whether economic conditions in homelands are good or bad. In both situations there is growing indifference toward emigration and the establishment of diasporic communities. Probably the most striking documented example of such changed attitudes is the case of Israel, where emigrants are no longer regarded as "deserters" who betray the nation and country (Damian 1987; Yaar 1998). Societies in less developed countries where poverty reigns and economic needs cannot be met locally now condone and tacitly encourage such emigration.

Moreover, poverty in homelands tends to promote chain migration. In turn, that pattern influences the nature of the diasporic entities that such migrants establish, and they tend to be more cohesive and supportive. The Christian Palestinian, Ghanan, Filipino, Moroccan, and Mexican societies provide good examples of that pattern.

Whenever migrants leaving their homelands and returnees from host countries are not severely restricted by governments because of political considerations (which usually is the case in authoritarian countries), the motivation to migrate arises from within individuals, their immediate families, and their social circles. Despite the lack of detailed polls and surveys concerning such trends, as far as can be ascertained, that is the case now in most eastern European, Asian, Middle Eastern, and North African sending countries. In some cases the drive to migrate is augmented by social and economic conditions and new societal attitudes. In poorer countries, particularly, those changed societal attitudes include increasing legitimization for individuals' rights to freedom of choice and for their attempts to better their economic conditions, as well as recognition of the collective need to alleviate the appalling economic conditions of those remaining in the homelands.

Taking advantage of the new opportunities created by those recent trends, some cynical rulers and governments serve as agencies to facilitate and encourage migration as a new source of corrupt income, especially the "export" of their unemployed to serve as menial guest workers abroad. Thus legal and illegal trafficking has become an important factor in facilitating the movements of numerous migrants (Widgren 1995, pp. 19–23; Van Hear 1998, pp. 57–61; Campani 2000).

Migrants' families, friends, and other relevant social groups remaining behind in the homeland expect that their migrants will maintain ongoing contact with them. Moreover, migrants' families firmly expect that as soon as their kinfolk reach a host country and find work there, they will transfer money back home. Indeed, remittances from that source are estimated to exceed $150 billion each year (this aspect of diaspora relations with the homeland is discussed further in Chapter 7). Although those who remain in the homeland may initially dislike seeing their relatives emigrate, so long as those migrants maintain regular contact their families are not greatly averse to the next, almost inevitable steps taken by the migrants: first, the formation of incipient diasporas, and later the establishment of fully fledged, permanent organized diasporas. After the formation of such incipient diasporas, gradually most homeland societies develop an indifferent attitude toward them. That further reflects the changing national attitudes about the moral, social, and political issues involved in accepting and justifying the existence of diasporas. During later stages in the development of diaspora–homeland relationships, families and other social groups remaining back in the homelands tend to become more concerned about the personal fate of their relatives abroad, particularly those who never intended to assimilate into their host societies and who always maintained close contact with their homelands. That is, at a later stage, homeland societies lose some interest in those who integrate or assimilate into host societies and do not maintain contact with their kin in the homeland. That, for example, has been the case with the changing societal attitudes toward Israeli migrants who have decided to settle permanently in the United States, Canada, South Africa, Australia, Britain, and, more recently, Germany (Sheffer 1998).

Homeland governments' attitudes toward "their" embryonic and incipient diasporas are quite a different matter. Generally, those political actors prefer that their emigrants retain their original citizenship and accept only temporary status in the host countries. They hope that retention of the homeland citizenship will allow them to have some control over their emigrants. Moreover, homeland governments tend to believe that during the initial period of their tenure in new host countries emigrants should continue to maintain close contact, be ready to serve their homelands' interests, and regularly remit money to their relatives back home. When their emigrants' begin to show signs of permanent settlement in host countries, home governments hope that for as long as possible those will remain incipient diasporas rather than permanent diasporas. The rationale behind that attitude is clear: Homeland governments hope that incipient diasporic entities can be more easily manipulated and thus serve their homelands' interests.

Usually that is indeed the pattern of development. The principal reason is that during the initial stage of diaspora emergence, the difficult conditions that migrants encounter in most host countries force them to depend on their homelands for substantial amounts of political and cultural support, especially support from their homeland governments. That has been the case, for example, with the Turks in Germany: Despite statements of noncommitment and indifference toward their emigrants, successive Turkish governments have provided such support. Those governments have defined fairly clear goals, designed proper strategies for achieving those goals, and acted accordingly (Chapin 1996). More specifically, successive Turkish governments have tried to control their

citizens' migration, encourage the establishment of diaspora organization in host countries, and influence their emigrants' behavior and activities. For example, Turkish governments have tried to minimize the
influence of the Islamic fundamentalist movement on diaspora communities by financing religious leaders who have opposed that fundamentalist movement. Successive governments have encouraged activities
intended to counter Kurdish militants in host countries, and on the other
hand they have created procedures to facilitate transfers of remittances,
which are important sources of foreign currency.

During the initial period after migration of large groups of their citizens and the formation of incipient diasporas, most home governments
will carefully monitor the development of those diasporas and, as the
Turkish case shows, on certain occasions actively meddle in the conduct
of their affairs. However, during later stages of their development, especially when incipient diasporas are slowly maturing into full-fledged
established diasporas, homeland governments usually begin to change
their attitudes, increasingly expressing ambivalence toward those
diasporas.

Some homeland governments reveal an attitude of cynicism in dealing
with their incipient diasporas. Once again, the history of Israel's relations with Israeli emigrants and the Romanian and Turkish governments'
relationships with their migrants in Europe well illustrate that pattern.
The most salient reason for such ambiguities and cynicism is the strong
possibility, almost a certainty, of the emergence of something less than
total loyalty among members of those entities vis-à-vis their homelands.
Because that is a highly sensitive issue, the more sophisticated home governments tend to be cautious in dealing with such diasporas.

A second factor contributing to homeland governments' caution and
reserve vis-à-vis their diasporas is related to their attempts to exercise
political influence over those emerging diasporas. Even in cases in which
it is clear that members of incipient diasporas are reasonably loyal to
their homelands, such homeland governments show caution and ambivalence in dealing with their diasporas, probably because of self-doubt
about their ability to closely control the diasporas' activities. And in
some cases there are reasons for home governments to be apprehensive
that their incipient diasporas will turn against them: dissatisfaction with
homeland governments' policies, the influence of opposition factions
within diaspora communities agitating against homeland governments,
resentment of their manipulation by host governments. Such patterns
have marked the relationships between the Cuban, Chinese, Iranian,

Iraqi, and Vietnamese diasporas and their respective homeland governments.

A third reason for homeland governments' ambivalence is genuine concern that as incipient diasporas develop and adopt behavioral patterns and policies that may benefit host countries' interests more than those of the homeland, significant segments of those diasporas may assimilate into the host societies and thus be lost to the homeland nation. Furthermore, homeland governments have some pragmatic reasons for being ambivalent and cynical. First and foremost, they are apprehensive about the possibility of being asked to help incipient diasporas in times of distress. For example, that was the case for the Italians in Switzerland in the early 1970s, the Turks in Germany in the 1980s, the Russians in the former Soviet republics, and the Romanians in Israel in the 1990s.

Despite their profound, almost inherent ambivalence, arising from the intertwined emotional, political, and economic issues involved in those relationships, home governments cannot totally ignore their emerging diasporas nor their established diasporas. Hence, it is rare to detect total apathy in those relationships. Although the relationships may fluctuate, in the final analysis most governments continue to hope that in the long run they may benefit from those relationships. Rather than ignoring or alienating emerging diasporas, they usually try to cooperate with the more important diaspora associations and their leaders, hoping for at least a "peaceful coexistence" and a reasonable degree of interaction with their diasporas. In any event, though apprehensive and suspicious, in almost all cases homeland politicians will pay lip service in declaring their unity with and responsibility for their co-ethnics in their diasporas.

Unlike the situation in homeland–diaspora relations, where the main actors are the migrants, the migrants' relatives, and the home governments, in the realm of host-country–incipient-diaspora relations things become more complicated, and there are additional actors: social and political groups, which are the main sources of opposition and sometimes hatred and violence. Although more host governments are demonstrating greater acceptance of pluralism in general, and greater tolerance toward diasporic entities in particular, social backlashes against migrants, especially against members of incipient ethno-national diasporas, still occur and are disruptive (Rogers 1993, pp. 133–7; Hanf 1999, pp. 12–14; Sen 1999). Such backlashes have occurred not only in Germany, Britain, and France but also in other countries that in the past often have boasted of their liberal attitudes and policies toward refugees and asylum-seekers, such as the United States. Hence it is not all that surprising that in the 1990s, California, which long had liberal attitudes toward migrants, was leading an anti-migration and anti-settlement movement (Bandhauer 1999). Similar developments have been seen in Canada, Holland, Denmark, and Norway. On the surface, the reason for those backlashes would appear to be mainly economic. It has been said that the cyclical economic recessions and the resultant high unemployment rates in those countries have triggered outbursts of hatred toward migrants and diasporans. Actually, however, such hostile attitudes persist even when economies improve, as seen in the cases of the United States, Britain, Austria, and France in the late 1990s. The recurrent riots and clashes in Oldham, Bradford, and Birmingham in Britain are good illustrations of such trends. They show that rather than arising from purely economic causes, hostile attitudes toward migrants and diasporas stem from renewals of conservatism, nationalism, and even racism in certain segments of those and other societies.

An additional source of tension and hostility affecting incipient diasporas is the competition among various emerging diasporas, as well as that between diasporas and indigenous minorities. That has been particularly evident in California, Florida, and elsewhere in the United States, where fierce competition involving Vietnamese, Koreans, Cubans, and Mexicans, and occasionally involving African-Americans, has resulted in tension and periodic violent confrontations. It should be emphasized again that such clashes have occurred not only during periods of economic recession but also during periods of growth and prosperity in the United States. Similar incidents have occurred in large cities in Britain, Germany, and France: Birmingham, Paris, Milan, and Berlin have all seen savage fighting between migrants and members of incipient diasporas and between local minorities and foreigner-bashers (Comparative Documentation Project 2001).

Judging from their behavior and responses to those developments, host governments and local authorities in the mega-cities are well aware of the problems posed by the arrival of migrants and by the formation of new diasporas: As newcomers try to openly organize in order to protect their interests and rights in their host countries, that further fuels societal discontent and hostility toward those migrants.

However, it is not only members of indigenous minorities and other societal groups who express hostile attitudes. Various host governments and municipalities are becoming quite apprehensive that the formation of permanent diasporas is increasing the demand for allocation of substantial resources to cater to the welfare needs of the members of those emerging diasporas. In the same vein, those governments and municipalities are aware that divided loyalties usually prevail among diasporans, so that when incipient diasporas are serving the interests of their homelands, their actions may run counter to the interests of their host societies. Yet, given the current circumstances, some host governments and municipalities have made an insightful choice: They see the emergence of organized diasporas as a lesser danger than what would result from attempts at repression. The main reason is that when migrants establish their diaspora organizations and pledge a certain degree of loyalty to their host societies and authorities, those organizations are easier to monitor than are innumerable individuals, and therefore they provide a means to keep tabs on the activities of the entire diaspora community, as well as a conduit for conducting negotiations with it and eventually for exercising some control over it. Thus, rather than dealing with numerous individuals or amorphous groups, host governments find it more convenient and efficient to deal with organized diasporas.

In some cases host governments have granted diaspora organizations and their leaders the right to establish formal corporations that officially represent their members. That has been done with the Jewish communities in France and Britain and with various Asian incipient diasporas in Britain. The diaspora communities in Birmingham and in some other cities in Britain are good examples of that pattern. In turn, the fact that those groups are so well organized tends to make them more successful in extracting from their host governments and local authorities various concessions concerning their own status and their homelands' interests in the host country.

Migrants as Social Actors

Against that complex backdrop it is now possible to turn to the main argument of this chapter. It concerns the emergence of new diasporas and the decline of some long-established diaspora communities. The crosscutting and overlapping pressures on migrants that emanate from their homelands, from their host governments and societies, and from other minorities in the host countries have not been completely offset by the recently more favorable global and local liberal trends, but they constitute only intervening factors that play lesser roles in an assessment of the causes for and the patterns of the emergence of ethno-national diasporas, their persistence, and their decline. Thus, in Chapter 1 the question was posed whether or not there are basic factors in addition to globalization, migration orders, and the attitudes of host countries and homelands that encourage migrants to become members of organized diasporas. This section deals with that issue.

The argument here is that we should digress from the traditional view about the close connection between (a) migrants' backgrounds and their reasons for emigrating and (b) the nature of the diasporas they will establish. The traditional view about the establishment of new diasporas has a long academic tradition and was an element in the thesis about "mobilized" and "proletarian" diasporas (Armstrong 1976), which claimed that migrants' reasons for migrating and the backgrounds of the migrants would determine their decisions about what kinds of diasporic entities they would form. Though it has been widely accepted and is reflected in the analyses of various writers in this field (Marienstras 1989; Esman 1994; Tololyan 1996; Cohen 1997; Van Hear 1998), the first element in that assertion is questionable. The second part of the thesis – that the cultural backgrounds of migrants will influence the nature of the diasporas they establish – is valid in certain cases. Therefore the following analysis deals mainly with the first element in that thesis.

The argument of this book is that with the exception of a few cases, the decision to establish or join a diaspora is made predominantly as a result of the migrants' own experiences, needs, and inclinations. Furthermore, those decisions are made only after a certain amount of time spent in host countries, and they are greatly influenced by the social and economic conditions prevailing in those countries. Thus, this view strongly emphasizes the fact that many migrants are not simply pawns in games conducted by an invisible hand or by systemic forces either in their homelands or in host countries. Even the poorer and less well educated migrants are not passive ciphers to be totally manipulated by states or by any other agencies. Rather, they are active social and political actors, which means that the establishment, maintenance, and dismemberment of diasporas are results of relatively autonomous decisions that individuals and small groups make in their host countries. Those decisions are not based solely on rational considerations. Subjective primordial and emotional considerations and feelings are also involved when such decisions are made. This alternative explanation is based on a number of observations concerning the emergence and development of diasporas in general, and incipient diasporas in particular.

The first observation in this regard is based on many stories, articles, books, and poems, as well as hard data showing that when leaving their homelands, most migrants respond to the question whether or not they intend to settle permanently out of their homelands with utter non-commitment. At that critical point in their lives, most migrants are not sure whether they will settle permanently in a host country and form or join diaspora communities or will return to their homelands. Although in many cases the chances are that they will indeed settle permanently in a host country, their initial noncommitment should be taken seriously, not as merely lip service to their relatives remaining in the homeland, nor as an attempt to satisfy the authorities allowing them to exit and to enter. Nor should their responses be regarded as stemming from self-deception, or as hiding different intentions. The anguish involved in individual and group decisions to leave their homelands, the conflicting pressures exerted on migrants by families, friends, and associates, and the uncertainty about the outcome of the decision to emigrate are so palpable that they lend credence to the migrants' reserved responses to questions about their intentions and their future choices.

At the bottom of the uncertainty about their permanent settlement in their prospective host countries lie doubts about the actual conditions there and also about their basic attachments to relatives, nation, and homeland. However, those kinds of ambiguous sentiments are not expressed by the much smaller numbers of migrants who leave their homelands because of profound social disappointment, because of severe political persecution, or because of overwhelming economic burdens. Among that minority of emigrants who leave their homelands because of utter desperation or disgust, most have no intention of returning (on the various studies of such attitudes among Israeli emigrants, see Krau 1991 and Sheffer 1998).

Another significant quantifiable indication that the decisions to settle in host countries tend to be made only after some period of residence in host countries and experience of the conditions prevailing there is that recently fewer migrants have been giving up their homeland citizenship and trying to acquire host-country citizenship (Castles and Miller 1993; cf. Brandt 1999). Also, decisions concerning citizenship depend not only on host countries' policies but also on homelands' policies. Moreover, many migrants say that in addition to the family and personal ties that account for their strong attachment to the homeland, they feel an attachment to the "country" and to the "people" at large. That is a crucial indicator of an identity orientation and an initial inclination to establish new diasporas or join existing diaspora communities and to maintain contact with the old homeland. As mentioned in Chapter 3, the decision to maintain contact with the homeland, which is among the most important characteristics of diasporans, should be attributed to a combination of primordial (Geertz 1963, 1973; Kellas 1991; Grosby 1994, 1995; Connor 1994), psychological-symbolic (Armstrong 1982; Smith 1993), and practical instrumental factors, rather than to purely instrumental economic considerations.

A third observation concerning the delayed decisions about settling in host countries – decisions that are reached only after assessing the conditions prevailing there – concerns the fact that many migrants, especially guest workers, leave their countries of origin intending to remain abroad only for a time that is specified beforehand. Today many people migrate under inter-governmental agreements or visa limitations that formally dictate that they must leave the host country after a specified time. That has been the case for Egyptian guest workers in Iraq, Yemenites in Saudi Arabia, most Asians (Thais, Filipinos, Koreans, and Chinese) in the Persian Gulf region, some Turks in Europe, Romanians and Thais in Israel, and so forth. As viewed by the migrants on leaving their homelands, those arrangements and limitations are major obstacles that may preclude any hope of settling permanently in host countries and establishing diaspora communities there (Weiner 1993). Thus, only after living for some time in host countries and becoming acquainted with the conditions there can migrants make firm decisions about breaking their contracts and later about permanent settlement.

Finally in this context, a related group of potential diasporans should be mentioned: the "circular migrants." These are groups of people who continually move between their homelands and host countries. They do so because of ethno-national sentiments, family and economic needs, and political and economic pressures in the host countries. Studies of Puerto Ricans, especially businesswomen, who continually move from their birthplace to New York and back have shown that they have a remarkable ability to cope with such frequent changes in context. They really feel at home both abroad and at home. Thus they remain members of established communities in both places (Scheff and Hernandez 1993). Those persons, as well as some Ukrainian entrepreneurs in Poland (Gorny 2001) and Israelis in high-tech firms in the United States, have firm roots in two worlds, and they probably provide the best illustrations of the phenomenon discussed in this book. There are indications that this phenomenon is spreading. Thus not insubstantial numbers of Turks, and Irish-Americans, as well as millions of Europeans, belong in this category of people who regularly move back and forth between their homelands and host countries. As for the future scope and nature of this type of ethno-national diaspora in the twenty-first century, it appears that their numbers will increase and that consequently they will form highly dynamic trans-state political systems.

Various groups of migrants import with them their habits, mores, patterns of behavior, forms of organization, and leaders. Those imported artifacts and persons contribute to the shape of their diaspora organizations and to their behavior. That pattern is particularly clear in the cases of the Pakistanis in Britain, the Palestinians in North America and South America, and the Latinos in the United States. Yet those organizational and behavioral patterns are continually being reshaped in host countries after the formation of organized diasporas. That is particularly the case in view of the gradual development of diasporas that feature amalgamations of "imported" and "local" patterns of organization and behavior, a process known as the hybridization of diasporas (Werbner 1997).

Migrants into Incipient Diasporas

Migrants coalesce into incipient diasporas in a staged process. During the first uncertain period of their residence in new host countries, the natural inclination of most migrants is to maintain contacts with their nuclear families and other relatives in their homelands. During that period, individual migrants regard their kin in their homelands and also, to a certain degree, their homeland governments as their main sources of moral and practical support. During that first stage in their host countries migrants face substantial uncertainty, and they harbor expectations that if worse comes to worst both their relatives and homeland governments will come to their rescue. On the collective level, they still perceive their homelands as the undisputed centers of their nations. Therefore, for as long as possible, most migrants put off decisions about permanent settlement in host countries and about their future relations with their homelands. An important reason for doing so is the considerable uncertainty about their abilities to reach positions where they can feel secure in their host countries. Hence their initial inclination is that they must first become better acquainted with the conditions there. As noted, it seems that homeland governments implicitly are also interested in prolonging that stage. Those governments want to maintain contacts with their migrants as closely as possible for as long as possible.

During that initial period of adjustment, while migrants try to sort out the intricacies of the new cultural, social, political, and economic systems confronting them and gradually learn to cope with the new factors and actors, they tend to join existing *Landsmanschaften* and other diaspora organizations or hesitantly begin to establish such bodies in order to facilitate their initial adjustment in new host countries and to maintain contacts with homelands (Elazar 1995; Gold and Phillips 1996; for historical perspective on this issue, see Soyer 1997). In addition to the moral encouragement and material assistance that migrants receive from those support organizations, such organizations provide literature, communications facilities for contacts with homelands, access to television and the Internet, and venues for meeting with other migrants or visitors from the homelands.

Quite naturally during that significant formative period, most migrants feel a need for contacts with kin, associates, and supportive agencies in both homelands and host countries. Usually they do not regard their reliance on both lands as contradictory. In some cases, however, therein lie the roots of problems they will later face while living in two worlds and wishing to feel at home abroad. Therein also can be found the roots of the ambiguous, dual, or divided loyalties of diaspora members.

Eventually, many migrants, though by no means all of them, decide to remain permanently in their host countries. Though there are no accurate figures, a common rough estimate is that the numbers of migrants who, after relatively short periods, return to their homelands do not exceed 20% of all those who entered host countries.

There is, however, nothing deterministic or irreversible about migrants' initial decisions to stay. That is, the reasons for their migration notwithstanding, the migrants' initial decisions are only tentative. Moreover, for most migrants, their wishes and hopes of returning to their homelands do not fade, and whenever those are expressed they are genuine. That is not lip service to the people back home nor to host governments (such as immigration authorities) and social agencies in host countries (such as local organizations that have to pay the costs of "absorbing" migrants). Except for the minority who are totally committed from the outset to remain in their host countries, the yearning to return to their homelands is experienced by many migrants and endures for long periods after their arrival in their host countries. In the late nineteenth and early twentieth centuries, for example, though they emigrated voluntarily, Irish, Italian, Greek, Polish, and Scandinavian migrants to the United States retained a sense of being there for only a short period, and that subjective sense remained alive even among second and third generations. That was the case even though they had become firmly rooted in their host country's cultural, social, economic, and political systems. The Tibetan diaspora provides a more recent example: Despite the fact that the Chinese have firm control over Tibet, many members of the Tibetan diaspora are imbued with a very strong sense of being in a transitory period. Many truly believe that they are on the verge of returning to their homeland.

Some groups of migrants and members of incipient diasporas maintain close ties with their homelands because they arrive in host countries accompanied by their spiritual and social leaders, or because those leaders later join the first waves of migrants in the host countries. Those leaders serve to import and consolidate homeland cultural, organizational, and behavioral patterns in the host countries. That has been the case for the Turks in Germany and Sweden and for other Muslim groups such as the Egyptians, Palestinians, and Moroccans who have migrated to the United States, Canada, France, and other European and Latin American countries, as well as for Pakistanis in the United Kingdom. The large numbers of mosques that have recently been built in most states in the United States, Australia, and European countries are indicative of that trend. That has also been the case for the Tibetans, Koreans, and Filipinos who over the past two decades have migrated to various Asian countries, the United States, and the Middle East, as well as for Sikhs who have migrated to Britain. Nevertheless, though all those groups establish and operate places of worship and cultural centers in their host countries, usually those institutions undergo clear processes of adaptation and adjustment to local conditions in the host countries.

During the initial difficult period of adjustment in any host country, religious sentiments and affiliations, fostered by religious leaders who accompany and follow the migrants, play meaningful roles in maintaining contacts among migrants who are members of incipient diasporas and between them and their homelands. Yet in that situation, religious sentiments and affiliations do not become autonomous factors in the lives of migrants. Just as in antiquity and during the Middle Ages, those affiliations rather reinforce migrants' ethno-national identities, protect the group boundaries, foster group cohesion, and reinforce the inclination to maintain contacts with homelands. The attitudes that are promoted by religious leaders are intended to prevent and in many cases do prevent hybridization of migrants and incipient diaspora communities. Thus,

Greek Orthodox and Polish Catholic priests, Lebanese Sunni and Iranian Shiite imams, Jewish rabbis, and Tibetan monks have significantly contributed to the persistence of ethnic feelings and love for homelands, and thus to the endurance of ethno-national diasporas (e.g., on the role of religion and the religious leaders in the Tibetan case, see Anand 1999; on the role of religion among Turkish youth in London, see Enneli 1999). During later stages in the development of diaspora communities, religious feelings may wane and affiliations cease. Though at first that process indicates the "normalization" of diaspora groups and adaptation to local social conventions, increasing secularization may lead to assimilation or full integration and eventually to weakening of the ties with the wider diaspora community and the homeland (Hammond and Kee 1993, pp. 56–8). In any case, the debate about the role of religion in sustaining diasporas lingers on among both practitioners and scholars.

The new media facilitate migrants' initial contacts with their homelands and somewhat reduce the need for intermediaries, such as religious and spiritual leaders. That is certainly true on the individual level. The ties of individuals to their homelands are reinforced through movies, television, videocassettes, the Internet, electronic mail, faxes, books, and newspapers that are produced either in homelands or in host countries. It is sufficient to check newsstands and bookstores that sell foreign publications, cassettes, and CDs, especially in densely populated ethnic neighborhoods in global cities and smaller towns, to grasp the full scope of that phenomenon (on the Kashmiri case, see Nasreen 1999; regarding this aspect in the white Rhodesian "diaspora," see King 1999). By any measure, the numbers of such publications sold have increased dramatically over the past decade. It is no wonder that the ease with which migrants can make such a wide range of contacts with their homelands complicates their decisions whether to settle in their host countries or to return to their homelands.

A further indication of the need and desire to maintain contact with homelands is the fact that many migrants continue to speak their native languages in their new host countries. In many situations newcomers are able to live and work among their own people without ever finding it necessary to learn the host country's language. Recently, a new pattern has emerged in this sphere: Even after learning the language of the host country, migrants show a strong tendency to remain bilingual. They tend to use their mother tongue in private domains (at home, in clubs, in religious centers, and in exchanges with other members of their diaspora) and the host-country language at school, in the marketplace and work-place, and in their dealings with the authorities (Citrin 1990, pp. 17–19; Alba 1995, pp. 8–10). Although that is not an absolute requirement for maintaining their ethno-national identities and contacts with their countries of origin, it certainly helps to preserve those identities and contacts. Experience in various American universities, especially in Florida, New York, and California, shows that that pattern is being maintained by second- and third-generation descendants of migrants, especially those from Asia and the Middle East.

The use of homeland languages, the presence of spiritual and social leaders among the migrants and diasporans, and the availability of cultural and political materials related to homelands all contribute to a solid foundation for setting up cohesive entities in host countries and for maintaining ties with homelands. That does not mean, however, that those factors are solely responsible for the patterns of diaspora organization and behavior that will be followed later.

Invariably, whether migrants' spiritual and social leaders encourage those migrants or whether they act spontaneously, the decisions whether or not to organize coherent diasporic entities or to join such entities are individual decisions. In other words, essentially those decisions result neither from manipulation by homeland authorities and by the religious and cultural leaders who accompany migrants nor from coercion by host societies and governments. Decisions in that intimate sphere originate at the individual and grassroots levels. Whereas usually the elites and the stronger elements among migrant groups can manage independently in host countries, the majority will need the support of their co-ethnics. Yet even those elites and stronger groups need such affiliations and connections for other reasons, especially for maintaining contact with the ethnic nation's cultural, political, and economic center.

Part of that spontaneous bottom-to-top process is related to the rise of new leaders after migrants settle in host countries. Many of those new leaders will be younger people who either migrated with their parents or were born and educated in the host country. Some of those young leaders will be among the more successful members of incipient diasporas, especially in the economic sphere. Yet many will be students and academics (as is the case among Palestinians and Kurds in Europe and the United States) or young and enthusiastic laborers (as is true among Asian diasporans in the United States and the Middle East) (for an analysis of the behavior of young Greeks, Italians, and Turks in Germany, see Weidacher 1999). Intelligence, dedication, and resourcefulness are the personal qualities that are most essential for becoming leaders capable of dealing with the substantial difficulties that migrants face even after they have solved their initial psychological and emotional problems and have decided to settle permanently in a host country. Resourcefulness enables rising young leaders to adjust more easily than most to the conditions in host countries, to locate the best sources of information on the social and political systems and institutions there, and to select the most appropriate strategies and tactics for dealing with them. They also tend to develop the ability to communicate more confidently with homeland governments.

The spontaneous and sometimes chaotic nature of the effort to establish and organize incipient diasporas does not diminish diasporans' willingness and capacity ultimately to meet the goals of the diaspora communities. The ready availability of the sophisticated new media can reduce the time and costs spent in nonstructured community-building and in chaotic and unplanned activities. In other words, today there is no longer an urgent need for a comprehensive blueprint for setting up such communities and institutions, nor is there any longer an essential requirement that rich migrants be involved in forming such organizations. Thus, unlike the situation during the late nineteenth and early twentieth centuries, when it seemed that only experienced, wealthy, well-known diaspora leaders and their followers could succeed in organizing and achieving communal goals (that was the pattern for the development of the American Jewish diaspora, as well as the Chinese diaspora in the United States and elsewhere), today even relatively poor groups of migrants can organize incipient diaspora communities. Later, they can also succeed in institutionalizing those communities (for the experience of the Turkish diaspora in Germany, see Hoch 1993). As far as the collective ability to establish such organizations and communities is concerned, because of the current trends in economics and communications technology, migrants' socioeconomic status and their motivations for emigrating out of their homelands play diminishing roles in determining the shape of their diasporic entities.

The ability of diaspora members to set up their organizations is further facilitated by the fact that, unlike the situation for migrants' entry into host countries, which to some extent can be controlled, in most receiving countries, and especially in democracies, there are no insurmountable formal or informal barriers prohibiting such organizations. That is a result of the greater acceptance of the idea and practice of particular-interest associations, which are becoming more widespread in Western countries, and which migrants regard as preferred channels for their activities in their host countries. That trend is not confined to democratic states, for authoritarian governments are encountering difficulties in suppressing the development of such organizations by incipient diasporas, especially when such efforts are led by diasporas' religious and spiritual leaders and are implemented in conjunction with religious institutions.

Finally, in this context, models for diaspora organization and operation are readily available and can easily be emulated. Thus, for example, Jewish diaspora organizations in the United States have served as models for a number of ethno-national diasporas in that huge country, such as the Greek diaspora. Similarly, the Chinese patterns of organization and behavior have served as models for Asian incipient diasporas. In that respect, international and local contagion is evident and influential. Moreover, today the Internet offers easy access to numerous sites operated by diaspora organizations that serve as models for other groups (Dahan and Sheffer 2001).

The Not-So-Unique Cases of the Roma Gypsy and the Russian Incipient Diasporas

There are two interesting cases of incipient diasporas that, regardless of their different historical backgrounds and characteristics, fit the general profile of modern diasporas presented in Chapter 3 and the main patterns of diaspora formation discussed earlier in this chapter: the 20–25 million Russians in the former republics of the Soviet Union and in its satellites (such as the independent Baltic countries) and the Roma Gypsies. Because both groups constitute diasporas that are in the midst of some quite noticeable processes of shaping their identities and establishing themselves as organized entities, analytically and theoretically it should be informative to examine their recent experiences. The discussion that follows should be regarded as an illustration of the general patterns seen during the emergence of organized diasporas.

The Russian Incipient Diaspora
The Russian incipient diaspora did not arise from expansion of a homeland (had it done so, it would not be included in this analysis), but rather from the collapse of the Soviet Union and its empire. It was created when

the Soviet empire began to contract and ultimately shrank to the territorial size of historical Russia. It should be noted that most Russians now residing in the former Soviet republics voluntarily migrated to those countries during the time of the Soviet regime. And it should further be noted that since the collapse of communism, most of those Russians do not constitute an ideological diaspora. Apparently they also do not have strong ties to the revived Russian Orthodox church.

Although present-day Russia maintains a semi-hegemonic status within the Commonwealth of Independent States (CIS), especially in some former Soviet republics, it has faced substantial difficulties in protecting the interests of the Russians in the various new ethno-national republics, especially in the Baltic region. Actually, Russians who have remained in some of those newly independent states have become a repressed minority (Kolsto 1993; Brubaker 1996, 1999; Vishnevsky 1999; Bodryte 1999). Indeed, the Russian government, certain groups in Russian society, particularly those who have relatives among the members of the Russian incipient diaspora, and the Russians in the emerging diaspora themselves have good reasons for worrying about the future. Even though most of those Russians have not suffered brutal repression, in some of their host countries their situation is still precarious. The reasons for their hostile treatment by host societies and governments are clear. First, among large groups in those host societies there is understandable resentment and even hatred of the Russians, who are regarded, with some justification, as the former local representatives of the brutal Soviet regime. Second, the Russians are regarded as actual and potential agents of their homeland, which is still perceived as a menacing power that is determined to maintain its regional hegemony. Third, some of the Russians are regarded as agents of the Russian Mafia and Russian economic conglomerates that intend to further exploit those host countries. It is therefore not surprising that in some of the independent or semi-independent states the Russians have been relegated to the status of second-class citizens, and in other countries they suffer from various forms and degrees of discrimination.

Whereas concern about the security and status of the Russians in various host countries is substantial and frequently discussed, another aspect has barely been mentioned: the Russians' individual and collective psychological trauma of being abruptly demoted from the status of masters to that of equals and in some cases to that of pariah second-class citizens. The difficult adjustments involved in that transformation are comparable to those involved in migrating from a homeland, as experienced by all other migrants who have formed incipient diasporas. That experience is relevant to the discussion here because it affects the decisions that the "Russians abroad" must make regarding the establishment of local diasporic entities, or a return to Russia, or migration to western Europe or North America. In the late 1990s, the reasons for the insignificant numbers wishing to return to the homeland were the harsh economic situation in Russia, on the one hand, and what appeared to be increasing chances of migrating to and settling in the West, on the other.

To the chagrin of those Russians, because of security, political, and economic reasons the Russian government does not encourage a massive return. It rather encourages them to stay put in their host countries and establish diaspora communities there. Again not surprisingly, because of the fact that about half of those Russians have no support organizations and networks, they have had to rely on the Russian government for assistance with their immediate and longer-term problems. In that respect there has been a certain amount of continuity of the patterns that existed in the Soviet Union, that is, considerable reliance of all citizens on central authorities. But also, like the authorities in many other homelands, the Russian government is showing noticeable ambivalence toward those groups and their demands and expectations.

Those developments notwithstanding, there are clear signs that, again like other ethno-national groups in voluntary or imposed permanent residence in host countries, many Russians in the newly independent host countries are determined to act on their own. They are organizing embryonic diaspora communities that may improve their chances of withstanding further explicit oppression and implicit threats from their hosts. Moving in that direction, they will encounter the same choices faced by most migrants and diasporans in other places and under different circumstances. In short, though some observers argue that the Russians are still a long way from organizing and forming diasporic entities (Vishnevsky 1999), it seems that actually they are following the lead of all those who live permanently in host countries but maintain close connections with their homelands (McLaren 1999).

The Roma Gypsies

Though some observers argue that the case of the Roma is totally unlike any other, actually in certain respects that ethnic group is not so different from all other incipient diasporas. In any event, it is extremely interesting to follow the unfolding case of that very old dispersed ethnic group whose leaders are now in the initial stages of putting together some

intra-state and trans-state organizations and networks. A better understanding of that process may be informative with regard to similar
processes that are being initiated and carried out by other incipient
diasporas.

As is well known, during the past millennium the Roma have existed
as a wandering, widely dispersed, largely unorganized, and severely persecuted stateless diaspora. Like some other historical and modern stateless diasporas, especially the Jews, Armenians, and Kurds, the Gypsies
have survived despite enormous hardships inflicted on them by extremely
hostile societies and governments, including the Holocaust in Europe
launched by Nazi Germany. However, until the late 1980s the characteristics of their ethnic diaspora were different from those of other stateless diasporas. First, the concept of a homeland was, and still is, very
fuzzy and highly controversial among the members of that group (in that
respect they resemble the African-Americans). The second difference
is that as a result of their anarchic life-style and their highly diverse
traditions, the Gypsies have been neither interested in nor capable of
establishing coherent institutions and forming unified communities in
their host countries. And third, the Gypsies have been unable to form
coherent trans-state organizations and networks.

More recently, however, chiefly as a result of intensive efforts by an
emerging group of younger and better-educated leaders, they have begun
a new movement toward the establishment of communal organizations
and networks in certain countries where there are large Gypsy concentrations and where host governments do not put insurmountable obstacles in their way. Such new developments have occurred primarily in
Romania, Bulgaria, Spain, Hungary, France, and the Czech Republic
(*Economist* 1999, 2001). Those young leaders have been engaged in
promoting more ambitious "national" projects, such as reshaping and
clarifying perceptions of the Roma identity, introducing new patterns of
organization, and establishing comprehensive trans-state networks.
Thus, those emerging leaders are engaged in a serious attempt to organize what has been an unruly ethnic group and turn it into a more cohesive and efficient entity capable of political action (Mirga and Gheorghe
1997; Curry 1999; for a report on an attempt to organize the Roma in
Israel and Palestine, see *Jerusalem Post* 2000). Thus a certain active core
of the Gypsy "nation" has recently emerged, and it can be regarded as
an incipient global diaspora. Following recent exchanges between young
Roma Gypsy and Jewish leaders and academics, it appears that like the

leaders of other incipient diasporas, the Gypsies are inclined to model their trans-state organizations on those of the Jewish diaspora.

Judging from a number of such activities, it is clear that those young, activist Gypsy leaders have reached an important crossroad in their own journey and in their nation's history. As expected, they are now facing dilemmas in regard to their organization and strategy much like those that confront other historical, modern, and incipient diasporas, especially the African-Americans and blacks. Thus, for example, Roma leaders must begin to decide about autonomy and corporatism versus full integration in their host countries (Mirga and Gheorghe 1997).

Furthermore, because of the new political patterns emerging in many states, after centuries of passivity and apathy among Gypsies, many younger and better-educated Romas are now deciding to engage in political activity. Their purposes are to work to safeguard their existence as a distinct ethnic group and to improve their political standing in their various host countries. In order to promote those interests, among other things, they have been approaching regional and international organizations (Jaroka 2000). Probably more than anything else, that initial arduous process of clarifying the identity of the Gypsies reveals that they have much in common with most of the incipient ethno-national diasporas.

Incipient into Mature Diasporas: A Developmental Perspective

The foregoing analysis shows that a significant aspect of the diaspora phenomenon is that diasporas are far from being idle and stagnant entities. Like many other social and political formations, most diasporas grow, decline, and disintegrate as a result of phased dynamic processes. Those phases will be discussed in the following paragraphs.

The first stage in the dynamic development of diasporic entities begins when a core group of migrants make firm decisions to settle permanently in a host country. Before that stage in the development, migrants who still hold homeland passports and are connected almost by umbilical cords to family and relatives there will rely mainly on their relatives and, to some extent, on homeland governments to assist them if they encounter severe difficulties. Thus homeland embassies in host countries are expected to serve as first responders in case of any urgent need. To a lesser degree, during that phase migrants may approach various non-governmental organizations (NGOs) and religious institutions in host countries and ask for their support.

Because in many instances chain-migrants tend to reside in enclaves, mostly in the global cities in host countries (the Vietnamese, Iranians, and Koreans in Los Angeles and Sydney, the Pakistanis in Birmingham, people from the West Indies in London), they have learned that by joining forces with their co-ethnics to create support groups and associations, they have effective supplements and substitutes for their earlier reliance on homelands, on host-country governments, and on NGOs in their host countries. The establishment of such support groups is the initial step toward the formation of organized diasporas.

The next phase in the process begins when migrants formulate their goals, become better acquainted with their new social, political, and economic environments, and become aware of the advantages that would be offered by further organization. At that point, they will also begin to ask questions pertaining to identity, identification, solidarity, and loyalty. If they decide to settle permanently but to reject full integration or assimilation into host societies, they are ready to embark upon the third phase of diaspora development.

The third phase in diaspora development can be protracted and arduous. During that phase, the committed members will gradually work out their main strategies vis-à-vis their homelands and host countries. They also will adjust their goals to account for the circumstances prevailing in homelands and host countries, agree on operational procedures, determine the structure for their organizations, build those organizations, and establish the patterns of their relationships with all relevant actors. In short, during that phase incipient diasporas mature.

Those are not necessarily linear and sequential processes. Thus, in some situations and during certain periods, diasporas may become dormant. That is, during such periods they may integrate into host societies, show less interest in their homelands, experience hybridization processes, reduce the activities of their diaspora organizations, and so forth. Between the 1940s and the late 1970s that happened, for example, to large segments of the Polish-American diaspora, and after World War II and until the mid-1970s it also happened to Americans in Lebanon. That can occur not only during periods of tension but also during periods of stability in both homelands and host countries. Yet, when circumstances change, their commitment to the diaspora can be renewed.

In view of those kinds of fluctuations in the active membership of a diaspora, one of the most important indicators that a diaspora has become firmly established in a host country is its ability to continue to reach out and mobilize core members and motivate them to act on behalf of the needy segments of the dispersed nation, including its dormant communities.

Diasporans into Migrants and Returnees

Like other aspects of contemporary diasporism, secondary and tertiary migrations, both forced and voluntary, by members of established ethnonational diasporas are not recent phenomena, nor is it a new development that diasporans sometimes decide to return to their old homelands. As discussed in Chapter 2, such return movements occurred in antiquity and during the Middle Ages (for earlier return movements by Turks and Germans, see Brubaker 1996). Though they were not recorded or documented, such movements apparently were not confined to European and Middle Eastern diasporas, but also occurred in other parts of the world. And, of course, they are still happening today.

When considering the issues of deportation, expulsion, imposed repatriation, and forced return of members of established diasporas, we must ask not only what happened and still happens in those situations but also why such transport of people took place. According to the profile presented in Chapter 3, most members of contemporary established diasporas do not regard their host countries as places of exile, and they intend to remain permanently in their host countries. And in host countries where they are socially, politically, and economically integrated they have little incentive to leave of their own volition. Therefore, the reasons for return movements, which often are forced repatriations, should be sought chiefly in the policies of their host governments. Reviewing the long and tortured history of diasporas that left their host countries, it seems that most such exits were imposed by authoritarian rulers and governments (Ther 1999; on the legal aspects of this issue, see Helton 1999). Only in rare instances were such exits necessitated by spontaneous grassroots sentiment in their host societies or prompted by explicit invitation from homelands.

Because most state-linked diasporas make substantial efforts to behave according to the rules of their host countries, to contribute to those host countries' well-being, and to avoid major confrontations with host societies, the main reasons for forced exits would not appear to be diasporas' disobedience. Similarly, worsening economic conditions in host countries do not seem to be among the major reasons for diaspora departures. Rather, the reasons seem to lie in deeper layers of the host-country–diaspora relationship: The main reasons for repatriation of diasporas appear to be the suspicions and enmities that are inherent in many inter-ethnic relations hips in host countries.

Whereas the reasons for forced exit of well-established state-linked diasporas are multiple, complex, and implicit, the reasons for expulsion of entire stateless diasporas or large segments thereof are clearer, and host governments have a much freer hand to carry out their decisions concerning those diasporas. First, because stateless diasporas have no access to recognized sovereign agencies in their homelands that could come to their rescue, host governments feel little constraint about ejecting them. Second, a stateless diaspora's unequivocal support for that part of their nation still in the homeland and still struggling for independence or autonomy, which might involve subversive activities in host countries, often has been regarded as sufficient reason for expulsion. Thus, for example, in the early 1980s, under Israeli military and political pressure, the Lebanese government decided to force the departure of Yasir Arafat and his colleagues, the leadership of the Palestine Liberation Organization, from Beirut, which was under siege by the Israeli army. Arafat and his colleagues moved to Tunisia and there established their new headquarters.

For the sake of theoretical clarity, it should be emphasized that voluntary exit of members of established diasporas should be regarded in the same way as emigration out of a homeland. The rationale behind this observation is that most members of an established diaspora (certainly the historical and modern ones) do not regard their host country as a place of exile, but rather as a second homeland or even their only homeland. Although diasporans usually maintain regular contact with their homelands, most of them feel a considerable degree of loyalty to their host countries. Therefore, the motivations for returning to homelands are varied and complex. Above and beyond "migration orders and crises" and unfriendly attitudes of host societies and governments, all of which indeed contribute to decisions about returning to homelands, in the end those decisions are made by individuals and small groups of diasporans.

When there is a massive expulsion or voluntary exit of a diaspora from a host country, not all members will leave. Even under the harshest conditions in host countries, almost always some diasporans will remain behind. The history of the Jewish diaspora in Europe just before and during World War II illustrates such a situation. Similarly, even after the massive exits of Jews from Arab countries in the late 1940s and early 1950s, there are some Jews remaining in Yemen, Egypt, Syria, and Lebanon. More recently, despite worsening security and economic conditions, Jews and Israelis have remained in South Africa, in various countries in Latin America, and in most of the former Soviet republics. The same applies to other diasporans that have been forced to leave or have voluntarily left their host countries. Thus, in the wake of the wholesale expulsions of guest workers just prior to the war in the Persian Gulf, some integrated Palestinians remained in Kuwait, Egyptians in Iraq, Yemenis in Saudi Arabia, and so forth. The current situations of those who remained will serve as a litmus test for changed circumstances in those host countries, and when the situation is deemed appropriate, they will serve to attract their co-ethnics seeking to make first or secondary migrations to those countries. In many cases, the newcomers will be relatives of those who remained in the host countries during the war. Those who remained can provide the necessary cultural, social, and economic infrastructure for revival of those diasporas. The Palestinians who remained in Kuwait after the Persian Gulf war, the Jewish refugees in Germany after World War II, and the Turks in Germany all serve as examples of those patterns.

The Implications

The recent, seemingly unstoppable waves of migration that have been facilitated by modern transportation, electronic communication, the new media, and the increasing tolerance toward pluralism and multiculturalism have contributed to the overall proliferation of ethno-national diasporas. The emergence of coherent incipient diasporas that have been able to overcome the initial difficulties that confront migrants in most host countries supports one of the most significant theoretical conclusions in this context: Those diasporas are neither "imagined" nor "invented" communities. As has been shown here, the decisions to form incipient diasporas and the motivation to maintain them do not depend only on economic considerations or calculations about social and political benefits. If such migrants were to decide to relinquish their ethno-national identities, which most of them decline to do, both as individuals and collectively some of those migrants might fare better in their new host countries. Rather, the evidence concerning that aspect of the general diaspora experience further supports the view advanced herein concerning the nature and identity of diasporas. Namely, the proliferation, organization, and endurance of those diasporas depend on a combination of primordial, instrumental, and psychological/symbolic factors.

A second significant conclusion is that although the primordial elements in their identities do influence the behaviors of such ethno-national groups, the migrants' persistence and hence their transformation into significant political actors will depend on cumulative individual and collective decisions made in the host countries. Thus, our findings emphasize the importance of determined, but not necessarily rational, choices in the life of most diasporans and diasporas. Members of those entities who are autonomous social actors make those tough decisions, rendered even more difficult because from the viewpoint of those groups, conditions in the local and international social and economic arenas have improved. Without firm personal and small-group decisions to join or form diaspora organizations, those groups could not have persisted, and consequently the chances that such diasporas would endure would have been minimal.

A third interlinked conclusion pertains to the particular roles of the elites and the rank and file. Although, as the case of the Roma Gypsies has shown, resolute decisions by the elites are necessary to launch the formation of diaspora organizations, the heavy lifting involved in the organization, mobilization, and functioning of those social and political entities requires spontaneous grassroots decisions and readiness to implement those decisions on the part of the rank and file. That does not mean, of course, that the elites do not take active roles. When there are enough demands to be met and initiatives to be undertaken, the elites often become involved in the details of forming diasporic entities.

The following are some further conclusions that have influenced the emerging theory of ethno-national diasporas: The greater openness and tolerance recently evident in host countries, on the one hand, and the ambivalent attitudes of most homelands toward their diasporas, on the other, tend to motivate migrants and members of incipient diasporas to opt for integration into host societies. Yet the primordial and psychological/symbolic elements of their ethnic identities, and particularly their membership in organized communities, are sufficient to guarantee the continuity of substantial core groups in diasporas. Therefore, in the future, those entities will tend to acquire more autonomy vis-à-vis their homelands and also their host countries. There is increasing evidence that ethno-national diasporas will continue to defy predictions about their demise and disappearance. As things stand now, it seems that despite some return movements to homelands (such as in the cases of the Irish, Jewish, Armenian, German, and Greek diasporas) most diasporas will overcome the many difficulties they face and will remain permanent features of national, regional, and global politics – and forces that will have to be reckoned with.

6

Stateless and State-Linked Diasporas

Fewer Stateless Diasporas

We have seen that some currently existing diasporas arose in antiquity or during the Middle Ages and despite enormous hardships have survived until today – those are the historical diasporas. The diasporas that arose much later, from the seventeenth century onward, many of which resulted from the great waves of migration that took place from the middle of the nineteenth century to World War II – those are the modern diasporas. Finally, all other diasporas either have been formed recently (i.e., since World War II) or are still in various stages of evolution – those are the incipient diasporas.

In Chapters 1 and 3 a further distinction was proposed: that between state-linked diasporas and stateless diasporas. It should be noted that although there are obvious differences between those two categories, most diasporas in both categories are similar in their attachments to their ethno-national identities and to their homelands and in regard to the problems they face in host countries. During certain periods in their histories, some diasporas were not connected to sovereign states, so at certain times those were stateless diasporas. For example, during long periods the Jews, Greeks, and Armenians (historical diasporas) and the African-Americans and Poles (modern diasporas) each had no sovereign national state in the territory they regarded as their homeland. Also, the Gypsies have no clearly defined homeland, and they have never had a state of their own. In other cases, such as those of the Palestinians and Tibetans (incipient diasporas), the homeland has been occupied and dominated by another state. Nevertheless, during such periods of statelessness, some groups and individuals in each of those diasporas have maintained contact with that segment of their nation remaining in the homeland. Some stateless diasporas have nurtured real histories or imagined legends about their homelands.

After World War I, that is, during the first wave of establishment of independent national states in the twentieth century, a period that saw the crystallization of the modern nation-state, some historical diasporas, such as the Armenians and Jews, still remained stateless. Despite the fact that most members of such diasporas either integrated or assimilated into their host societies, certain "nationalist" groups in those entities fervently maintained their ethno-national identities. Moreover, the core members of such diasporas – that is, those who permanently resided in host countries but continued to treasure their ethnic origins – cherished memories of their homelands, mourned the fact that their nations were stateless, and were ready to mobilize to fight for independence for their homelands. Some of those core members continued to look forward to ingatherings in their homelands in order to facilitate the achievement of national independence there. For them, their homelands became essential not only for defining their identities but also as the goals toward which their political orientations and activities were directed.

Regardless of determined efforts made by such diasporans to promote the cause of national independence in their respective homelands, some remained stateless until the middle of the twentieth century, which witnessed the second wave in the emergence of independent states. Most notably, during that period the Zionists in the Jewish diaspora achieved their goal of an independent state. The Zionist and pro-Zionist elements in the Jewish diaspora played important roles in establishing Israel and providing assistance during the critical stages of that struggle for independence. The 1948 Middle East war that resulted in establishment of the independent Jewish state uprooted many Palestinians and caused both forced and voluntary increases in the Palestinian diaspora. Prior to World War II the Palestinians had established proto-diaspora communities, especially in various parts of the Middle East, Africa, South America, and Latin America. Thus, the transformation of the Jewish diaspora into a state-linked diaspora caused the emergence of a substantial stateless Palestinian diaspora. Other diasporas, such as the Armenian, have remained stateless for longer periods, though statelessness ended for some with the collapse of the Soviet Union late in the twentieth century (Hovannisian 1997).

One of the more notable consequences of the "new world order" that has emerged following the collapse of the bipolar global system of the cold-war era is that additional stateless ethnic nations and minorities have been able to establish their own independent national states or regain control over their homelands. Among others, the Ukrainians, Latvians, Lithuanians, Estonians, Croatians, and Albanians have realized their hopes of founding, or reestablishing, independent national states. Many, but not all, members of those national diasporas supported their co-ethnics' demands and struggles for independence and sovereignty.

The political struggles going on around the world between minorities seeking separation, secession, or independence and those who oppose them are reflected in the dilemmas now facing even the most liberal politicians, political philosophers, and sociologists. Despite their moral and intellectual commitment to the ideas of personal and collective freedom and self-determination, some of those theorists regard the ambitions of the smaller ethnic minorities to gain independence as dangerous. That position is diametrically opposite the stand they had on that issue prior to the collapse of the Soviet Union. During the Soviet period, such theorists strongly supported the principle of self-determination, especially for ethnic nations under the Soviet yoke, with some even manning the front lines of the protest movements against Soviet treatment of ethnic nations and minorities. However, when the cold-war system collapsed and stateless ethnic nations and their diasporas began to demand independence in their homelands, the support of such theorists for indiscriminate application of the principles of self-determination faded when they saw the wars, massacres, and ethnic cleansings in the former Yugoslavia, Azerbaijan, Nagorno-Karabakh, and other ethnic hot spots. They realized that the situations in those places were so laden with danger to international and regional order and stability that some joined the neo-realists in arguing that equilibrium had to be reestablished in international and national politics, and then strictly maintained (Posen 1993; Van Evera 1994). Those theorists and politicians added that any further disintegration of states, the essential building blocks for a rational international system, had to be prevented in order to ward off even greater global chaos. They concluded that the right to self-determination for ethnic groups and ethno-national diasporas would have to be limited and sometimes even denied (Nye 1993; Chipman 1993).

Others from that school of thought suggested that the new world powers, that is, primarily the United States, should intervene in areas of instability and ethnic conflict with the aim of managing or solving such conflicts, but without splitting existing states. The most obvious example of such conflict management has been the U.S. policy toward Iraq under Saddam Hussein. Despite the considerable American interest in toppling Hussein and his dictatorial regime, the U.S. government, fully supported by the United Kingdom, did not like the idea of splitting Iraq and granting independence to the stateless Iraqi Kurds. The United States and its main allies faced a similar dilemma when formulating their policy concerning recognition of the independent republics of the former Soviet Union (for an analysis of some of those cases from the point of view of diaspora involvement, see Shain 1999, pp. 55–66), as well as in the more recent crisis in Kossovo. There was similar ambiguity in the official U.S. attitude toward establishment of an independent Palestinian state. Since the 1970s, when the Palestinians forced their issue onto the international agenda, successive U.S. administrations have carefully avoided explicit statements about the desirability and feasibility of such an independent state. Yet a close review of official statements toward the end of the Clinton administration shows that the president and his advisors were inching toward a clear recognition of that Palestinian right. Finally, in January 2001, just before leaving the White House, President Clinton stated that the solution of the Palestinian-Israeli conflict should include the establishment of an independent Palestinian state. The new Bush administration has reluctantly followed that line. Attainment of independence and sovereignty by the Palestinians will, of course, further reduce the number of stateless diasporas. It remains to be seen whether or not the remaining entities in that group will be able to fulfill their dreams of establishing national states.

The History and Identities of Stateless and State-Linked Diasporas

For both stateless diasporas and state-linked diasporas, identity is neither a given nor an immutable factor. Because it is based on a combination of contributing factors, some of which are subjective, an identity can change over time. Variations in psychological inclinations, situational factors, and practical instrumental considerations can produce changes in diasporans' identities. Yet, as maintained throughout this book, probably to a greater extent than the identities of other ethnic nations and ethnic minorities, the identities of diasporas are relatively rigid, for they are more firmly based on primordial components, including biological relationships (partly the result of deliberate decisions to maintain ethnic purity), similar physical characteristics, belief in common ancestry, adherence to certain communal norms, and, of course, strong sentiments about an ancestral homeland. Predominantly, however, the identities of diasporas are based on shared symbolic and cultural elements that are firmly anchored in the history of those groups and are still vivid in the minds and memories of their core members. Those elements are almost unaffected by diasporans' integration into their host societies.

In analyzing the African diaspora's identity, influential scholars have strongly emphasized the importance of certain traditional cultural assets, such as music and dance, in shaping and maintaining that identity. According to that approach, ethnic identity is the historical product of expressive rites and customs that individuals and groups follow and repeat. Thus identity can be altered by changes in the social and political environment, and to a certain degree the cohesion and continuity of diasporas will then depend on the development of cultural assets such as traditional rites and customs. Development in too many different directions can harm a diaspora's chances for survival (Gilroy 1994).

In this context, a distinction should be made between established and incipient ethnic diasporas. Among members of an incipient diaspora there will be individuals whose identities will have been shaped in the homeland before their migration. They will still have personal attachments to the homeland people and to their homeland and culture, and from among them will come the elders and the spiritual and political leaders, the bearers of the ethno-national torch. Often despite unpleasant memories of their earlier life in the nation's homeland, those leaders will work hard to inculcate a favorable opinion and salutary sentiments about the homeland in younger members of the community. By doing so, they serve to strengthen the diaspora's cohesion in its host country and to maintain its loyalty to the homeland. As noted in Chapter 5, consequently some members of incipient diasporas nurture hopes of returning to their homelands: Russians in some Baltic states, Turkish and Iraqi Kurds in Germany, Tibetans in India, Palestinians in Middle Eastern countries and elsewhere, some African Americans, and, to some degree, also Israelis, who now constitute an incipient diaspora that is separated from the historical Jewish diaspora (Sheffer 1998).

Wishes, some vague, some steely, to return to homelands are not confined to incipient stateless diasporas. Although it is true that the vast majority of the members of historical and modern diasporas do not entertain the hope of return, there are some groups in those diasporas who are inclined toward such dreams. Those dedicated individuals and groups may resist the forces pushing them toward evolution of a hybrid identity based partly on the host-country culture and partly on their ethnic background (on the concept and debate concerning "hybridity" of ethnic groups, see Werbner 1997).

Yet no matter how members of a given diaspora hold on to their ethnic identity, none of them will be completely immune to the influences of the host-country culture and norms. That problem particularly affects long-standing state-linked diasporas whose members have won recognition and legitimacy in their host countries as well as in their homelands. If a diaspora's experience in its host country is relatively painless, and its homeland is in no major danger, the chances are that gradually the memories of the homeland will fade. When that occurs, it becomes difficult to maintain the community's cohesion and active membership. Success in counterbalancing such trends will depend on the dedication of diasporas' leaders and the strength of their organizations, as well as on positive grassroots reactions, rather than on situational factors such as the political, legal, and economic conditions prevailing in host countries and homelands.

The need to keep a diaspora's primeval roots and recent history constant and vivid in members' minds is particularly important in the case of stateless diasporas. As long as a struggle for independence is continuing in the homeland of a stateless diaspora, its members will be particularly torn between memories of their homeland and the wish to recapture the past, on one hand, and the need to comply with the norms of their host country, on the other. For that reason, diaspora leaders and their organizations invest considerable time, effort, and resources in trying to convince younger members not to give up their identity and not to defect from the group. Whenever members of a stateless diaspora are emotionally involved in their nation's struggle for independence and sovereignty in their homeland, the tendencies urging them to assimilate and integrate into the host society are counterbalanced by their strong sentiments toward their homeland. As part of their efforts in that context, the younger leaders, intellectuals, and other activists will be intensively involved in reviving their nation's past, and if necessary, re-imagining and re-inventing it. Then political leaders, religious functionaries, intellectuals, and activists will disseminate the results of such endeavors among the largest possible number of diaspora members. Both the Jews and the Palestinians, among others, have experienced such developments.

Yet neither the members of state-linked diasporas nor the members of stateless diasporas will have uniform attitudes toward their national histories. Narratives adopted, elaborated, and cherished by various segments of a given diaspora are never identical (Skinner 1993). Attitudes will differ according to the extent to which identities in various segments of the diaspora have been hybridized – the extent to which their experiences in the host country have begun to take precedence over memories of their experiences in their homeland. The existence of such competing narratives can lead to controversies within diasporas and occasionally to severe schism, thus hampering any concerted action on behalf of homelands and national movements for liberation or independence of those homelands. Such cultural controversies have existed among the Armenians, and now they are splitting certain Palestinian communities in the West, especially in the United States.

Stateless Diasporas in the New Global Environment

The recent establishment of some new, independent ethnic states, most often despite the ambiguous attitudes of the United States and other Western democracies, has had at least two major consequences for contemporary diasporas. First, it has reduced the number of stateless diasporas. Second, it has led to a clear change in diasporas' strategies toward their host countries and their homelands. Thus, the reestablishment of independent Armenia, Ukraine, Latvia, Estonia, and Lithuania, which transformed their stateless diasporas into state-linked diasporas, gradually changed their principal political orientations and spheres of activity. Instead of focusing most of their efforts on matters related to their homelands, now those diasporas are devoting more attention and resources to solving their own problems in their host countries. In other words, they are trying harder to feel at home abroad. To some extent, that is their reaction to the increasing reluctance of some newly independent homelands to permit their diasporas to have a voice in their domestic and international affairs. That new ordering of priorities and consequently the new patterns of resource allocation are evident, for example, in the behavior of the Armenian diaspora. Because of the delicate circumstances prevailing in Armenia after independence, the Armenian government wanted Armenian-Americans to cease their attempts to remain involved in homeland internal affairs. Also, it seems that the Armenian diaspora has lost some of its earlier emotional zeal and practical motivation to pursue the activist strategy that had served its political agenda. Among other things, they no longer have any reason to initiate or support terrorist activities in Western host countries (Hovannisian 1993, 1997). Since Armenia gained independence, the Armenian diaspora has not pursued subversive policies anywhere. In other words, the homeland's new status has transformed the "overseas Armenians" into a "normal" state-linked diaspora. Like other established state-linked diasporas, the Armenian diaspora has turned its attention to recruitment of political support, lobbying efforts, and some fund-raising for the homeland and has directed most of its resources to solving diaspora problems (Tololyan 1991, 1995). Though important segments in that diaspora continue to be concerned about the fate of their co-ethnics in Nagorno-Karabakh and to support their struggle, in the late 1990s they were primarily enlisting political and diplomatic support and providing some economic assistance, rather than engaging in clandestine subversive activities.

Similar processes have characterized the Albanian diaspora in Western host countries, especially the United States. In the late 1980s those Albanians were supporting the homeland struggle to gain full independence. Later the diaspora supported the transformation of the Communist regime into a democratic system. Simultaneously, more resources were invested in the diaspora itself. By the late 1990s, however, in view of the ethnic cleansing directed against the Kossovar Albanians, again that diaspora redirected its activities and resources. Reacting to those new developments in what they regard as part of their homeland, certain groups in the Albanian diaspora used their political clout and economic resources to assist their endangered compatriots. Indeed, the immediate response among members of the Albanian diaspora to the unfolding horrors in Kossovo was to raise substantial funds for the homeland. Later their activities were extended to include intensive political lobbying in Washington, western European capitals, and the United Nations. Yet it seems likely that once the Kossovo problem is resolved, the diaspora will redirect its attention and actions to its communal affairs.

Usually, as soon as stateless diasporas achieve their goals of independent national states in their homelands, thus becoming state-linked diasporas, most of them tend to pursue a "communal strategy" in their host countries. As indicated in Chapter 3, that strategy is intended primarily to strengthen diaspora communities. When diasporas shift to that strategy, they place new emphasis on reinforcing their solidarity, preventing population losses, increasing the membership in diaspora organizations, expanding the activities of those organizations, maintaining a high degree of readiness for mobilization, and ensuring the availability of resources for communal continuity. Adoption of that strategy is most appropriate following the establishment or reestablishment of independent national states. It allows for more efficient utilization of the resources needed for ongoing economic, political, and diplomatic support for homelands during the formative period of state-building. Simultaneously, it can produce sufficient resources to ensure the diasporas' own well-being without provoking much opposition from their host countries, which otherwise might try to restrict diasporas' efforts to assist their homelands. That is, of course, just another of the many problems faced by those trying to be at home abroad.

Now it is possible to proceed to an analysis of the various strategy choices made by the remaining stateless diasporas. Here the focus is on stateless diasporas that have relatively well defined homelands. Despite the fact that African-Americans continually grapple with the issue of the historical location of their homeland and with questions pertaining to their best strategy toward Africa, and despite the fact that in the late 1990s various segments of the Roma Gypsy diaspora have also been engaged in internal debates about their country of origin and in organizing worldwide diaspora institutions intended to unite their entire ethnic group, the discussion here does not apply to those two large stateless diasporas. That is primarily because of lack of consensus among the members of those two diasporas regarding the application of the diaspora concept to their situations. The flip side of the coin is that among those diasporans there has been a very long tradition of perceiving themselves as indigenous ethnic minorities in their host countries.

Politically, the more active groups in the stateless-diaspora category are the Palestinians, Kurds, Sikhs, and, in their particular style, also the Tibetans. Because of a deeply ingrained veneration of the idea of the nation-state, the ultimate goal of those diasporas is still to establish or re-institute sovereign states in their homelands, and in that sense they are not conducting post-national struggles (on the notion of post-nationalism, see Soysal 1996). Majorities of the Palestinians living in the United States, Canada, Latin America, and Europe, the Kurds residing in the United States and western Europe, the Tibetans in India and in adjacent states where they have found refuge, and the Sikhs in the United States and Britain support that orientation. Nevertheless, in all those cases, internal debates continue over the main orientation that those diasporas should adopt regarding the future of their homelands. The integrationists in each of those diasporas would settle for cultural and economic autonomy of their homeland; more radical elements would argue that a separatist strategy should be followed by that segment of their nation residing in the homeland, with the diaspora providing substantive support for such an effort.

Usually such splits over the chief goals that should be pursued in the homelands are reflected in the main strategies that those groups advocate and pursue in their host countries. Certain segments, probably the majority of those residing in host countries, behave like members of state-linked diasporas – that is, they usually opt for the locally oriented and more moderate strategy of communalism. For example, among the Palestinians in the diaspora there has been consensus that the nation should establish a sovereign state. In practice, however, Palestinians in the United States, Europe, and Latin America have behaved like other similar entities there – they have developed communal diaspora organizations and have pursued communalist policies. As will be seen in Chapter 9, that controversy carries over into debates in such diasporas concerning the question of loyalty.

From a security point of view (i.e., regarding the possibility that members of stateless diasporas might support and actually engage in subversive acts and terrorist activities), diasporas that pursue or support secessionist and separatist movements in their homelands have the greatest potential to cause trouble for those in control there. By the same token, they pose real and potential threats to their host societies and governments, to international organizations, and, through their occasional participation in terrorist trans-state networks, to fourth and fifth parties. Thus, for example, when some extremely militant Palestinian groups and individuals formed an alliance with the radical Red Army in Japan and the German Baader-Meinhof gang, they trained together and cooperated in various clandestine activities directed not only at Israeli and Jewish diaspora institutions but also at host countries. Later, those Palestinians and some of their German and Japanese associates participated in guerrilla and terrorist activities organized by the PLO, Hamas, and other Palestinian organizations in Israel and Western countries, such as the bombing of the Israeli embassy and Jewish institutions in Buenos Aires and Jewish facilities in Paris. Eventually, after gaining military experience in their struggle against Israel, those Palestinians trained members of other diasporas and ethnic groups who became involved in conflicts in their various homelands, including Shiite Lebanese, Kurdish activists in Europe, and Albanian and Irish freedom fighters.

Militant leaders and members of such stateless diasporas know full well that clandestine terrorist and guerrilla activities per se cannot win independence for their homelands. The main purpose of their violent activities is to draw the greatest possible general attention to their national plight and struggle. Those activities also are intended as public expressions of their unequivocal determination to see the establishment of their independent national states. Sometimes such signals are particularly directed at their own people back in their homelands and are intended to encourage them to escalate their struggle for independence. Another goal of those activities is to exert pressure on host governments and societies, as well as on international organizations, to respond to the diasporas' demands or to act in their support.

In a sense, all of that resembles the radical strategies of special-interest groups trying to influence the foreign policies of their countries. In the case of such diasporic entities the purpose is to pave the way for independence in the national country. In some cases, the purpose of violence is rather to punish all those whom the diasporans regard as causing military, political, and social harm to the interests of their communities and homelands. Sometimes there are more specific aims: to gain the release of some of their people in prison, or to obtain ransom money and acquire other resources. The Palestinians, the Sikhs, the Basques, the Irish supporters of the Irish Republican Army (IRA), and the Jews and Armenians before the establishment of their own independent states have all been involved in the entire spectrum of such activities. In retrospect, it seems that those actions tended to be directed against opponents in their host countries and in their homelands. And here it should be noted that in certain situations those kinds of violent measures were directed against co-ethnics who cooperated with actual and perceived enemies of their nations.

When some segments of a stateless diaspora and their leaders are territorially concentrated, particularly in areas close to the homeland, it becomes easier for them to organize and execute subversive and terrorist activities. That was the case for the Palestinians in the 1970s, when the PLO's leadership and headquarters were situated in Lebanon. It happened again in the 1990s, when the Hamas leadership operated out of Jordan. There have been similar situations involving the Turkish Kurds in Berlin and, to some extent, the Irish-Americans, especially in New York City. It is difficult to imagine, though not entirely inconceivable, that a vastly dispersed stateless diaspora with no established centers, such as the Gypsies, would be able to enunciate a separatist strategy and demand an independent state somewhere in Europe. It would be even less feasible for Roma Gypsies to try to claim territory in northern India, which many of them regard as their ancient homeland. Nonetheless, once that diaspora becomes better organized and establishes a center or centers, it will be capable, if it so chooses, of acquiring the tools of violence to try to achieve political goals in its various host countries.

Terrorism is only the visible tip of the much larger iceberg of stateless diasporas' activities directed at satisfying their national aspirations. The range of diasporas' nonviolent activities is substantial. Those activities are implemented through elaborate trans-state networks that both poorer and richer stateless diasporas establish. Through those trans-state networks diasporas transfer to people back in their homelands various seditious resources, including combatants, weapons, military intelligence, and money (Angoustures and Pascal 1996). When the security of nation-states is defined in broad terms so as to include cultural, political, and economic aspects and interests, stateless diasporas can pose real challenges to those states and state agencies that they regard as opponents, including those in control of their homelands.

State-linked diasporas, on the other hand, usually engage in perfectly innocuous exchanges through similar trans-state networks. It should be pointed out, however, that state-linked diasporas have also been involved in subversive activities directed against host governments on behalf of their homelands. Probably the best example of that pattern concerns the secret activities the German diaspora carried out for its fatherland on the eve of World War II. Nazi Germany coordinated and financed espionage and sabotage activities by that diaspora in the Americas and around the Middle East. Similarly, Fascist Italy tried to mobilize and make use of Italian emigrants and the Italian diaspora in the United States, Latin America, and the Middle East (Cannistraro and Gianfausto 1979).

Stateless diasporas' trans-state networks have also been used as conduits for transferring resources needed by the liberation fighters and terrorists of other ethnic groups. Thus, for example, such networks have been used by the governments of Libya, Syria, and Iran to coordinate activities, transfer resources, and supply information to the PLO's constituent groups, to Hamas, and to the Islamic Jihad in the Israeli-occupied territories, to the Hizbullah in Lebanon, to the Japanese Red Army, and to Kurdish and Armenian international clandestine organizations.

Efforts made by single host governments, by coalitions of host countries, and by international organizations such as Interpol to contain such networks and put an end to their activities have been almost futile. Because of globalization in so many realms and the new ease of transportation and communication, especially the availability of relatively inexpensive sophisticated electronic means of communication, the use of those networks by stateless diasporas for both legitimate and nefarious purposes can perhaps be slowed, but not stopped. Just as it is impossible to arrest the flow of migrants and refugees and prevent their settlement and eventual establishment of diasporas, it is equally impossible to destroy or paralyze those networks and stop the transfer of resources through them. Attempts by British, Jordanian, Israeli, Iraqi, Sri Lankan, Indian, and other governments to halt or significantly curb the transfer of such resources to the ethnic groups bedeviling them have been largely unsuccessful (Angoustures and Pascal 1996, pp. 529–36).

Moreover, as difficult as it is to slow illegal migration and impede the transfer of resources and information through faxes and the Internet, it is even more difficult to interrupt the flow of matériel, messages, sensitive intelligence, and ideas through those trans-state networks. By the late 1990s, that had been well demonstrated by a modern diaspora that had become engaged in such activities: the Albanians, who provided massive support for their co-ethnics in Kossovo.

The main conclusion to be drawn from the analysis in this section is that the only way to stop such activities or even slow them is to meet the basic demands of stateless diasporas, that is, independence for their homelands, which means that the stateless will become state-linked diasporas.

State-Linked Diasporas' Strategies, Tactics, and Organization

The greater tolerance that democratic host governments now show toward all ethnic minorities influences the stance of state-linked ethnonational diasporas in those countries. In various Western countries, those groups are gaining relative freedom, at least to pursue "cultural autonomy," namely, to maintain their own traditions, mores, and customs. That relative freedom is further enhanced by the increasing inclination, albeit a reluctant one, of host governments to accept as faits accomplis cultural diversity and plurality, but not necessarily multiculturalism (Darby 1998; Van den Berghe 1999; Rex 2000). Because some ethnic diasporas are quite active politically, that tendency toward cultural pluralism is augmented by the presence of such political activism in the midst of host societies. That trend is reflected in the attitudes of receiving governments toward language requirements for entry of immigrants, which are increasingly becoming less rigorous. That is paralleled by the aforementioned attitude change among migrants such that today many are not bothering to learn the host country's language, which limits their relationships with their hosts.

The developments that have resulted in greater respect for ethnic culture, as reflected, albeit somewhat superficially, in the popularity of ethnic food, fashion, festivals, and pop music, make it easier for diaspora members to maintain their identity. But it should be emphasized that those more liberal inclinations are not shared by all members of those host societies. In most Western countries, countervailing societal forces are emerging. In those countries, racism is again on the rise, anti-foreigner sentiments are widely expressed, and acts of violence against those perceived as foreign are increasing.

Here it should be added that the effects of the increasing rates of intermarriages – for example, in 1994, 18% of first-generation Asian-Americans, 29% of the second generation, and 42% of the third generation, and in the same year, 8% of first-generation Hispanic-Americans, 27% of the second generation, and 33% of the third generation (Rodrigues 1995) – can be either positive or negative from the diasporans' viewpoint. That is, sometimes that purportedly integrationist mechanism can rather increase the hostility toward diasporans.

The increasing freedom of diaspora groups to determine, maintain, and display their identities and cultures and to join local social and political groups and parties, as well as diaspora associations, without excessive host-government pressures (Patterson 1975, pp. 305–13) also increases their opportunities to develop and maintain regular ties with their homelands. The scope and intensity of diaspora–homeland contacts do not depend on geographic proximity, nor on the goodwill of host governments. The continuing existence of those entities and the maintenance of their varied contacts depend mainly on the inclinations and strategy cumulatively chosen by individual members and groups within diasporas. And, as will be argued later in this section, the strategies that state-linked diasporas can employ are numerous and quite varied.

Maintaining diasporic entities hinges on the choices made by leaders and members. Those choices will change with circumstances. In turn, such decisions are based on the general strategies that diasporas employ to promote their interests. The following subsections describe the main strategies that diaspora groups can pursue. They compose a spectrum, beginning with benign strategies designed to achieve maximal integration and accommodation with host-country governments and societies, and ending with radical strategies intended to force the granting of independence in homelands.

A preliminary observation concerns the attitudes of newcomers and members of state-linked incipient diasporas regarding the choices of their main strategies in host countries: On their arrival, newcomers prefer to reside or are pushed to reside in cultural and residential ghettos and create support groups or join such associations already established by those who preceded them. Those arrangements used to be the standard way for migrants to settle in receiving countries and integrate into host societies. Increasingly, however, migrants do not find it essential to establish social contacts with host societies. That is particularly true in cases in which large outspoken groups in a host society display overt hostility toward migrants, other foreigners, and incipient and established diasporas. Hence, in such host countries there are mutually reinforcing processes: Societal hostility increases the newcomers' inclination to stick together, and in turn that trend among migrants intensifies their hosts' fears and enmity toward them. Those trends explain why newcomers who join existing diaspora communities usually go along with the main strategy of the more experienced leaders in those communities. That has been the case, for example, with Moroccan Jews who in the 1950s migrated to France and with most of the Chinese immigrants to the United States and Canada. Those trends also influence the decisions of the more experienced leaders in incipient diasporas about their own preferred strategies.

Mindful of these preliminary comments, we now turn to discussion of the main strategies employed by those entities.

The Assimilationist Strategy

Today an assimilationist strategy is adopted by relatively few international migrants and members of incipient diasporas. It is adopted mainly by members of established diasporas who firmly intend to settle and do not intend to cultivate their connections with their homelands. Full assimilation, however, means more than just total identification with a host society and indifference to connections with one's homeland. It means eradicating one's own ethnic identity and adopting that of the predominant sector in the host society. As the events of the twentieth century have shown, however, that is not an easy transition, for it is extremely difficult, often impossible, to shed one's primordial and psychological/symbolic identity and adopt a new one. That is the case particularly because individuals and groups within host countries have long memories that relish the enduring subtle distinctions between "us" and "them," between "us" and all "others."

It is, however, important to note that the foregoing observation is hotly debated among academic observers and diaspora members. It is debated on both the theoretical level and the practical level. Some diasporans and academics believe that assimilation not only is possible but also is highly desirable. Consequently, such diasporans try hard to assimilate. The view here is that although individual assimilation definitely occurs, it does not include entire diaspora communities, which means that despite demographic losses, relatively large core groups maintain their ethno-national identities and connections with their homelands. Also, assimilation is becoming less appealing to members of incipient diasporas (on the situation among Irish migrants to the United States, for example, see *Economist* 1994). Moreover, as noted, many "assimilated" diasporans are "rediscovering" their old identities, rejoining their diaspora communities, and identifying as such.

The Integrationist Strategy

The integrationist strategy is aimed at substantial degrees of social, economic, and political participation, but not assimilation, in the host society. Its meaning is that diaspora members strive to gain the same personal, social, economic, and political rights as the majority in the host society, and recognition of their equal status. When pursuing that strategy, some diasporans may try to decrease the visibility of their ethno-national traits and characteristics and sever ties with official institutions in their homeland. Nevertheless, they will maintain some of their ethnic cultural features and admit their origin. Members of entities that adopt this strategy may visit their homelands, and some may even return to their homelands. White South Africans who migrated to Britain, Canada, the United States, and Australia, and Russians in some of the former western republics of the Soviet Union, are among the emerging diasporas that employ the integrationist strategy.

As mentioned earlier, certain long-established diasporas that have successfully implemented the assimilationist and integrationist strategies should be viewed as dormant diasporas. Under certain circumstances, those entities can reawaken. Indeed, many in such entities have shown renewed interest in their origins, become active members of diaspora organizations, and consequently reestablished contacts with their homelands. That trend has been noticeable among some Americans of German and Scandinavian origins.

The Communalist and Corporatist Strategies

As we begin discussion of these strategies, it should be noted that probably more than any other aspect of modern diasporism, adoption of these strategies illustrates the main thesis of this book: that members of most current diasporas do their utmost to be at home abroad.

Thus the communalist strategy is intended to lead to a voluntary and relatively loose framework for preserving ethno-national identity, for defending the diaspora, and for organizing members' activities vis-à-vis the host country, the homeland, and the other fragments of the dispersed nation. In other words, the strategy aims to achieve a reasonable degree of "absorption" of diasporans into the host society, but not full integration, which might lead to assimilation – all the while maintaining continuous and unwavering relations with the homeland. To a great extent, implementation of that strategy depends on the creation of elaborate diaspora organizations and trans-state networks to connect the diaspora to its homeland and to other dispersed segments of the same nation.

Basically, the corporatist strategy is much like the communalist strategy. It also is based on maintaining the ethno-national identity and on nurturing communal organizations and activities that will promote identification with the group and provide services complementary to those supplied by the host country. The main difference between these two subtypes is that the latter is based on formal status for communal organizations vis-à-vis the host country's legal and political systems. Those organizations officially represent affiliated members in their dealings with host-country authorities (Weiner 1991). Various diasporas in Britain, France, and Germany enjoy such status.

The choice of either the communalist or corporatist strategy will be influenced by the political conditions prevailing in host countries. In liberal democracies where there is an inherent tradition of associationalism, such as the United States, Canada, and the Scandinavian countries, the natural choice would seem to be the communalist strategy. In such democracies, where voluntary association is legal and widely practiced, diasporas' communal organizations can thrive without having to apply for formal status sanctioned by state authorities. In neo-corporatist democracies, that is, less liberal democracies, such as Germany, France, Spain, and to some extent Britain, diaspora members will tend to opt for the corporatist strategy. That was the route to the formal status that the

Jewish communities were granted in those host countries. Other diasporas in those host countries have been striving, with various degrees of success, to attain similar status. Host countries' influences on the behavior of such diasporas, especially on their attitudes toward their homelands, on the types of organizations they create, and on the tactics that those organizations pursue, are related to the form of recognition that host countries confer on those communities and their organizations. In the Ottoman Empire, the corporatist arrangement was widely implemented and was known as the millet system. A similar arrangement was introduced in the Hapsburg Empire, and to an extent also in czarist Russia.

As the experiences of diasporas in those empires and the history of diasporas in other countries have shown, formal recognition of those communities as corporate bodies representing their diasporas tends to moderate and channel the political activities of such diasporas and contribute to their feelings of security. Hence, within some militant diasporas there have been disagreements concerning the advisability of adopting that strategy. That was the case in the Jewish community in France following the arrival of a relatively large wave of Jewish migrants from North Africa in the 1950s and early 1960s. Whereas the old established Jewish community (mostly Ashkenazi, that is, Jews of European background) wished to continue with the corporatist strategy, the newcomers (mostly Sephardic, that is, of North African origin) preferred a more militant communalist strategy. That led to an intra-communal split and to the emergence of virtually two separate entities, which demonstrates the fact that despite inherent communal solidarity, many of those entities can be ideologically and practically split. Such differences notwithstanding, the two strategies can be regarded as variants of a single general strategy, and therefore here they are dealt with as virtually a single strategy.

The choice of communalism or, to a lesser extent, of corporatism as a main strategy has become almost universal among state-linked diasporas that remain relatively small minorities in host countries (some observers refer to a 2% law, meaning that diasporas usually do not exceed 2% of the total population in their host countries). Yet there is a significant factor that entails reasons both for and against choosing those strategies: the geographic dispersal of a diaspora in its host country. There was a time when members of state-linked diasporas were inclined to concentrate in the political and economic centers – the global cities, the capitals, and large urban centers – but today they are more widely dispersed within their host countries. That new pattern of settlement makes those strategic options that require high population concentrations to facilitate mobilization less feasible. At the same time, their substantial geographic dispersal in host countries makes it more difficult for them to establish cohesive diaspora communities. To overcome those difficulties, diaspora leaders today try to promote the use of modern means of communication and the new media in the intra-state networks that they organize.

Two additional factors contribute to the popularity of the communalist and corporatist strategies among state-linked diasporas. First, they are the optimal strategies for promoting diasporas' vital interests in the regional and global arenas. Second, although those strategies can lead to clashes with both homelands and host countries, overall they have been found to be the strategies least objectionable to most host societies and homelands. Compared with the more radical separatist, irredentist, and autonomist strategies discussed later, they appear less menacing to host countries because they do not entail any actual or potential challenge to either authoritarian or democratic states in regard to their sovereignty and territorial integrity – the two attributes of the nation-state that are considered sacred by receiving governments and societies, even in the most liberal Western countries. The more nationalistic and chauvinistic host societies in Asia, in the Middle East, and to some extent in Africa are even more fanatical about sovereignty and territoriality (Smith 1986; Young 1986).

Though rather quiet about it, host governments also show greater tolerance toward diasporas' communalism because it provides them adequate means for monitoring and controlling those groups' activities, which, notwithstanding the increasing tolerance toward them, are almost always regarded with some suspicion. Thus, host governments have realized that although allowing diasporas their organization and institutionalization may involve some inconvenience with regard to host-country sovereignty and freedom of action vis-à-vis those ethnic entities and their homelands, in the final analysis, allowing diasporas their communalism is the least unfavorable arrangement. Moreover, in some cases it is also the most beneficial to the host countries. Furthermore, perceptive host governments know that such arrangements foster moderation and responsibility on the part of diaspora leaders and their rank and file. All those benefits are obtained without endangering the vital interests of the host country. That attitude of toleration has caused internal debates in diasporas and in host societies, sometimes leading to radicalization of certain segments in diasporas and thus causing security problems for host societies: France in the wake of the Muslim

Moroccan and Algerian influx has been an example of that problem. Generally, however, tolerance in regard to a communalist strategy has proved to pose the smaller risk, and most host countries have been willing to assume such risks.

Hence, use of the term "diaspora communities" is neither accidental nor entirely misleading, for the strategic aspiration of most of the established state-linked diasporas is to establish cohesive communities that can implement a moderate communalist strategy. Subsequently, that pattern determines the nature of the entire structure, organization, and activities of those diasporas. Therefore diaspora leaders and activists who are strongly inclined to establish and maintain such cohesive communities invest considerable energy and resources in promoting solidarity, recruiting members and mobilizing them, and gaining legitimacy for their operations from host authorities and societies.

The next role for those leaders and activists is to preserve the diaspora communities they establish. Many observers of diaspora affairs have discussed the various roles of religious leaders who accompany migrants to their new host countries and there provide initial guidance and support for the migrants. Such leaders work to strengthen migrants' connections to their entire nation, to their homeland, and to their religion. Some of those religious leaders commute between homelands and host countries, not only providing religious continuity but also maintaining political contacts. That has been particularly true for Turks, Pakistanis, Iranians, Sikhs, Jews, and Palestinians. In some of those cases, religious functionaries have served as homeland governments' agents and emissaries to their diasporas – the Iranian and Turkish mullahs and imams are good examples of that pattern.

It is less widely known that intellectuals, artists, musicians, and academics play significant roles in establishing diasporas, maintaining their cultural traits, and furthering the communalist strategy. Writing and communicating in their native tongue, in the languages of host countries, or in English, which has become the current lingua franca, such influential people communicate their opinions through a diaspora's traditional media outlets as well as the new media, and they can gain considerable influence over its cultural, social, and political development in its host countries and in the homeland. They also can be quite useful in fostering close contacts between diasporans and their homeland and in helping diaspora communities adjust to host countries.

Such intellectuals can have significant roles in the creation of incipient diasporas and in their transformation into established entities. For example, the well-known scholar and activist W. E. B. Du Bois was instrumental in founding the African-American diaspora movement, and the orientalist Edward Said was influential not only in the development of the Palestinian diaspora and in shaping its main political orientation but also in spreading the idea of a global Muslim diaspora. Many other intellectuals have carried the torch of ethno-national diasporism in the effort to maintain or reshape ethnic identities. Such people use their renown to exert influence, but in some cases they can cause adverse consequences. When expressing views critical of either their homelands or diasporas, some Turkish intellectuals in Germany, Cubans in the United States, Armenians in the United States, and Jews and Palestinians in the West have been viciously attacked by their fellow diasporans and by homeland politicians and agents.

Partly spontaneously and partly because of the influence of their religious and secular elites, the more determined and activist diasporans have created close-knit communities that employ a variety of political mechanisms, such as building political parties, seeing to it that their members vote, lobbying, and mass protests, to promote the interests of diasporas and homelands. As would be expected, most of those close-knit communities are in smaller and geographically concentrated diasporas. Albanians in the United States, Ukrainians in the United States, Canada, and Australia, Hungarians in Australia, and Jews in Australia (Rutland 1997) and Germany have all followed that strategy, and with good reason the lay leaders and professional functionaries of those communities boast of their success.

Still, success in establishing activist communities encompassing large segments of a nation's diaspora permanently residing in a given host country is not necessarily a good indicator of homogeneity and cohesion. Therefore it is a legitimate question whether or not groups such as the large Jewish entities in the United States and in Russia indeed constitute such cohesive communities. The same applies, for example, to the Chinese, Polish, and Greek diasporas in the United States. That issue has not been properly studied and should be further explored. In particular, the nature of diaspora sub-communities in its various host countries and their connections to the core group and the homeland should be reexamined. That will involve the development of clear criteria for judging the cohesion of ethno-national diasporas. Thus far, such criteria have not been formulated.

A further examination of this issue is needed not only because of the general debate about ethnic "imagined communities" but also because of the more tightly focused arguments about cultural hybridity that have been applied to ethnic groups and ethno-national diasporas. The notion of hybridity holds that ethnic identities are constructed through negotiation of differences and that the presence of cultural contradictions in a community is not a sign of weakness or failure. The concept of hybridity also stresses that identities are not created by a "mechanical" fusion or synthesis of many elements, but result from intensive exchanges between various social and cultural actors. In that vein, it has been argued that the process involves substantive encounters between the different subgroups that can transform various viewpoints (Papastriyadis 1997; Werbner 1997). Other observers of that phenomenon have suggested that we should think of identity as a process of "production" and "reproduction" that never ends, that always develops, and that invariably is constituted within and not outside representation (Hall 1990). In sum, the cohesion and hybridity of diaspora communities should be reexamined from two viewpoints: the cohesion of those communities within and vis-à-vis their host societies, and their intra-communal cohesion.

The Autonomist Strategy

The autonomist strategy is intended to gain special political and cultural rights and freedoms for diasporans within host countries' polities. To a great extent the feasibility and efficacy of that strategy will depend on two factors: the extent of the territorial concentration and cultural homogeneity of diaspora groups, and the willingness of host countries to allow some of their powers to be exercised by such ethno-national groups. Both factors can prove to be major obstacles in the way of achieving such rights. In the past, various diasporas were granted certain degrees of political autonomy, such as the Jews within the framework of the millet system in the Hapsburg and Ottoman empires, and Soviet Jews, particularly in the "autonomous republic" of Birobidzhan. Currently, however, there are almost no formal autonomist arrangements for diasporas. Yet those entities can and do achieve de facto cultural autonomy. That is expressed in explicit and implicit authorization to establish special schools, to practice their religions, to establish and operate religious institutions, to run radio and TV stations, to create Internet sites, and to render other cultural services to their members. In a sense, diasporas' quest for cultural autonomy overlaps with their pursuit of the communalist strategy, for communalism facilitates a substantial degree of cultural autonomy.

The Irredentist Strategy

In the context of ethno-national diaspora politics, the irredentist strategy seeks to achieve separation of that part of a diaspora's former historical homeland currently under the control of a host country and join it to adjacent segments of that diaspora's nation in order to establish a national state within the boundaries of the diaspora's historical homeland (Chazan 1991). The most obvious example of a group some of whose members in western European diaspora communities have pursued that strategy is the diaspora of the Iraqi and Turkish Kurds.

The Separatist Strategy

The separatist strategy and the irredentist strategy are the most radical political strategies followed by diasporas. The separatist strategy is intended to establish an independent state in a diaspora's former historical homeland and facilitate the return of all or most segments of its ethnic nation (Smith 1986; Weiner 1991; Sheffer 1991). The latter two strategies are employed either by stateless diasporas or by diasporas whose historical homelands have been taken over by other ethnic groups and host countries.

For practical reasons, state-linked diasporas do not choose either the secessionist or irredentist strategy. Because most leaders of state-linked diasporas are realists and pragmatists, in most cases (even those cases in which the homeland borders on the host country, as is the case with Mexico and the United States, Sri Lanka and India, and the Basques in Spain and France) such strategies are not considered feasible options. There is one exception to that pattern: diasporans supporting the IRA's demand that Northern Ireland be returned to the Irish republic. It seems that they may eventually succeed in achieving their goal. Similarly, as diaspora leaders are fully aware that no host society or government would seriously consider granting them formal territorial autonomy within host-country boundaries, full autonomy within a host country is not a realistic option.

Historically, from the middle of the nineteenth century until the late 1930s (the period of massive waves of migration from eastern and central Europe to western Europe and then to North America and Latin America), and then from the late 1940s until the 1970s, most immigrants and the diasporas that they established pursued assimilationist, integrationist, or, in a few cases, corporatist strategies. After arriving in their final destinations, the purpose of most migrants was to assimilate, or at least to integrate and obtain formal recognition of equal political and social rights. The decisions of the members of those groups were motivated in part by profound dissatisfaction with the political and economic conditions prevailing in their homelands (hence their desire to begin a new life in host countries) and in part by unpleasant encounters with the notions prevailing in their host countries, strongly emphasizing homogeneity and sovereignty. Thus, in order to survive and prosper in their new environments, diasporans usually pursued one of the two acommodationist strategies. However, since the 1970s, as a result of the major transformations that have occurred in world affairs, which, among other things, are encouraging pluralism in democratic host countries, both established and incipient diasporas have been altering their attitudes toward the fundamental dilemmas of their existence in host countries. Consequently, they are also altering their strategies. Because members of such diasporas are no longer embarrassed by their origins and feel confident and secure enough to maintain their ethnic identities and identify as such, more diasporans are discarding the assimilationist and corporatist strategies and adopting communalism instead.

Both historical and modern diasporas that had become dormant but recently have been awakening in response to new realities in their homelands and in their host countries show clear indications that they, too, are inclined to adopt the communal strategy. In so doing, they join the Jewish, Indian, Chinese, and Greek diasporas that have always preferred to pursue that strategy.

Following are some observations about the tactics used by the various types of diasporas. Much like the choice of a strategy, to a great extent the choice of tactics will depend on self-perceptions of diasporas' capabilities. Specific tactics are chosen with an eye to, among other things, the population densities and the numbers of the diasporas' members. Thus, although the population numbers of the larger diasporas are growing, still they usually constitute only relatively small segments in their host societies. Furthermore, despite the fact that pockets of diasporans can be found concentrated in global cities and large urban centers, in terms of total membership most diasporas are geographically dispersed in their host countries. Their relatively small percentages in the population and their territorial dispersal are not conducive to adoption of radical tactics that could seriously challenge strong host countries. Those and additional systemic constraints, such as the limitations imposed on diasporas by their hosts and the demands from their homelands, lead to self-imposed restraints regarding diasporas' willingness and capacity to generate and use various resources and tactics for both offensive or defensive purposes within host societies. Leaders of those communities are well aware of such constraints, and that tends to infuse further restraint into their decisions about the strategies and tactics they adopt.

Earlier in this chapter it was posited that stateless diasporas pose greater potential challenges to the sovereignty of whoever controls their homelands than to those who control their host countries. And indeed, depending on their geographic concentration/dispersion within their host countries, and especially when large concentrations of diasporans are close to the borders across which their co-ethnics are residing, radical stateless diasporas that have chosen the separatist and irredentist strategies tend to use aggressive and violent tactics. That was the case for the Palestinians during the first *Intifada* (uprising) that they launched in the middle and late 1980s, when occasionally they resorted to violence against Israeli and against Jewish targets outside Israel. In that case, substantial resources and logistical support for those who actually carried out those attacks were provided by the Palestinian diaspora in the adjacent Arab countries. Such patterns also apply to the Sikhs, who have employed violent tactics both within India and abroad, and to the Kurds, who are engaged in a protracted, sometimes violent struggle, especially against the Iraqi and Turkish governments, including their legations abroad.

The main goal of the communal strategy, which is pursued by the majority of state-linked diasporas, is to achieve a secure and respected existence within host countries. Thereby those diasporas hope to gain and maintain various rights and freedoms, including the right to establish relationships and carry on exchanges with their homelands. Adoption of that strategy dictates moderation and the use of nonviolent tactics and means. Therefore, the most important tactics that those diasporas use are political, economic, and occasionally also social in nature. In the political sphere, diasporas establish and operate promotional, advocacy, and lobbying organizations. In that respect, they act like many other interest groups, including indigenous ethnic minorities. In the economic sphere they tend to establish and operate fund-raising and investment organizations, as well as political action committees (PACs) in the United States and their equivalents in other host countries. Those PACs serve as conduits for distribution of some of the monies diasporas raise or earn, including to candidates running for political offices in host countries. Other financial resources are used to assist diasporas' protective and promotional endeavors in the political and economic arenas. In the societal sphere, diasporas establish organizations for the promotion and maintenance of bilateral and multilateral inter-communal associations. The function of those organizations is mainly to build relationships with majority groups, but also to achieve and maintain peaceful coexistence and cooperation with other minorities and diasporas within and outside their host countries.

Diasporas invest substantial efforts in protective and promotional measures in the economic sphere. The Jewish, Chinese, Armenian, Greek, Korean, and Japanese, to mention only a few notable diasporas, all are very active in advancing and defending the economic interests of their homelands in their host countries, especially the United States. That, however, is not a one-way process. Diasporas also advance and facilitate the economic interests of their host countries in their homelands. Those activities are aimed at securing economic aid, investment, particularly investments in critical industries, debt cancellations and moratoriums, tax reductions, and so forth. With considerable degrees of success, diasporas try to serve as credible mediators and facilitators between their homelands and host countries to the benefit of all sides, including the diasporas themselves. Some diasporas are involved in the promotion of new political and social ideas, such as liberalization of governmental procedures and standards, privatization of some governmental functions, and equal opportunities for all ethnic groups.

Finally in this context, a few words about the tactics used by dormant diasporas. Even more than active diasporas that have had long experience in pursuing the communalist strategy, dormant diasporas that had become integrated into their host societies and now are experiencing revival are far from being inclined to use aggressive and violent tactics. In that vein, it would be difficult to envision Swedish-Americans or Polish-Americans, who are now renewing their interest in their homelands and in diaspora affairs, using violent or aggressive tactics. Consequently, they, too, invest effort in reviving or establishing their communal organizations and use nonaggressive tactics.

The Functions of Diaspora Organizations

Because of their multiple interests, diaspora communities function on five levels in politics: the domestic level in host countries, the regional level, the trans-state level, the level of the entire diaspora, and the level of homeland politics. On each of those levels, a diaspora's functions fall into three broad categories: maintenance, defense, and promotion of its communities' multifaceted interests.

Whereas interactions between members of diaspora communities and their host societies usually are carried out directly by the rank and file on both sides and by general communal organizations, most of the important interactions and exchanges on all other levels are performed by specialized communal organizations or by units in those organizations.

On the first level, the host-country level, diasporas' communal organizations deal with issues pertaining both to diasporas' internal affairs and to their relations with host countries' political and economic institutions. On the second level, the regional level, diaspora organizations have mainly been involved in economic matters, but increasingly also in the political arena. On the third level, the global level, the communal organizations' functions pertain mainly to interactions with global organizations such as the United Nations and its functional agencies (the International Labor Organization, the International Monetary Fund, and the World Bank) and to a lesser degree to "bystanders" or fourth and fifth parties who show interest in the affairs of a given diaspora or in the diaspora phenomenon at large. For example, in the case of the complex multifaceted relationships involving Israel, the Soviet Union, and Russian Jewry, the U.S. government, which was deeply involved in the issue of Russian Jews' emigration, was a fourth party, and the Palestinians and the Arab countries constituted the fifth party. On the fourth level, the entire diaspora, usually the interactions are with very similar or sister organizations. Finally, on the fifth level, diaspora–homeland relations, the interactions are mainly with governmental and public organizations.

The diaspora organizations' maintenance functions include fundraising, carried out through general or special-purpose organizations, routine administration of cultural, economic, and social functions, such as schools and community centers, oversight of religious institutions, such as mosques, churches, synagogues, and theological schools, and supervision of universities and colleges and research institutions. Long-established communities, such as the Jewish and Greek diasporas, also support elaborate health and welfare services, such as hospitals, clinics, psychological services, and senior citizens' homes.

The communal defense functions are performed mainly through specialized organizations that provide physical protection for diaspora members when that is found to be necessary. South Korean, Chinese, and Jewish communities in the United States, Jewish communities in South

America, North Africans in France, Turks in Germany, and Pakistanis in Britain all have established such self-defense organizations. They are responsible not only for the communities' defense vis-à-vis hostile segments of the dominant societies in host countries but also for defense against other ethnic minorities or diasporas. Such formal organizations and small groups of vigilantes have been involved in clashes between Vietnamese and South Koreans in California and between Pakistanis and Indians in Britain.

Frequently the defense function also entails political and legal activities to secure personal, social, and political rights, as well as educational, employment, and welfare opportunities for their members. Thus most diasporas now establish organized lobbies that unabashedly act in most democracies to obtain and secure their members' rights. The literature on this aspect of diasporas' activities is vast, but it focuses mainly on a few diasporas. For some general analyses, see Esman (1986), DeConde (1992), Connor (1993b), Ifestos (1993), Huntington (1997), Shain (1999), and Demetriou (1999).

The promotional and advocacy functions fall mainly into three frequently overlapping subcategories: cultural, political, and economic. The communal organizations responsible for performing those functions deal with issues such as recruiting new members (certain diasporas, such as the Jewish, Greek, and central and eastern European, actively reach out and locate newcomers and other non-registered co-ethnics) and persuading them to become activist members ready to contribute intellectual, political, and financial resources to facilitate communal activities. Of even greater importance are the promotional activities that are intended to increase ethnic awareness and a sense of identity among diasporans. Many of those activities are in the cultural sphere. Thus, the organizations coordinate ethnic festivals, exhibitions, and lectures and operate via traditional and new media. All those functions are intended to increase membership, advance diaspora communities' visibility and stature, and consolidate diasporas' contacts with their homelands.

Better-organized and richer diasporas also engage in elaborate advocacy activities intended to increase acceptance of the general diaspora phenomenon and tolerance of specific diasporas and their respective homelands. A relevant example concerns the efforts made by the rather small American Turkish community and the countermeasures taken by the much larger American Greek community during various stages of the Cyprus crisis in the 1970s and later (on the Greek diaspora organizations that were involved during that period, see Watanabe 1993).

Further examples of such activities are the extensive efforts by the Palestinians and other Arab diaspora groups in the United States and by the North African diasporas in western Europe to enhance their stature, improve their images, and promote specific interests of their respective homelands.

In this context, a primary concern and an important sphere of activity for organized diasporas encompasses a whole spectrum of interests and activities: providing generous economic aid to their homelands, making investments there, promoting cooperation between host countries and homelands, lobbying for liberalization of tariffs, and so forth. That is especially the case for diasporas residing in the United States, which has become the only remaining global superpower. The United States claims to be and sometimes has been the main defender of human rights and of the security of threatened nations and ethnic groups. It is also the main financier for homelands in need, as well as a market for the products of those homelands. It should be emphasized, however, that by no means are such efforts made only by diasporas in the United States. Similar activities are conducted by the Turkish diaspora in Germany, and to some extent by the Pakistanis and Indians in the United Kingdom. In any case, intensive lobbying, cajoling, and persuasion in and around the U.S. Congress and White House in regard to economic issues that affect their homelands can be "profitable endeavors" for diasporas. Such lobbying can elicit not only direct American support but also aid and investments from the G8 nations, the World Bank, and the International Monetary Fund because of the decisive U.S. role in those organizations. After World War II, the Greek, Polish, Jewish, and Irish diasporas in the United States, all succeeded in obtaining generous economic and financial aid for their homelands. More recently, the incipient Palestinian, Vietnamese, and Korean diasporas in the United States have successfully engaged in similar lobbying and persuasion efforts.

Diasporas sometimes try to influence host countries' policymakers also to agree to moratoriums on loans to their homelands. The Mexican diaspora in the United States has been successful in that respect. Yet another of the various activities in this sizable sphere is lobbying intended to end economic boycotts and limitations on exports and imports to and from host countries. For example, some Jewish organizations in the United States lobbied for an end to the economic boycott of South Africa during the apartheid era, their purpose being to assist the Jewish community in South Africa, which was facing economic difficulties there. Those efforts to sway international policies toward South Africa led to heated controversies among various groups and movements in that diaspora. They also led to tensions with African-Americans, who were working to intensify the boycott against South Africa. Also, certain parts of the Chinese diaspora in the United States have been involved in similar activities regarding policies toward mainland China. On the other hand, occasionally diasporas will become involved in lobbying to impose boycotts and sanctions on their homelands. The cases of certain groups in the Cuban and Iranian diasporas in the United States and the Iraqi diaspora in Europe come to mind in that connection.

Furthermore, diasporas often take on the middleman function in regard to promoting industrial, commercial, and banking cooperation and investments between their hosts and homelands. The Jewish, Irish, Japanese, Chinese, and Korean diasporas all have played significant roles in that sensitive sphere of economic exchanges. Because of the dramatic changes that have occurred and others that are expected in the financial sector of the "global village," it is reasonable to assume that those and other diasporas will play even greater roles in the future.

On the extra-communal levels, diasporas' maintenance activities include remittances, personal and collective donations and other kinds of unilateral transfers of economic and financial resources, and the supply of other political and social "services" to homelands and other communities of co-ethnics living in other host countries. That latter category of activities includes individual and group visits to homelands and coordination of social, economic, and political actions vis-à-vis homelands.

The defense functions on the extra-communal levels usually include lobbying for protection of the political and economic interests of the entire diaspora against attacks by fourth and fifth parties. The American Jewish community's negotiations with the Soviet Union and Ethiopian governments in regard to the fate of those two harassed Jewish communities are good examples of recent successful actions by the defense organizations of a highly organized diaspora on behalf of its co-ethnics. The mediation of PLO leaders with the Iraqi and Kuwaiti governments during the Persian Gulf War in regard to the well-being of the Palestinians in Kuwait is a second example of such activities, and a third is the intercession of Greek-Americans regarding the fate of the Greek Cypriots.

Among other things, the promotional and advocacy functions of diaspora organizations on the extra-communal levels involve efforts to organize campaigns to engender favorable attitudes toward their homelands and other parts of their diasporas. The efforts of Turks, Greeks, Palestinians, Croats, and Kurds in the United States and the European Union come to mind in this respect. In promoting the interests and rights of minorities in general and of ethno-national diasporas in particular, organized diasporas increasingly are using, sometimes in a quite sophisticated manner, the most advanced means of communication. Thus, although diasporas usually are not inclined to try to increase their visibility, certain communities have conducted carefully planned and professionally executed radio, TV, and Internet campaigns. Those will be further analyzed in Chapter 7.

As far as their particular interests will permit, diaspora leaders tend to cooperate with leaders of other ethnic minorities and diasporas in organizing and carrying out demonstrations and protests against the oppression of particular diasporas and for the granting of individual and collective political rights to other minorities and diasporas. Thus, for example, leaders of various established diasporas supported the Jewish campaign on behalf of Russian Jews, and leaders of Jewish diaspora communities in western Europe supported the struggles of North African migrants. Yet it must be added that sometimes relationships between diasporas deteriorate into competition, tension, and conflict, and that has sometimes been the case for African-Americans and American Jews (Shain 1999, pp. 132–64), as well as for the Greeks and Turks in the United States. However, in many other cases, when the immediate causes for such tensions and clashes are removed, attempts at rapprochement will follow. Following reestablishment of the status quo in Cyprus, American Jews and Greek-Americans resumed their contacts and cooperation.

As a rule, the more firmly established and the richer the community, the more elaborate and comprehensive its organizations become. The fact of being a long-established and rich community does not mean only the availability of financial resources for organization and action. It also means that the scope of the community's interests will expand, which will tend to bring easier access to powerful segments in host societies and governments. Consequently, the expertise, acumen, and dedication that are needed for such activities will increase and become more widespread among the members of the community. Among the best examples for such development are the American Jewish (Elazar 1986, 1995), the overseas Chinese (Esman 1986), and the American Greek communities (Constas and Platias 1993).

But contrary to a widely held view about diasporas, communal affluence is not an absolute prerequisite either for the establishment of successful communal organizations or for their effective operation, though ample financial resources, elaborate communal structures, and developed organizations certainly do not hurt the cause. But more important by far are determination, experience, and hard work on the part of activist members and leaders of diasporas. Thus, contrary to the arguments of those who follow the lead of Armstrong (1976), it is not only the long-established, richer "mobilized" diasporas that can be successful in such efforts, but also the more recent, less well established, and poorer diasporas. Certain segments of the Turkish, Kurdish, Algerian, Albanian, and Moroccan diasporas have clearly demonstrated that they can create thriving organizations and launch effective activities on their own behalf and on behalf of their homelands. Moreover, even the most "proletarian" diasporas can succeed in organizational efforts and subsequently in other activities. That has been clearly demonstrated by the Turks in Germany and Sweden, the Palestinians in Latin America, and the Mexicans and South Koreans in the United States. In most of those instances, enthusiasm, resourcefulness, and zeal proved to be no less effective than the routine workings of large, well-endowed diaspora organizations. Whenever those attributes are in evidence, diasporas' efforts to organize can be successful even if they are intended to be for only a short duration, or arise from ad hoc situations. In most cases, those efforts are not confined to the organization of institutions in host countries, but also entail determined efforts to establish elaborate trans-state networks. Those are discussed in Chapter 7.

7

Trans-state Networks and Politics

Diasporas' Trans-state Networks

It is no surprise that two related phenomena that are at the center of our discussion at this stage – ethno-national diasporas and distance-shrinking technologies – are today attracting great attention. Although the world is fully aware of the significance of each of those phenomena, not all observers of the world's affairs are aware that they are inter-connected phenomena and that to some extent they influence each other in a circular feedback manner (for elaboration of all points made in this section, see Dahan and Sheffer 2001).

The simultaneous developments we have been discussing, such as distance-shrinking technologies, increasing globalization, and increasing diasporism, do not serve only to enhance the peaceful existence and pros-perity of all parties involved in or affected by the exchanges between diasporas and other parties. It is quite true that large portions of all com-munications and resources that diasporas exchange with other actors inside and outside their host states are harmless. Yet the existence of extensive diaspora networks and the various communications and resources that are transferred through them can also lead to tensions and contribute to conflicts involving diasporas, host states, homelands, and other interested parties. Some of those conflicts challenge the sovereignty of host countries, some exacerbate inter-state relationships, and some have even wider regional and global ramifications.

The first question that will be asked here is whether or not the inten-sive use of distance-shrinking communications systems by diasporas is a recent development. The answer is, of course, negative. In fact, throughout their historical existence, those groups have been making extensive use of "old," then "more modern," and now "new" distance-shrinking communications technologies. Like other social groups and state governments, diasporas long used, and some still use, old forms or means of communication, such as messengers on horseback, communication via drums and signal fires, homing pigeons, and letters carried by boats and ships. One of the best historical examples of that pattern is the system of rabbinical *responsa* (questions by the rank and file and answers by rabbis concerning all aspects of Jewish life in the homeland and the diaspora) that was established by the Jewish religious leadership in ancient Babylon and other Jewish diaspora communities. Those questions and answers were communicated to near and far communities through the old forms of communication. Similarly, rulers of states, especially those with vast empires, in antiquity and during the Middle Ages established widespread networks and used whatever distance-shrinking means of communication were available to maintain their rule over remote territories and to ensure their interests. Various diasporas used those and related means of communication to promote their own interests.

During much later periods, in addition to those older means of communication, diasporic entities progressively used railroads, the telegraph, the telephone, wireless radio, and the automobile for the purpose of faster interchanges with their co-ethnics, with other ethnic groups and organizations, and with various rulers and governments. Also, *Landsmanschaften*, that is, organizations of migrants, in the United States and Europe used whatever means of communication were available to rapidly transfer information from homelands to dispersed groups and back.

More recently, especially since the late 1970s, those groups have begun to use modern information-communicating technologies (ICTs), such as continuous global coverage of news by radio and television, and newer inventions, such as faxes, to facilitate exchanges of information between geographically dispersed ethnic groups. At about the same time, ideas about creating local and trans-state communications networks began to percolate, and soon plans for such networks were coordinated by various diasporas and put into operation (Brunn 1981; Brunn and Leinbach 1991; Brunn and Jones 1994).

As in other related spheres, such as electronic banking and commerce (e-banking, e-commerce), the most recent development in communications, which began in the late 1980s and gained momentum throughout the 1990s, is the explosive increase in the use of the Internet. That has substantially changed the nature of interactions in all fields, including interactions between diaspora groups and governmental and non-governmental organizations, both at home and abroad.

Consequently, the range and quality of diasporas' activities have been increased by the availability, low cost, and, most important, the reach and interactivity of this medium, thus increasing their number of audiences, their efficacy, and the impact of their media. Those activities now include dissemination of news and cultural artifacts to local communities in host countries, improvements in education in those communities, mobilization and transfer of economic, cultural, and political resources to homelands and other diaspora communities, creation of trans-state political communities, and communication with local and global NGOs and IGOs. All of those contribute to the emergence of a global civil society, which in turn will strengthen diasporism and specific diasporas.

Globalization has expedited the development of noticeable similarities among the various Western democracies, among many developing societies, and between indigenous ethnic minorities and ethno-national diasporas. Moreover, the propagation of liberal social, economic, and political ideas has been greatly increased by the new means of communication. Similarly, people's exposure to ethnic food, fashion, and pop music has been facilitated by the new media. Consequently, those trends have affected and continue to influence most social, economic, and political systems. There is no doubt that those developments are having substantial ramifications for current processes of economic liberalization, political democratization in many countries, and empowerment of various minorities, including ethnic groups and ethno-national diasporas.

Some politicians and political analysts have expressed the view that as a direct result of globalization, regionalization, and the emergence of cross-national and cross-state similarities, national and ethnic identities may be eroded and membership in social and political entities based on such identities may substantially, or even critically, decline. A further concern is that "identity" may cease to be defined by members of such a group themselves within the context of their immediate environment, but rather that it will come to be defined in conjunction with new regional and trans-national cultural and ideological trends, or defined by global movements and organizations. From the viewpoint of such groups, if indeed the media blur specific group identities, then ethnic affiliation, like age, gender, and personality, will be nothing but an abstract variable in a fuzzy pattern of information processing and dissemination.

Despite such a possibility, which still lingers, those new equalizing trends have not yet caused the disappearance of tribal groups, ethnic minorities, and ethno-national diasporas. Quite the contrary, as noted earlier, ethnicity and ethnic affiliations have persisted, and, both socially and politically, ethnicity is still with us and is flourishing (for a discussion of "cyber-Balkanization," see van Alstyne and Brynjolfsson 1996). One of the consequences of our transformation into a post-modern society, characterized by global flows of wealth, information, power, and images, is that the search for identity, collective or individual, primordial or constructed, becomes the fundamental element in social meaning (Castells 1996). In that vein, it is argued here that the Internet promotes globalized diffusion and localized appropriation (Slevin 2000).

The emergence and spread of the new media, as well as our easy and inexpensive access to them, are tending to obliterate the gap between urban, rich, sophisticated diasporas and rural, less well educated, poorer ethnic groups. That is, the availability of these new means of communication has at the very least created the potential for all diasporas to have equal access to public opinion and to policymakers, regardless of diasporas' economic and political resources and regardless of their central or peripheral location. Like most other social and political groups, diasporas use the new media to increase their access to homeland and host governments and to facilitate communication among their members. In addition to the traditional purpose of sharing information about current affairs, dangers, and opportunities, those groups use the media to ensure continuity of the diaspora and to preserve their cultural heritage, history, and particularly language. That is becoming a significant concern because of the greater opportunities for integration and assimilation into the dominant societies in host countries and because of the tendency to begin taking on the cultural and political traits of the host society, a tendency that is reinforced by the messages and influences disseminated through the host-country media.

Diasporans actively and passively participate also in general networks that promote the ideas and practices of "new politics." Members of such entities support and advocate issues such as equal rights for all minorities, affirmative action to right old wrongs, social and economic justice for all disadvantaged groups, and the return of land to native nations. For example, the American Jewish Anti-Defamation League directs its efforts to an ongoing public campaign against racism in general and anti-Semitism in particular. Diaspora defense and promotion organizations also work toward achieving equal access for all and use all existing means of communication to advance their agendas (Mele 2000). Yet substantial portions of diasporas' communications via the new media are directed at placing their plight and grievances on the public agenda.

In addition to those uses of the new media, diasporas often are responsible for introducing and implementing such new technologies in their homelands, particularly in less developed countries. In some cases diaspora communities have financed the purchase of needed equipment and the training for its use. Diasporas use communications technology extensively and intensively and on a number of levels. On the host-country level, they use new technologies for communication between members of various local communities and for contacts with other ethnic groups. On the trans-state level, they are used for communication with homelands and other communities living in other host countries. On the global level, they are used to promote contacts with other diasporas and global IGOs and NGOs, such as the Red Cross, Amnesty International, the United Nations, and human-rights groups. Often the new communications technologies offer the only means available for diasporans to express their concerns and voice their opinions, especially when they have no access to the media controlled by unfriendly governments and unsympathetic social groups.

Basically, diasporas create trans-state communications networks because of their members' existential need to maintain contact with their homelands and other dispersed communities of the same origin. Although those are the networks' most basic functions, they increasingly are connecting diasporas with other diaspora systems, with ethnic networks, and with regional and global IGOs and NGOs. Like all other organized entities, most diaspora organizations prefer to communicate with institutionalized counterparts and through formal channels. Yet the opportunities offered by such networks are attracting the attention of individuals and non-establishment groups that increasingly are using those trans-state networks and systems.

As noted earlier, the emergence of such networks is not a recent phenomenon, nor has their use been limited to the long-established rich diasporas. Such networks were created in the earliest days of ethno-national diasporism. They have served ancient and medieval diasporas, especially those engaged in international trade, commerce, and financial services. They have not been unique to archetypal diasporas such as the Jewish, overseas Chinese, and Armenian. In ancient times the dispersed Phoenicians, Nabateans, Akkadians, and Greeks established and operated such networks. They were, of course, using much simpler means of communication, such as drumbeats, vocal signaling, signal fires, and messengers using horses, coaches, and ships. Also, diasporas that arose during the Middle Ages, such as the Mongolian, Indian, and Japanese, maintained such networks to try to ensure their continuing existence and well-being. Recently, Greek, Armenian, German, Kurdish, Turkish, Palestinian, Korean, and even Sardinian diasporas have established and operate such networks using modern technologies (Brunn 1996, pp. 266–70; Elkins 1997, pp. 140–1; on the Sardinian diaspora networks, see Cappai 1999; for an overview of Arab diaspora networks and the new media, see Anderson 2000).

Without taking an overly strict institutional and organizational approach, it seems that to a large extent the nature of those networks is determined not so much by the content of the information and resources transferred through them as by the way they are formed and administered. Because some diaspora organizations are now conducting cultural, political, and economic transactions using the most up-to-date means of communication, they have completely replaced their old networks by new ones that are operated according to post-modern ideas and practices (Elkins 1997, pp. 148–51).

In the past, the creation and operation of such networks were generally left to the diasporas' elites. Those elites operated the networks through the communal organizations they headed. Only recently have homeland rulers and governments realized the significance of those networks and begun to take part in their operation and maintenance. In some cases, especially those of loyal and cooperative diasporas, such homeland governments have significantly increased their contributions to the maintenance and operation of the networks, though primarily to serve their own interests. Despite denials from homelands, the net result is that some of those networks have become governmental or semi-governmental operations or joint ventures with diaspora associations.

In view of their proliferation and greater political, diplomatic, and economic significance, diasporas' trans-state networks must figure prominently in any analysis of the general global diaspora phenomenon, taking into account the fact that in addition to their positive roles in facilitating trans-state exchanges, occasionally their actions can create tension and lead to conflicts between diasporas and host countries and homelands.

The political exchanges carried out through those trans-state networks are conducted largely by diaspora defense organizations, as discussed in Chapter 6. Such exchanges include detailed reports about the diaspora organizations' activities in host countries, requests for assistance from homelands and other dispersed communities, and calls for intervention on behalf of other diasporic entities of the same origin. For example, in the late 1980s, Russian Jews used such networks to communicate information about their situation and seek support for their demand that they be allowed to leave the Soviet Union. Palestinians used similar networks during their two *Intifadas* (in the 1980s and early in the twenty-first century). Iraqi Kurds have used such networks and means of communication during the recurrent Iraqi offensives against them, and East Timorese outside their homeland have used such networks during their struggle against the Indonesian government.

As a result of diasporas' increasing self-confidence and assertiveness, their networks are also carrying criticisms of their homelands and even transmitting demands concerning the expected behavior of homeland societies and governments. Thus, both liberal Jewish organizations and ultra-religious and rightist Jewish associations in the United States transmit their criticisms of Israeli government policies regarding the peace process, a process that involves the fate of another diaspora: the Palestinian. Similarly, using such networks, liberal South Africans abroad demanded an end to apartheid, some Irish-Americans tried to moderate the IRA's behavior, Palestinian-Americans urged tougher PLO positions vis-à-vis Israel, and overseas Chinese and Cubans spread anti-homeland-government propaganda in the context of the struggle for human rights.

Those exchanges are significant because they are not confined to material matters such as political and diplomatic representations, remittances, financial contributions, trade contracts, and economic joint ventures. Some of the exchanges concern major long-term issues of diasporas' identities and continuity and the politics of homelands and host countries. In short, such communications are attempts to sway the political and economic power bases of those groups.

No less important are the sensitive and sometimes secretive exchanges that are carried out through those networks. Among those, the exchanges of economic and financial resources between homelands and their diasporas are more tangible and therefore also more quantifiable. That category includes unilateral financial transfers (donations and remittances), investments in the homeland, and resources for other joint ventures either in homelands or in other host countries. Some of those transactions, however, are extremely intricate, involving more than two parties. Occasionally such transactions are conducted in the gray area between the legal and illegal.

By no means are such transactions one-way, originating in diasporas and directed at their homelands. Money and other tangible resources are transferred out of homelands to diaspora organizations for financing their maintenance and especially promotional activities, including propaganda campaigns on behalf of homelands. In some instances homeland governments also finance and assist their diasporas' defense organizations and activities. Thus, it is known that the Israeli secret services, especially the Mossad, maintain ongoing contacts with the security officers of major Jewish organizations all over the world. Through those networks, warnings about possible terrorist attacks and other disruptive activities against the homeland and the diaspora are exchanged. The same or similar networks are used for the transfer of educational and other cultural resources in which homeland governments are interested.

Although it is impossible to obtain full and accurate information on such matters, it is more than just conceivable that embezzlement is carried out and money is laundered through such networks and transferred to secret bank accounts outside the homeland. Similarly, Mafia-like organizations in homelands maintain close connections with their counterparts in diasporas. Through such networks, crime organizations in homelands establish and maintain what can be called branches or affiliated organizations in their diasporas. Money generated in homelands has been laundered through those networks by the Russian and Colombian crime rings and the Japanese yakuza. But again, by no means are those one-way networks – criminals also transfer money and information from diasporas to homelands (Angoustures and Pascal 1996).

For reasons that have to do with political, economic, and legal considerations of both host countries and homelands (such as general restrictions on foreign exchange and investments, limitations on minorities' economic and commercial activities, and the battle against terrorists and organized-crime gangs), exact figures concerning donations, investments, and joint ventures with homelands are difficult or impossible to come by. However, there is one notable exception: the Jewish diaspora. In that case, the data on unilateral transfers from the diaspora to the homeland are available and relatively accurate (Raphael 1982; Sheffer 1986c; Stock 1987; Kaufman 1996; Shain 1999). Thus, in the late 1980s the annual transfer from the principal Jewish fund-raising organization, the United

Jewish Appeal in the United States (UJA), to Israel was about $500 million. Ten years later, only about $250 million were transferred to Israel from that source. In the late 1980s, Jewish fund-raising organizations in other countries transferred to Israel about $300 million yearly, but toward the end of the 1990s, only about $120 million. The decline in funds transferred to Israel is explained not by a drastic decrease in the total amounts raised in the diaspora but rather by the decisions of diaspora donors and leaders to invest more in their own communities in order to ensure their continuity. Estimates of the donations transferred to the PLO during the same periods are about one-tenth of the sums that the Jewish diaspora transferred to Israel, that is, about $50 million yearly. Other diasporas, even smaller ones, such as the Armenian, Albanian, Serbian, Croatian, and Slovenian, also transfer substantial sums of money to their homelands. As far as can be ascertained, the amounts that homelands transfer to their diasporas are substantially smaller. For example, only in the late 1990s, for the first time since its establishment, did the Israeli government allocate funds (about $10 million) to finance cultural centers in various Jewish diaspora communities.

It should be noted that such data as are available concerning donors in various diasporas clearly show that small numbers of rich people contribute most of the money to those organizations. In the American Jewish community, about 6 percent of the donors contribute about 80 percent of the funds.

As indicated earlier, fluctuations in the sums raised by diasporas and transferred to homelands are caused by multiple factors. Those fluctuations are indicative of the internal situation in the diaspora and the dynamic relationship between those two parts of the ethnic nation. Increasing transfers may reflect a problematic situation in a homeland, on the one hand, or a revival of a wealthy and generous diaspora, on the other. Furthermore, a substantial reduction in the amount of financial resources that a diaspora transfers to its homeland does not necessarily mean impoverishment of the diasporas. Rather, it may mean a change in the priorities of diaspora organizations and rich donors. That has been a significant factor in the dramatic reductions in donations that the Jewish diaspora has sent to Israel and the Armenian diaspora has sent to Armenia.

The financial resources provided by fund-raising organizations are not the only financial support that diasporas send to their homelands through their trans-state networks. Important sources of support for homelands are the remittances by individuals and families.

Remittances and Other Exchanges

Remittances by individuals and families play a major role in migrant–homeland and diaspora–homeland relations. Table 7.1 illustrates the magnitude and changes that have occurred in that phenomenon from the homelands' viewpoint, and Table 7.2 presents data from the host countries' perspective. Because of the paucity of official data, the figures are based on information from various reports released by the World Bank, the International Monetary Fund (IMF), and host countries, as well as information from recent academic publications and news media.

Five aspects of the remittance phenomenon are particularly striking. First, according to various analysts, remittances soon may outstrip the

TABLE 7.1. *Estimated Annual Remittances to Selected Homelands (Amounts in Billions of Dollars and Percentages of Total Imports)*

Homeland	1984 ($ billion)	1994 ($ billion)	1984 (%)	1994 (%)
Former Yugoslavia	4.0	5.0	28	40
Pakistan	2.5	4.0	36	75
Mexico	0.2	3.5	2	10
Portugal	2.1	3.5	29	30
Egypt	3.6	3.0	39	40
India	2.2	3.0	16	15
Italy	1.4	3.0	18	7
Poland	3.0		12	
Turkey	1.8	2.5	18	20
China	2.5		7	
Greece	1.3	2.0	10	12
Philippines	0.5	2.0	15	25
Spain	2.0	1.7	10	7
Morocco	0.8	1.5	23	40
South Korea	0.5	1.5	1	2
Lebanon		1.2		17
Thailand	0.1	1.2	1	15
Bangladesh	0.5	1.0	20	70
Jordan	1.0	1.0	41	17
Yemen	0.9	0.8	71	20
Albania	0.6		35	
Israel	0.2	0.5	6	7
Ghana		0.5		60

Sources: Data from various sources, including Keely and Tran (1985), reports from the World Bank, the IMF balance-of-payments data, and *Economist* (1994, 2001).

TABLE 7.2. *Estimated Annual Remittances from Selected Host Countries, 1994*

Country	Amount ($ billion)	Country	Amount ($ billion)
United States	12.0	Israel	0.7
Germany	5.0	Italy	0.7
Saudi Arabia	4.0	Venezuela	0.7
France	3.0	Japan	0.5
Switzerland	2.5	Austria	0.5
Britain	2.0	Ivory Coast	0.4
Kuwait	1.0	Belgium	0.3
Gulf states	1.0	Holland	0.3
		Sweden	0.3

Sources: Data from various sources, including Keely and Tran (1985), reports from the World Bank, the IMF balance-of-payments data, and *Economist* (1994).

financing provided to homelands by multilateral institutions like the World Bank and the IMF and the aid given by rich countries.

Second, there is no doubt that proletarian migrants and members of incipient diasporas remit substantial sums of money to their homelands, but as there are almost no records of those remittances, it is difficult to compare their remittances and those by established and organized diasporas. Generally, however, it seems that members of established diasporas, such as the Indian, Italian, Turkish, Chinese, Greek, and Lebanese, remit more money to their homelands than do proletarian migrants, guest workers, and members of incipient diasporas.

Third, although remittances are only the tip of a tremendous financial and economic iceberg, and despite the fact that Tables 7.1 and 7.2 provide only a very partial picture, the estimates that remittances amount to more than $500 billion per year serve as eye-openers about the scope of that aspect of modern diasporism (Keely and Tran 1985; cf. Russel and Teitelbaum 1992; Van Hear 1998).

Fourth, the fact that Mexico, Yugoslavia, Portugal, Morocco, Tunisia, China, the Philippines, Bangladesh, India, Pakistan, Sudan, Turkey, and Egypt get between 10 and 70 percent of their total income from such remittances indicates the significant dependence of those homelands on those sources.

Fifth, it should be noted that the annual volume of remittances transferred to homelands fluctuates and therefore is unpredictable. Changing circumstances in the diasporas, host countries, and homelands all influence those transfers, and just as remittances can rise rapidly, so they can decline sharply. Such fluctuations can be attributed to worsening economic conditions in host countries, shifts in the global work market, dwindling numbers of diaspora members as a result of assimilation and full integration in their host countries, return movements to homelands, and improving conditions in homelands.

There are two contradictory views about the desirability of the flows of money that result from migration and the consequent emergence of diasporas. The negative view of that phenomenon highlights the following aspects: Continued migration and remittances will increase homelands' dependence on their diasporas, encourage further chain-migration and consequently brain drain, create instability in homeland economies, stifle economic initiative, feed consumerism, increase inequality, and lead to developmental distortion and economic decline that may even overshadow the advantages for a minority of beneficiaries. It is clear that the negative view of remittances is predicated on a bias toward a statist-centrist approach emphasizing development of homelands.

The positive view of remittances seeks to turn each of the negative arguments on its head (Iglesias 2001). Thus, as a result of those trends, so it is argued, homeland economies will have to become responsive to market forces, homelands will get resources for development because those monies will have a multiplier effect, and the remittances will improve income distribution (poorer families in homelands will receive otherwise unattainable resources) and contribute to a higher standard of living, including better education, sustenance for elderly people, and adequate housing for families in homelands.

An analysis of the data on remittances shows that neither the negative view nor the positive view of those flows is totally accurate. Generally, the volume of remittances has not diminished, and in certain cases it has increased. Thus it is difficult to argue that income from that source is responsible for economic crises or recessions in homelands. Yet it is equally difficult to say that remittances have become reliable engines that can sustain economic growth or narrow social and economic gaps in homelands. In the absence of a clear theoretical conclusion that would support either view, analysis indicates that because of the great differences in the volumes of remittances to various homelands, homelands and diasporas must consider the implications of dependence on that source and make their own decisions whether or not to encourage those transfers.

As far as other exchanges are concerned, it seems that state-linked diasporas usually engage in relatively harmless transfers of resources through their diaspora trans-state networks (though there are some exceptions). Stateless diasporas, as well as organized groups of refugees that support irredentist, secessionist, or national liberation movements, such as the Palestinians, Kossovar Albanians, Turkish Kurds, Sikhs, and other militant groups, potentially can use those networks to transfer less benign resources.

Those networks can also be used for communications and for shipment of resources needed by international networks of intransigent ethnic groups, and in some extreme cases also transport of terrorists (e.g., to coordinate activities and supply information to the Palestinian rejectionist organizations, such as bin Laden's al-Qaeda and Hamas, and to Kurdish and Sikh underground international organizations). Obviously the existence of those networks entails considerable potential for conflict between diasporas and host-country governments and militant xenophobic groups in host societies. Host countries, coalitions of host countries, and international organizations such as Interpol make substantial efforts to monitor and control the flow of resources. Usually those efforts are futile. Diasporas using those networks for clandestine activities are almost always successful in pursuing their goals.

The Triangular Relationship

In the recent past, almost no confrontation between a host country and a state-linked diaspora has deteriorated into total conflict, or a zero-sum game. That is in contrast to the trend in earlier periods, when host-country–diaspora conflicts led to massacres and expulsions of entire diasporas from their host countries. Some of the better-known historical examples include the expulsion of Jews from England in the twelfth century, the Jewish expulsion from Spain toward the end of the fifteenth century and from Portugal soon thereafter, and the expulsion of Bulgarians from Turkey. More recently we have seen the expulsion of Asians from eastern Africa, the large-scale expulsions of Egyptians, Yemenites, and Palestinians from Saudi Arabia, Iraq, and Kuwait during the Persian Gulf War, and the largely unsuccessful attempts to deport and expel guest workers from Britain, France, Switzerland, Germany, and Spain.

Despite many instances of racism and anti-foreigner policies and actions around the world, in recent years there have been no instances of alienation between ethnic diasporas and host countries that have led to total breakdown of communication between the two sides. Even in the most bitter and protracted conflicts, like those between the Tamils and Sinhalese in Sri Lanka, the Palestinians and Israelis, and the Palestinians and Kuwaitis, or the Kurds versus the Turks and Iraqis, or during the bleakest periods of apartheid in South Africa and periods of high tension between the French government and North African groups residing in France, various channels of communication have always remained open and functioning. Furthermore, there is evidence of cooperation on various levels between such disputants even during acute crises.

The chief reason for those patterns is that leaders of host countries and diasporas have come to realize that, as in the economic and cultural spheres on the global level, their political symbiosis is inescapable: Host-country–diaspora interdependence ultimately compels the two sides to limit the escalation of their conflict and temper their harsh rhetoric, for the social, political, and economic risks involved in all-out conflict are high for both sides. Recognition of that interdependence usually forces them to acceptance of the advisability of maintaining certain rules of conflict and some standards of decency, even though partial. Accordingly, on the one hand, host countries increasingly are tolerating diasporas' wishes to sustain their ethno-cultural identities and to organize and maintain contacts with their homelands, and on the other hand, except for stateless diasporas and some incipient diasporas, most diaspora communities are avoiding excessive conflict over the question of their loyalty, especially when issues of the sovereignty and security of their host countries are at stake. Also, except for ethnic Mafia-type groups, diasporas usually are committed to obeying the laws and the basic economic rules in host countries.

It is true that tense confrontations still occur in those symbiotic but nevertheless potentially antagonistic relationships. Short of total breakdowns that might lead to genocide, detentions, or massive expulsions, or to intensive terrorism, there is a wide range of conflictual exchanges that take place in those relationships. The spectrum ranges from mild controversies to acute adversarial standoffs, usually involving the host government and the diaspora organizations. That is, the dissatisfaction of diasporans usually is directed at host governments rather than at host societies. On the whole, except for the extreme rightist parties and xenophobic groups that have emerged in almost all receiving societies, and except for occasional outbursts of grassroots hatred toward foreigners, especially when economic conditions deteriorate, most large segments of host societies are disinterested and almost uninvolved in those diaspora–host-government conflicts. At the same time, any expressions of hatred toward diasporas or violent outbursts directed against them, or even against other ethnic groups, are of major concern to all segments of those diasporas. That asymmetry in the attitudes of rank-and-file diasporans and the attitudes of most members of host societies has significant implications for the policy choices and action initiatives of both host governments and diasporas.

Consider the causes of open conflict between host countries and diasporas: The divergent ethnic identities of diasporas and host societies are the most basic causes of confrontation. Most conflicts that arise from those relationships are grounded in the emotional and cognitive loyalties to those different identities. All other sources of conflict are superimposed on that basic dichotomy. With certain modifications, the distinctions among economic, cultural, and security causes for conflict generated by recent international migration (Weiner 1993) are also relevant to the emergence of real or perceived risks that lead to conflictual relationships between ethnic diasporas and their host countries.

Accordingly, diasporas occasionally become involved in conflicts that are directly caused by real or perceived economic deprivation. Examples include the riots of Asians in Birmingham and London in the early 1980s and in the mid-1990s. Other examples are the clashes involving Muslims (Harkis and others) in France, Muslims in Brussels, Turks in Berlin and other German cities, and Latin Americans and Vietnamese in various cities in the United States. Numerous less widely known conflicts have been triggered solely by economic competition, and most of those have been local and short-lived and have not caused large-scale disturbances. Some spontaneous outbursts of militancy, especially in the United States and Britain, and the ensuing clashes between diasporas and host governments and their police forces have been triggered by tensions between various diasporas. Those have centered on issues of unemployment, housing, education, and access to welfare services. Thus the past decade has seen bitter clashes between the Korean and Vietnamese incipient diasporas on the west coast of the United States.

The disputes between diasporas and host countries that concern defense and security issues tend to be more serious. Some of those pertain to domestic affairs in host countries, but most concern the relationships between diasporas and their homelands. The mere existence of diasporas' defense and promotional organizations, and especially their trans-state communications and exchange networks, can trigger such confrontations. Yet in most cases the immediate triggers are explicit or implicit complaints about acts of homeland–diaspora cooperation that are alleged to pose dangers to the sovereignty of host countries and thus threaten their most vital interest. Major changes in foreign policy in either homelands or host countries can lead to such confrontations between hosts and diasporas, which usually feel that they have to protect the interests of their homelands. Such policy changes have been the root causes for disagreements between the American Jewish diaspora and various U.S. administrations, between Greek-Americans and Turkish-Americans and Washington, between the Moroccans and the French government, and so forth.

Host governments can be averse to the idea of permitting entry of poorer groups of migrants and may try to expel such refugees or migrants, whether immediately after their arrival in host countries (e.g., the Vietnamese boat people, the Albanians who have tried to find refuge in Italy, and the Moroccans who moved to Spain) or after longer periods in host countries (such as the Turks in Germany). Likewise, host governments may be opposed to the establishment of diasporas within their territories, as seen in the efforts of most Persian Gulf countries to avoid such a development. Nonetheless, basically, and as far as possible, host governments much prefer to avoid full-scale confrontation with all ethnic groups, including ethno-national diasporas, and when disputes occur, they seek reasonable solutions.

Host societies and governments are not always the innocent parties in such confrontations. Their inclination to take actions that may precipitate disputes will depend on the extent of host societies' openness and tolerance toward ethnic groups in general, and in particular on their inclination to make any concessions when diasporas make demands about matters concerning their homelands. Yet today, to a greater extent than only a few years ago, the responsibility for precipitating such confrontations and prolonging them falls on the diasporas and depends on their readiness to engage in conflict with host countries and governments. It seems that, within certain limits, that readiness has recently been reinforced by diasporas' increasing self-confidence and assertiveness.

Essentially, except for the temporary damage caused by terrorism and violent protests carried out by stateless and state-linked diasporas, such conflicts tend to be more intensive and destructive to both sides when the insurgent diasporas are well entrenched in host countries, when they are politically and economically strong, when they are strongly committed to homeland policies, and when they possess enough resources to launch protracted and expensive campaigns. The corollary of that observation is that though diasporas may try to confront host societies and governments over economic deprivation and other related social issues, and though they may mobilize active support from their homelands, those confrontations tend to be relatively marginal and less destructive than conflicts about identity or defense issues.

In any event, the most critical and most sensitive issues facing both host countries and diasporas are those pertaining to divided, dual, and ambiguous authority, and what that implies: divided, dual, and ambiguous loyalties, which will be discussed further in Chapter 9. True, the fundamental dilemmas that diasporas face arise from the basic issue of identity that confronts all ethnic minorities, but in the case of ethnic diasporas those dilemmas are magnified by the ongoing explicit and implicit forms of competition between homelands and host countries in regard to moral and corporeal authority over the diasporas. Those issues can be further exacerbated when diasporas' loyalties to their homelands are intense. In cases where membership in ethnic groups is determined according to undisputed primordial principles, homeland societies and governments will have no doubt about their supremacy in the diaspora–host-country–homeland triangular relationship. Given such circumstances, homelands will tend to demand total loyalty from diasporas, or, at the very least, half. As noted earlier, because of the primordial elements of their identity, the Nazis claimed full moral and practical authority over the German diaspora on the eve of World War II. And indeed they had the undivided loyalty and obedience of large segments of that diaspora residing in various host countries. Today, when decisions about becoming activist members of diasporas are made by individuals and small groups voluntarily and almost autonomously, homelands and diasporas whose identities are shaped according to the instrumental-environmental pattern find it more difficult to forge and maintain the kind of full loyalty that the overseas Germans displayed in the middle and late 1930s. Still, despite that changing attitude, there are always zealots and true believers in all diasporas whose allegiance to their homelands is such that they stand ready to engage in clashes with host countries on behalf of those homelands, which can be major sources of conflict that can yield acute inter-state ramifications.

The question of authority and loyalty is not critical in cases of homelands and diasporas whose identity is formed according to the instrumental-constructivist pattern. In those cases, the readiness of diaspora members to engage in conflict with their host societies over issues concerning their homelands and other diaspora communities of the same origin is more limited. But even in those cases homelands often try to exploit their ethnic bonds and myths as they campaign for diasporas' loyalty, demanding that diasporas act to promote and protect homeland interests in host countries.

When looked upon from the diasporas' point of view, the loyalty choices are difficult and usually involve considerable agonizing over many considerations. Whereas homelands try to cash in on the ethnic sentiments and whatever loyalties prevail among diaspora members, diasporans try to avoid expressing too openly where their loyalties lie. Most diasporans would prefer to maintain ambiguity concerning their loyalties. Hedging their bets, some state-linked diasporas, such as the American Jewish diaspora, will have formal or informal agreements with their homelands. Stateless diasporas, such as the Palestinians, may have similar understandings with the leaders of their national liberation movements about the need to avoid actions that might turn into serious confrontations between those diasporas and their host societies and governments. Yet clashes related to diasporas' loyalties cannot be completely avoided, particularly during periods of acute tension between homelands and host countries.

The consequences of such disputes can be costly for all sides involved. In the late 1990s, such disagreements occurred in the triangular relationship involving the United States, Israel, and the American Jewish community, particularly over the Pollard affair. Apart from the fact that the affair broke some of the ground rules between those two very close allies, Israel's actions caused great confusion for many American Jews, who found themselves torn between loyalty to the United States, which most of them regarded as homeland, and their support for Israel. Many in the American Jewish community were dismayed, for by using an American Jewish spy, Israel breached a long-standing agreement with the American Jewish community, the Ben-Gurion–Blaustein agreement, that the Jewish state would refrain from raising the issue of the diaspora's loyalty (Kumarasawamy 1996). The ramifications of that affair for the three parties involved have been profound, affecting not only the relationship between the two governments but also the individual Jews employed by the American government, especially in the State Department and the Pentagon.

An allegation that a diaspora is acting as a fifth column, working for its homeland to undermine the interests of the host country, can be used as a pretext for discrimination and persecution of the diaspora. Thus, when Uganda expelled Indians and other Asians because of economic considerations, the government attempted to pass that off as a reaction to threats to Uganda's security because of those diasporans' primary allegiances to foreign states. The manner in which the United States treated Japanese-Americans during World War II and the way that the Kuwaitis treated the Palestinians on the eve of the Gulf War arose from similar underlying considerations on the part of those two host governments.

Attempts by diasporas to act on behalf of their homelands or their co-ethnics in other host countries in regard to security issues will involve use of the diasporas' trans-state networks, and that can trigger confrontations with host countries. When those occur, host countries may try to keep diasporas and homelands from using those channels for transfers of information and material resources, and homelands and diasporas will try to protect those channels and ensure their continued regular operation. Such trilateral or multilateral disputes can create inter-state tension and sometimes provoke open hostilities between host countries and homelands. Moreover, before escalating disputes to higher levels politically or militarily, host countries may attempt preemptive strikes to take out or neutralize such networks (e.g., recurrent British attempts to wipe out the IRA's trans-state networks, or Israeli attempts to destroy the Hamas channels of communication). In that context, the mistaken-identity assassination of a Palestinian worker by the Israeli Mossad in Norway, which became known as the Lillehammer debacle and led to considerable tension between Israel and Norway, is a good example of how such attempts can go wrong.

In homeland–diaspora relationships, usually it is the homeland that is largely responsible for tension and discord. Often such quarrels are caused by egregious presumptions by homeland leaders that the very raison d'être of all diasporas is to maintain contact with homelands, continually expressing loyalty and contributing goods and services, particularly those related to defense and political and economic matters. When relationships between homelands and relevant host countries are friendly and cordial, then despite host countries' apprehensions about manipulation of diasporas and their networks by homelands, often a comfortable modus vivendi can be found and maintained.

Such superficially friendly relationships can be shattered when homelands alter their attitudes and policies vis-à-vis host countries or their diasporas, with the most extreme cases escalating to war between homelands and host countries. As has been well documented, during World War II the rights of American citizens of Japanese heritage were largely stripped away, and overseas Germans in host countries were adversely affected by the Nazi war of aggression. Chinese-Americans experienced such difficulties during the Korean War and later, and more recently, during the Persian Gulf crisis in the early 1990s, that was the case for 1.5 million Egyptians in Iraq. In extreme cases, such groups may become hostages in host countries (Weiner 1993) or may be expelled, as were half a million Yemenites living in Saudi Arabia and 300,000 Palestinians in Kuwait (Van Hear 1998, pp. 80–92).

Examination of the behavior of homeland governments shows that some have developed cynical attitudes toward "their" established diasporas. No homeland would go so far as to deliberately sacrifice its diaspora in order to protect and promote its own interests, but when the needs of the homeland and the needs of its diaspora conflict, the preference is clear: The homeland's interests, both security concerns and economic interests, come first. Only when those are secured and satisfied will the homeland entertain involvement on behalf of its diaspora, which in the meantime may find itself in considerable distress.

Thus, whereas some homeland governments have been quite willing to exploit their diasporas in an effort to use them for espionage and other covert operations affecting the security of host countries (during the coldwar era, East Germany, the Soviet Union, and Israel could not resist that temptation), they have been reluctant to engage in international confrontations or combat on their behalf. Such reluctance is seen with regard to all sorts of political and economic issues that could spark international confrontations involving homelands and host countries. Although homelands sometimes are dragged into situations in which they are compelled to protect their diasporas, they are not thrilled to do so. When they do become involved in such situations, homelands tend to be very cautious, often trying a variety of political and diplomatic tactics to diffuse situations that threaten to escalate into undesired warfare with host countries.

Taking Stock of Diasporas' Involvement in Trans-state Politics

The foregoing analysis shows that because of the nature of diasporic entities, their members tend to become deeply involved in the political affairs of host countries and homelands, as well as in regional and international politics. It is clear that the decisions to join such entities and act on their behalf, perhaps leading to serious political consequences, are voluntary decisions on the part of individuals and small groups. Such decisoins reflect increasing readiness to be known and identified as members of collectives that have roots in foreign homelands. No matter how far from their homelands migrants settle, and no matter how long they are away from those homelands, that connection is still a pivotal force in shaping the identities and affiliations of the members of diasporas. No matter whether their migration was voluntary or resulted from expulsion or from political, social, or economic pressures in their homelands, the core members of diasporas tend to retain deeply rooted loyalties to their homelands and often are ready to act on their behalf.

In the face of crosscutting and contradictory pressures, the processes of establishing distinctive ethnic communities in host countries, maintaining ethno-national identities, cherishing the links to homelands, and remaining ready to serve homeland interests are all crucial elements in determining the behaviors of diaspora groups. The precarious situations of those entities in their host countries pose difficult dilemmas that require complex solutions, including the ongoing task of carefully maneuvering between loyalty to homelands and loyalty to host countries. That is reflected in the strategy and tactics that diasporas choose to employ in dealing with the intricate situations confronting them.

As it turns out, most diasporas adopt the communalist strategy. Only certain radical groups within stateless diasporas will choose a separatist or irredentist strategy. Adopting the communalist strategy and moderate tactics will shape the structure and behavioral patterns of their organizations in such a way that many of their organizations will complement those of their host countries, and some will have no parallels in host countries' political and administrative systems. Those organizations will be designed to deal with issues pertaining to maintenance and defense of their communities, advancement of their status, and achievement of varied economic and cultural goals. Such organizations are essential not only for maintaining solidarity among the diaspora's members in the face of the unfriendly environments prevailing in many host societies (despite the increasing tolerance and acceptance of such entities in most Western countries), but also for ensuring mutual support, communal empowerment, and coordination of goals and actions. They are also essential for reinforcing members' ties with homelands and with co-ethnics in other host countries. Those features distinguish between ethnic diasporas and all other ethnic groups and activities.

The special status and precarious existence of diasporas and the patterns of loyalties that they develop can lead to tension and confrontations with their host societies, homelands, and other international actors. The main sources of conflict between diasporas and those other parties are not economic. Rather, their disputes arise against the controlling background of ethnic identities and pertain mainly to matters of host-country security and cultural differences. Host governments try to min-imize areas of friction with diasporas, but the commitments of diasporas to their homelands are ever-present threats to trigger confrontation when they conflict with host-country interests. In some situations host coun-tries will take advantage of diasporas' quarrels with the governments of their homelands, supporting their criticisms of the homelands and even encouraging activities directed against homeland governments, and such activities can easily trigger homeland–host-country confrontations.

The opposite is true regarding homeland–diaspora relations. There, homelands usually are the initiators of tension. That inclination often involves a cynical attitude that prompts homeland leaders to try to use "their" diasporas to further their national interests. Indeed, the increas-ing numbers of diasporas and diasporans, as well as the more elaborate and more efficient diaspora organizations, tend to increase the potential for and incidence of tension and discord with homelands. But just as there is no policy potent enough to prevent the arrival of migrants in host countries and the emergence of diasporas, there is no easy way to prevent the disputes that ensue. Nor are there any tested recipes for managing such confrontations when they arise. However, like most other social disputes, they should not be regarded as evidence of dysfunction. Rather, they are a given in today's domestic and international politics. Each society must try to cope with those controversies as best it can, and as boldly it dares.

Still, as paradoxical as it may sound, recalling the functions that his-torical diasporas performed in the days of the Hapsburg, Russian, and Ottoman empires, greater attention should be paid to the fact that with their trans-state networks and connections contemporary diasporas can also serve as mediators and bridge-builders between states and regions. In some situations, the diasporas, often portrayed as pernicious, can facilitate peaceful economic, commercial, and cultural exchanges, enabling them to fit in among the conceptions behind the expectations for a post-national world order.

8

Diasporas, the Nation-State, and Regional Integration

Diasporas and the Current World Order

There is wide consensus among political analysts and scholars that the new world order is leading to a marked decrease in the propensity of nations to go to war and to escalate their quarrels to violent confrontations. Whereas in earlier centuries such wars and confrontations were continual threats to the existence and sovereignty of nation-states, today the sovereignty of most established states seems to be assured. Despite continuing inter-state conflicts and tensions, today the likelihood of conquest and occupation of entire states and their annexation is negligible. That trend is partly attributable to a gradual increase in the number of functioning democracies, which tend not to fight each other, and in most cases they also refrain from the use of violence in their adversarial relations with non-democratic states (Doyle 1986; Maoz and Abdolali 1989; E. Cohen 1990; Maoz and Russet 1991, 1992). It is also attributable in part to the collapse of all empires and to a gradual liberalization and democratization of authoritarian regimes. Such transformations have reduced authoritarian states' inclination to wage war and consequently have reduced the number of instances in which democratic countries have to react to inter-state aggression. Most of those reformed and reforming states accept the new rules of the international game, including respect for states' external sovereignty.

However, the relative calm in the global system and the increasing stability of inter-state relationships have not resulted in elimination of tension, confrontation, and violence on the regional level and within nation-states. In fact, confrontations and internal "small wars" continue unabated, though today fewer of those encounters involve claims over states' territories and demands for boundary modification. Instead, those tensions and disagreements often are related to cultural, social, political, and economic rights and interests, issues that are more benign than disputes over territories.

Even a cursory review of the lingering confrontations and small wars that have recently ravaged and continue to bedevil various corners of the globe will reveal that the combatants involved in those conflicts have mostly been militant ethnic groups (Horowitz 1985; Montville 1991; Gurr 1993; Brown 1996). Paradoxically, in certain regions, such as eastern and central Europe, central Asia, Africa, Latin America, and to some extent the Middle East and the Balkans, the increasing involvement of ethnic groups in such hostile exchanges constitutes the other, less fortunate side of the democratization and liberalization process. That is due to the gradually spreading mood of political assertiveness and militant tendencies that are fueling the struggle for collective and personal rights and freedoms. Greater freedom and increasing democratization augment the ability and inclination of ethnic groups to express their views and undertake a greater variety of activities, including actions pursuant to their goals in their conflictual and adversarial relationships. It is thus not surprising that ethnic conflicts in general, and the combative activities of specific ethnic groups in particular, are attracting greater attention from politicians and scholars. Yet little has been done to distinguish between the involvements and roles of different types of ethnic groups in those feuds. The main reason is that most scholarly work in the field has been done with respect to particular states or regions, rather than on a comparative basis and with respect to various categories of ethnic groups.

This chapter tries to deal with those issues while distinguishing between ethno-national diasporas and other ethnic groups. In that vein, we shall examine diasporas' attitudes toward regional organizations and the nation-state and the extent to which various types of diasporas contribute to regional tensions and to instability within states. The purpose is to see if indeed such tensions and instability pose major challenges to the sovereignty and security of states, undermine the foundations of state governments, and frustrate efforts to achieve regional stability and integration. We shall further examine the question whether or not ethnic diasporas are as pernicious as French, German, British, Dutch, Danish, American, and other racists, xenophobes, and nationalists have asserted. Those opponents of large-scale international migration and its main consequences (the establishment and functioning of ethnic diasporas), as

well as some proponents of regional integration, claim that the mere existence of such "alien elements" in host societies endangers or at least neg-
atively affects their basic security and their foreign relations in general,
and in particular it frustrates attempts to achieve regional integration
(Weiner 1990; Tololyan 1994; Rollins 1995; Ruggie 1997; Huntington
1997; Shain 1999).

In some cases those arguments clearly are based on a preference for
cultural and ethnic homogeneity and for "realist" foreign policy – thus
ipso facto based on an unyielding objection to ethnic pluralism and multiculturalism. Those views are anchored in suspicion, in fear, and occasionally in hatred of others, especially international migrants and ethnic
diasporas, sometimes to the point that they echo some arguments used
prior to and during World War II, arguments that led to Nazi Germany's
genocide against the Jews and Gypsies. They also remind us of the
Soviets' forced transport and execution of ethnic Germans and the U.S.
internment of Japanese-Americans. Such emotional and ideological positions were echoed, too, in the expulsion of Asians from eastern Africa
in the early 1970s and the expulsion of the Palestinians from Kuwait in
the early 1990s.

Despite the fact that, in general, there is increasing acceptance of diasporas, recently antagonism toward migrants and diasporas has intensified in reaction to the alleged radicalization and growing assertiveness
of those entities. Those pernicious influences allegedly are "imported"
through their trans-state networks and connections with their homelands
and other diaspora communities. All such concerns are exacerbated
because of host countries' uncertainty about where the loyalties of those
diasporas lie. Thus, a common but usually unfounded accusation
directed at diasporas is that their primary loyalties are to foreign nations
and states and that they are capable of "stabbing their hosts in the back."
The argument has been that diaspora groups have the potential for fifth-
column activities in their host countries and that, at the very minimum,
they have dual loyalties (Walzer et al. 1982). The issue of diasporas'
loyalties is discussed in Chapter 9.

The discussion here begins with a look at the validity of those negative images and notions and proceeds to examine whether or not ethno-
national diasporas are indeed becoming more aggressive and whether or
not such allegations misrepresent their "natural" inclinations and behavioral reactions to their basically hostile surroundings. On the basis of a
consideration of the main strategies and tactics that diasporas employ to
ensure their survival and achieve their goals, we shall attempt to answer

the question of which groups actually tend to undermine the legitimacy and authority of established states, sway their foreign policy, and hamper the emergence of regional stability and integration. Then we shall turn to the opposite scenario: the actual and potential positive contributions of diasporas to cooperation on both the state and regional levels. In the final section we shall consider some practical and theoretical conclusions from the analysis.

Are Diasporas Inherently Militant?

Ingrained suspicions and negative views about diasporas still exist in most societies, whether they be liberal democracies or conservative authoritarian states (Cohen 1997, pp. 193–4). Those attitudes are based on emotions and on political philosophies and ideologies, such as neo-Marxism, neo-nationalism, and neo-conservatism. Rightist ideologues especially, but also radical leftist doctrinaires, still view diasporas as artificial and temporary social and political entities that can only cause trouble and disruption (on such attitudes among neo-conservatives in the United States, see Hu-Dehart 1993, pp. 7–8, and Shain 1999, pp. 204–7). As for the question of emotional factors, though in many instances diaspora–homeland relationships can turn hostile and cause problems for both sides (Sheffer 1993a), a tenacious myth persists that regardless of such quarrels and difficulties, diasporas essentially favor their homelands over their host countries. At best, so it is alleged, even diasporas that have become extensively integrated into host countries will have only a partial loyalty to their host societies (Walzer et al. 1982; Sheffer 1992). Such widespread negative perceptions prevail in Germany (Margalit, 1996), France, and Switzerland, and even in the purportedly tolerant Holland (van Amersfoort and Penninx 1994, p. 134) and Denmark (Hjarno 1994, 1996).

As is the case with other myths and many widespread perceptions, the actual situation is more complex than is indicated by the slogans used by the protagonists. Thus it would be difficult to name highly organized ethno-national diasporas that completely deny any loyalty to and reject the legitimacy of their host states and show absolute loyalty to their homelands. Diasporas are far from always being supportive of homeland interests. It is true, for example, that certain dedicated segments in the Irish-American diaspora have unequivocally supported the IRA, that most diaspora Palestinians support the PLO and its national demands, and that former Russian Communists in their incipient diasporas in the former Soviet empire are closely connected to their homeland. Yet only small minorities in diasporas would question the legitimacy and act against the fundamental interests of their hosts. Although most diasporas, including historical diasporas such as the Jewish, Chinese, Japanese, and Indian, do show loyalty to their homelands, it is also true that members of all four of those diasporas served in the armies of their host countries during World War II and in other wars involving their host countries. Moreover, contrary to prevailing perceptions, diasporans give only carefully measured support to their homelands. A partial proof of that observation is the fact that homeland governments, fearing that they command only partial loyalty from their diasporas, invest in efforts to increase that degree of loyalty. For example, the Greek, Turkish, and Israeli governments have undertaken such activities vis-à-vis their diasporas. With respect to loyalty issues, diasporas behave much like other indigenous ethnic minorities. Only under very unusual circumstances will diasporans be ready to serve their homelands without reservation and thus almost surely antagonize their host countries. The same applies to most diasporans' reluctance to serve other foreign states or groups with whom they establish and maintain close contacts through trans-state networks. An important implication of that observation is that not all tensions between diasporas and host countries arise from ideas and demands "imported" into diasporas. Indeed, diaspora members are quite autonomous in the decisions they make, including decisions about activities on behalf of their homelands.

To a great extent, the emergence of an acute case of divided loyalties will depend on the readiness of a diaspora to take a more confrontational position in the political sphere. Again, such assertiveness will depend not only on developments in homelands and on general global trends but also on developments in host countries and on regional politics. Only conditions of extreme deterioration in homelands can lead to a substantial increase in diasporas' readiness to act on behalf of their homelands. In some situations, such circumstances can lead them to pursue clandestine activities within host countries that may indeed pose challenges to host countries. Because Chapter 9 will deal in greater detail with the loyalty issue, here we shall consider some basic issues pertaining to diasporas' attitudes toward the statist ideology and ethos and toward regionalism. Hence the relevant questions here: Do diasporas pose a challenge to the basic ideas of the nation-state and regionalism? Which diasporas are more assertive and are ready to confront their host governments and regional organizations? Why do they adopt such stances, and in what direction do such attitudes lead them?

The most obvious examples of increasing assertiveness toward host states have occurred among members of the category of smaller stateless diasporas, including the Kurdish, Sikh, Palestinian, Kossovar Albanian, and Tamil diasporas, and to some extent the Gypsy diaspora. Prior to the collapse of the Soviet Union and the establishment of the free Armenian republic, that list would have included the Armenian diaspora, parts of which had been quite mobilized and activist on behalf of their homeland, carrying out, among other things, terrorist activities (Hovannisian 1997).

The chief reason that diasporas have assertive attitudes is, of course, their commitment to assist in the quest for statehood for their ethnic nations. In the 1980s that tendency increased dramatically, partly because of particular reasons internal to various diasporas, such as the emergence of younger and more militant leaders, creation of more elaborate organizations, better communications between diaspora members residing in various host countries, increasing contacts between the institutions of the various national groups, and so forth. Those recent developments allowed for greater mobilization for action and better-coordinated action. That assertiveness can be attributed to changes in the general international political atmosphere during the last years of the cold-war era that encouraged struggles for self-determination and independence. Thus, during that period, the stateless Armenian diaspora more persistently and militantly pursued its goals; the Iraqi and Turkish Kurds, strongly supported by radical elements in their diaspora in Europe, escalated their struggle against their oppressors; and Palestinians in Gaza and the West Bank launched the first *Intifada*, supported by various groups in their diaspora around the world.

A second group of diasporas that have become more assertive, and consequently more inclined toward direct action, includes historical and more recent dormant diasporas. Though some members of those diasporas had engaged in sporadic ethnic-cultural activities in their host countries, the majority had been almost impervious to developments in their homelands and participated only marginally, if at all, in activities on their behalf. Two primary factors explain that apathy. First, members of those diasporas were strongly inclined to assimilate or fully integrate into their host societies. Second, either the conditions in their homelands were satisfactory or, at the other extreme, there were substantial problems in their homelands because of the oppressive regimes there, which led to a sense of hopelessness and consequently limited their interest and involvement in diaspora affairs. In some cases, such as those of most Irish-Americans and Norwegian-Americans, diaspora members believed that their homelands had little to offer them in cultural, political, and economic terms, and they gradually lost interest in their homelands, even to the point of apathy and denial. In other cases, such as the Polish, Hungarian, and Baltic diasporas, their homelands spent long years in isolation under Soviet rule, and that eroded the contacts between homelands and diasporas. Recently there have been noticeable awakenings among members of all those diasporas, related to the collapse of the Soviet Union, to the establishment of the independent republics, and to the consequent emergence of the "new world order."

The economic situations in homelands also influence diasporas' attitudes and actions. Thus, when diaspora members become involved in extending aid to their homelands because of worsening economic conditions there, those renewed contacts tend to touch sensitive nerves and evoke memories and dormant associations. After 1975, for instance, members of the Lebanese diaspora in Latin America were suddenly awakened by the civil war in Lebanon. Consequently, they increased their involvement in developments there and in supportive activities, regularly remitting funds to their families and transferring financial resources to support their factions in Lebanon. But by no means were they posing any real challenge to their hosts. On the contrary, they offset their renewed involvement in their homeland affairs by increasing their charity donations and charitable activities in their host countries.

The processes of liberalization and democratization in homelands tend to make those states more open to new influences and more attentive to their diasporas, thus enhancing homeland–diaspora relations. Among others, that applies to the Chinese in the United States and Canada, the Turkish diaspora in the United States and Germany, and the Poles in the United States (Misztal 1990). Those processes also have considerably increased the number of dormant diasporas that are awakening. In addition to the aforementioned groups, this category includes the Latvian, Lithuanian, Ukrainian, Slovenian, Serbian, and Slovakian diasporas.

Composing a third group are incipient diasporas that have become more assertive and have increased their political and economic activities, though not necessarily exclusively for the benefit of their homelands, such as the Moroccans in Spain, Holland, Denmark, and France, the Algerians in France, the Koreans in the United States, Canada, and western Europe, and the Latin Americans in the United States. The principal cause of their new assertiveness is their need to defend against host countries' governmental and societal prejudice and intolerance, especially against cultural, social, political, and economic discrimination.

Yet another group of activist diaspora communities comprises those susceptible to confrontations with other minorities or diasporas in their host countries. Recent examples of that pattern include the Argentine Jews who took measures to protect their institutions because of Palestinian terrorist attacks in the mid-1990s and British, French, and German Jews who were prompted to intensify the activities of their defense organizations because of threats by anti-Semites in the late 1990s. The Israeli government provided political and logistical assistance to those Jewish diaspora communities in their endeavors to protect themselves and their interests, though for obvious reasons no details have been disclosed concerning the nature of that assistance. For understandable reasons, however, not always were those offers of assistance welcomed by the diasporas.

Host governments naturally resent allegations that they cannot protect their populations, whether they be members of the dominant ethnic group, diasporans, or other minority groups. By the same token, those governments resent and may oppose any inclination of diasporas to import assistance from their homelands. Because of the sensitivity of such matters and the secrecy surrounding how governments deal with such issues, it is not clear how host governments and other interested governments actually react in such situations.

Despite the prevalence of so many ambivalent or unclarified attitudes, as well as the confusing information and the secrecy surrounding actual developments, no diaspora has shown any blatant opposition to the idea of the nation-state. Consequently, no diasporas have challenged the fundamental bases of the sovereignty of their host countries, nor of their homelands. That is, it would be difficult to find any major diaspora group nurturing or acting from a position of anarchy. As noted earlier, that applies not only to state-linked diasporas but also to stateless diasporas that strive to establish their own independent national states. The almost unavoidable and somewhat paradoxical conclusion it that in this age of expanding post-nationalism, most, though not all, members of those truly trans-state entities strongly support the nation-state idea and practices.

As noted in Chapter 6, the survival and growth of diasporic entities hinge on the policy choices made in tandem by leaders and members, which in turn are determined by the strategies that those leaders and members employ to protect and promote their interests. To better understand diasporas' current positions vis-à-vis the nation-state and their consequences, it is important to examine the implications of the strategies that various diasporas pursue, that is, the assimilationist, integrationist, communalist, autonomist, irredentist, and separatist/ secessionist strategies we analyzed earlier. Unlike the majority of historical, modern, and incipient state-linked diasporas, stateless diasporas usually employ one of the two radical strategies – that is, the irredentist and separatist strategies – and they use aggressive and violent tactics that are directed primarily at host states and at oppressive governments in their homelands. That has been the case for the Sikhs, who occasionally have employed violent tactics both within India and abroad, the Basques fighting for independence from Spain, and the Kurds, who are engaged in a protracted struggle, especially against Iraq and Turkey. Yet such diasporas work very hard to try to help their co-ethnics living in their homelands to achieve their national goals, and they greatly cherish the nation-state idea.

Because the main goals of the communalist strategy, which is pursued by the majority of the historical, modern, and incipient state-linked diasporas, are to achieve a secure and respected existence for diasporas within host states and thereby gain and safeguard social and political rights and freedoms within the host states, including the right to establish relationships and conduct exchanges with their homelands, adoption of that strategy usually dictates the use of only nonviolent tactics and means. Therefore, the most important tactics that such diasporas employ in trying to achieve their goals are diplomatic, economic, and occasionally social in nature. Thus, in the political arena, essentially such diasporas will use various kinds of lobbying and attempt to exert only moderate pressure. In the economic sphere, they tend to lobby and to establish and operate fund-raising and investment organizations, such as political action committees (PACs) in the United States, and their equivalents in other host countries. To facilitate the activities of those organizations, their leaders comply, as far as possible, with the laws and regulations of the host states. Thus, diaspora members must conduct most of their organized activities legally, because those activities serve as vehicles for raising and distributing funds for the defense and promotional endeavors of diasporas within their host societies and for assisting their homelands. In the social sphere, the main tools for achieving diasporas' goals are bilateral dialogues such as those conducted among Jewish, African-American and Greek organizations in the United States, multilateral discourses, and direct personal persuasion.

Even more than active historical and modern diasporas that have long experience in pursuing the communalist strategy and using its tactics and tools, awakening dormant diasporas are far from being inclined to challenge the idea of the state and use violent tactics vis-à-vis their hosts. It would be difficult to envision Americans of German, Norwegian, or Polish origin questioning the right of their government to exist and rule, or using violent tactics on behalf of their ancestors' homelands. Consequently, they too invest considerable effort in either reviving or establishing their communalist organizations and in pursuing nonaggressive tactics.

Despite the difficulty of trying to identify all or even most of the sources of the disputes in which diasporas become involved, two conflictual situations in particular should be considered. The first is that in which the mere existence of "foreign" ethno-national diasporas in the midst of certain host societies causes tensions that can result in hostile confrontations, in most cases initiated by xenophobic elements in the host societies. On the other hand, certainly there are situations in which diasporas can cause tension and discord, either in the context of their activities on behalf of their homelands or because of their opposition to developments in host countries. A common feature in most of the recent altercations in host countries involving diasporas is that usually they seem to have been initiated by hostile elements in the host societies, rather than by diasporans. That has been the case in recurrent confrontations between German citizens and emigrant Poles and Turks, between certain local groups and North African guest workers in Switzerland and Austria, between British workers and workers from Pakistan and other Asian diasporas in Britain, between French rightists and Moroccans and Algerians, and between African-Americans and Koreans in Los Angeles. Those hostilities arose against a backdrop of worsening economic conditions, usually on the pretext that there was a need to reduce competition for jobs and for other scarce economic and welfare resources. In fact, however, those confrontations cannot be dissociated from other reasons and deeper sentiments: the wish for ethnic "purity" of host societies, and fear and loathing of the presence of "alien" groups within those societies.

Expulsions and repatriations of both established and incipient diasporas have occurred against a backdrop of rightist and racist militancy and explicit accusations that diasporas cause major disruptions for the polities and economies of host countries. According to such allegations, the presence of diasporas inherently leads to instability in host countries, damaging their defense and political interests as well as economic well-being.

Contrary to a widely held perception, the relatively few confrontations initiated by diasporas, such as those launched by the Pakistanis in Birmingham and the Turks in Berlin in the late 1980s and early 1990s, have had to do primarily with their need to defend themselves, rather than having any intent to challenge the sovereignty of their host societies and governments. Indeed, to try to cope with that danger, various diasporas, including the Greek, Turkish, Jewish, and very recently the Korean, have had to establish their own defense organizations, but even then they try to operate those organizations within the existing legal framework.

Diasporas and Regional Integration

Similar analysis is needed concerning the questions whether or not and to what degree diasporas oppose and can jeopardize regional integration and stability. Because most diasporas that have chosen the communalist strategy, such as the Muslims in western Europe, the Asians in the Middle East, and the Irish in the United States, have concerned themselves mainly with the politics of their host countries, their homelands, and their co-ethnics in other host countries, as yet most of them are only marginally interested and involved in the politics of regional integration.

On the other hand, because they have to be concerned that the actions of regional groups or major extra-regional powers might adversely affect their efforts to achieve their separatist and irredentist goals, stateless diasporas have a considerable interest in creating obstacles to regional integration and stability. The regional instability that led to the involvement of non-European states in the 1998–1999 Serbian–Albanian crisis in Kossovo, as well as the involvement of the Kossovar Albanian diaspora in that crisis, serve as good examples of such developments.

Only in cases in which homelands are locked into vital regional struggles will their diasporas consider becoming directly involved, thus adding further tension and instability to those charged situations. Nevertheless, examples of that pattern abound: the recurrent interventions of the American Jewish diaspora, on the one hand, and Palestinians in the United States, on the other, in the protracted Arab–Israeli conflict and in other regional affairs; the involvement of Cuban-Americans in Caribbean affairs; the historical role of the overseas Chinese in the politics of Southeast Asia, especially in Hong Kong and Taiwan; the Greek and

Turkish diasporas' roles in eastern Mediterranean affairs, particularly in connection with Cyprus.

In such situations, diasporas that pursue the communalist strategy tend to become only prudently and indirectly involved in such matters, mainly through political lobbying and diplomatic negotiations. Only infrequently will those diasporas get involved in such situations to the extent of direct and active support of their co-ethnics in their homelands. However, Armenian-Americans did become involved to that extent in the Nagorno-Karabakh crisis and in its regional ramifications.

The disintegration of the Soviet Union and the crystallization of the European Union have created special opportunities for diasporas. Like other ethnic minorities in western and eastern Europe, Africa, and central Asia, the established diasporas, and even more emphatically the incipient diasporas in those parts of the world, have been fully aware of the political significance and implications of regionalization, as well as the new opportunities and difficulties that regionalization places before them and their homelands. Although little information about the attitudes of specific ethno-national diasporas and their actual policies toward those developments is available (largely because of the recency of those developments), it seems that, like other militant ethnic minorities, diasporas are experiencing considerable ambiguity about the unification of Europe and the creation of associations like NAFTA. However, it looks as if diaspora leaders are speculating that because of increasing regional political unity and the strengthening of regional organizations, which they see as simultaneously weakening the traditional nation-states, they can gain greater elbow room for their clandestine and overt, illegal and legal activities.

Yet at the same time, diaspora leaders clearly are worried that the spread of regional values and loyalties may strongly appeal to their members, a development that could diminish rank-and-file commitment to their communities and shift their attention and loyalty to the newly emerging trans-national entities. Indeed, as a result of their homelands' desires to join the European Union, various diasporas that originated in Europe, such as the Hungarian, Polish, and Czech, have begun to show interest in European Union politics. Diaspora leaders are worried about an additional issue: the possibility of agreement on a joint regional policy concerning migration, settlement, citizenship, and the roles of diasporas in the new political and economic formations. In a number of agreements regarding those issues, the European Union has already shown the probable direction of future developments, namely, an inclination toward policies and regulations intended to curb migration and the emergence of new diasporas. Moreover, the rapid increases in illegal migration have already pushed member states toward bilateral and multilateral cooperation. Britain and Italy provide an example: They joined in an attempt to curb the migration of North Africans, Albanians, and Iranians to European Union states. Similarly, the United States, Canada, and Mexico have been engaged in negotiations concerning attitudes and policies toward migration and permanent settlement of migrants.

The situation in the former Soviet Union has been almost diametrically opposite. After the initial shock of the sudden collapse of the Soviet Union and its empire, many diasporas located there, such as the Pontic Greek diaspora (Bruneau 1998), the Gypsies, the ethnic Germans, and Jewish groups, were not at all interested in seeing Russia gain strength and establish hegemony in the areas of the former Soviet Union. The main reason was that they believed, correctly, that a weakened Russia would not try to stop their return to their respective homelands. On the other hand, it is no surprise that the large incipient Russian diaspora has been most interested in seeing a strong Russia establish regional hegemony. In view of the continuing regional instability, that incipient diaspora is facing the momentous dilemma that all diasporas face at the most critical point in their history: whether to return to Russia, where they will not be warmly welcomed, or adjust to the new regional conditions. Because of the local roots that the Russians had begun to develop in the new republics, and the appalling economic, political, and security conditions in their homeland, their choice is not easy. Like other diasporans, after making a decision in regard to that basic choice between remaining in their host countries or returning to Russia, they will have to plan their future strategy and tactics. It is highly likely that those who decide to stay put will join the family of ethnic diasporas, and it is equally likely that later they will adopt the communalist strategy.

Because it has not been adequately studied, it is still too early to fully report on a recent development in regard to diasporas' attitudes and activities vis-à-vis regional organizations. Yet there are clear indications that diasporas, such as the Roma, will seek to have regional organizations find remedies for their disputes with host-country governments. Apparently that has been occurring with the members of the European Union, the most extensively developed regional union: Whenever diaspora leaders disagree with the positions and policies of states that are members of the European Union, they try to bypass host-country governments and submit their grievances to various agencies of the

European Union. Though for obvious reasons the governments of member states have not been happy about that new development, they cannot do much about it. Those governments try to limit such cases, but the European Union has no choice but to continue to shape joint policies and regulations for the issues pertaining to those groups.

Additional Comments on Diaspora–Homeland Strains

The importance of all their exchanges with host governments, regional and global organizations, and other ethnic groups notwithstanding, still the quintessential dimension of the extremely complex diaspora phenomenon is the diaspora–homeland relationship. From the viewpoint of the diasporas, it would seem that diasporas can pose greater challenges to their homelands than to their host societies and governments. Whereas in most cases organized diasporas manifest affinity for and solidarity with their homeland societies, under certain circumstances they can demonstrate pronounced opposition to homeland governments. More specifically, diasporas often become critical of the political systems that prevail in their homelands and especially of the policies that the governments there pursue. The main reason for such criticism is the way in which homelands treat their citizens. Given such circumstances, members of diasporas sometimes will work to undermine the stability of homeland regimes, perhaps even helping to launch revolutions or coups d'état there. The following cases come to mind: the resolute opposition and overt and covert activities against oppressive homeland regimes conducted by the Latin American diasporas in the United States, especially the Cubans and Haitians (Pedraz-Bailey 1985; Malone 1997); the hostility of overseas Chinese toward Communist China, as expressed, for example, in their reactions to the Tiananmen Square massacre; the determined opposition and actions against apartheid on the part of South Africans in the United States and Britain; and the opposition of Iranians and Iraqis to the dictatorial regimes in their homelands.

On its own, no diaspora could overthrow a repressive regime in its homeland. Yet through the activities of their trans-state networks, through cooperation with other interested parties, and by lobbying in their host countries diasporans can help to foment internal instability and tension in their homelands and thus increase the difficulties with which such governments and rulers have to deal. The situation in Lebanon in the late 1970s is an example. In rare instances such efforts can prove to be the last straw on the camel's back, causing a government or regime to fall. The involvement of Greek-Americans in toppling the military regime in Greece and moving toward democracy in the 1980s is a relevant example.

The tactics and tools that diasporas can employ against oppressive homeland governments are varied and, within certain limits, often quite effective. For example, diasporas have supported their host governments in denouncing their homeland governments. They have lobbied for reforms and even supported revolts and revolutions in their homelands. Diasporas have lent legitimacy to boycotts and have supported other activist measures taken by host governments or international organizations against oppressive regimes in their homelands. Moreover, diasporas have served as valuable sources of information and intelligence about homelands in cases in which host governments have planned hostile actions against those homelands. Diaspora members have initiated propaganda campaigns and more subversive activities against homeland governments. And they have reduced their financial support for their homeland governments, or stopped it altogether. All those measures have been used by the Iraqi and Iranian diasporas.

However, it is important to reiterate here that diasporas are neither innocent nor subversive political actors by nature. Because of the special and difficult circumstances under which they persist and operate, until the early 1990s diasporas usually reacted to developments, rather than initiating insurgencies. More specifically, their hostility and militancy, on the one hand, and empathy and cooperation, on the other, at various times directed both at host countries and at homelands, usually emerge as reactions to the policies and actions of homelands and host countries. When left alone to pursue legitimate interests within their host countries and to maintain "normal" connections with their homelands, diasporas' energies are almost always directed to constructive enterprises.

Turning to the positive aspects of their activities, it should be noted that through their elaborate trans-state networks, contemporary diasporas can serve as political mediators between different societies and sometimes also between hostile governments. They can also serve as facilitators of commercial, financial, and trade ties between their host countries and homelands – the Japanese, Chinese, and Koreans in the United States are good examples of that pattern. Of even greater significance is the potential for ethno-national diasporas to serve as examples and champions of cultural pluralism and even multiculturalism. In that respect, they are well equipped to facilitate exchanges between cultures and help foster tolerance in their host countries, homelands, and regions.

In sum, diasporas occupy a special niche in the ethnic mosaic that is taking shape in the world today. Moreover, they are emerging as actors in regional politics. Their enhanced role is due mainly to their increasing interest in host countries' politics, and diaspora members are beginning to show much wider interests in global and regional affairs. As discussed in Chapter 7, their activities in those spheres are carried out through elaborate trans-state networks that in some respects are similar to those of multinational and global corporations and trans-state and trans-national interest groups.

Together with those large corporations and interest groups, diasporas serve as the precursors of the global and regional social and political arrangements of the future. As was shown in Chapter 6, because of the decreasing ability of most states to control their borders, their connections and exchanges through trans-state networks cannot be stopped. Nevertheless, though in certain instances they have contributed to instability in the global system at large and in particular regions and states, they can also serve as bridges between cultures, societies, and states.

Because ethnic minorities and diasporas will play significant roles in any global and regional regimes that emerge in the near future, these matters are of particular theoretical interest for students of international relations, politics, and ethnicity. The discussion presented here can serve as a basis for some preliminary answers to the questions posed earlier in the book about diasporas' roles and behavior in the new international environment. Thus, this discussion has shown that the mere presence of diasporas in the midst of host countries is a cause for some tension and unrest. Racist, nationalist, and rightist politicians argue that diasporas dilute ethnic purity and endanger the economic well-being of poorer groups within their societies. Moreover, because of diasporas' loyalty to their homelands, host governments have always regarded them as permanent sources of unrest. Diaspora members and leaders view the situation quite differently. Having migrated from their homelands and made their decisions to settle permanently and make a living in host countries, most of them also have made deliberate decisions to respect their host countries' laws. Generally speaking, they are interested in maintaining their ethnic identities, in defending their members, and in securing their rights and freedoms, including the freedom to maintain political and economic ties with their homelands and with their co-ethnics in other host countries. Hence, except for the more militant stateless diasporas, most diaspora communities do not pose major challenges to the sovereignty of their host states nor major security risks to their host societies and regions. If they were inclined toward disruption, diasporas' capabilities are of such a nature that the damage they could inflict on their home-land governments would be much greater than any they could inflict on host countries and their governments.

On balance, even though diasporas are sporadically involved in some bitter conflicts and confrontations, that is not endemic to their nature. Both their passive and active involvements in such conflicts would be significantly reduced if ethnic pluralism and multiculturalism were to gain greater acceptance as general norms in host societies and governments. That would especially be the case if it were more widely recognized that diasporas are quite capable of residing as peaceful and peace-loving minorities in host countries and as facilitators of cross-cultural, inter-state, and inter-societal dialogues.

9

Loyalty

The Context

The issue of diasporas' loyalties has been mentioned briefly in previous chapters. To accurately appreciate that issue, it must be discussed in the context of the various environments in which diasporas operate. Thus it should be emphasized again that the expanding roles and increasing involvements of ethno-national diasporas are not limited to political matters in their homelands, host countries, and surrounding regions.

As noted in Chapter 8, today diasporas are playing important roles in the ongoing global and regional processes of change in the cultural, social, and economic spheres. Both older and more recent diasporas are having important inputs into the development of pluralism and, to some extent, multiculturalism wherever they are evolving. More specifically, diasporas contribute to the emergence of new attitudinal and cultural patterns. Thus, for example, they have helped to change attitudes toward food and fashion. Likewise, they have contributed to the increase in multi-lingualism and to new developments in literature: Poets and writers who are members of the Indian, Chinese, Japanese, Pakistani, black West Indian, and Caribbean diasporas in the United States and Britain are enriching the English language and its poetry and literature. Much has been written about the major cultural contributions of African-Americans and other segments of the black diaspora. Among other things, that diaspora has contributed significantly to contemporary music, cinema, literature, and poetry. In the social realm, some diaspora communities, particularly the Jews, Latinos, and Africans, have long been involved in the ongoing struggle to gain wider acceptance for pluralism and multiculturalism. That has particularly been true in the United States (*Economist* 2000). In the economic sphere, the Greek, Indian, Armenian, Korean, and Chinese diasporas, to mention just a few, are active in international trade, shipping, and financial affairs. Those and other diasporas have certainly contributed to globalization and liberalization in a number of spheres, such that, in many respects, ethnonational diasporas are closely identified with those two processes.

As noted in earlier chapters, the close connections between members of diasporas and many individuals and collective parties in and outside their host countries have considerable potential to trigger suspicions, tensions, and confrontations between diasporas and their host countries, their homelands, and other bystanders. Also as discussed in earlier chapters, the increasing role of the ethno-national diaspora phenomenon in present-day cultural, economic, and political developments has reopened some sensitive practical issues that have significant theoretical implications. They include issues pertaining to the identity, identification, status, organization, and behavior of diaspora elites and rank and file.

However, one very sensitive issue has been largely neglected: that of diasporas' loyalties. That neglect has in part been due to the social and political sensitivity of the issue, as well as to difficulties in obtaining detailed information and data. Thus, for example, it is well known in political, bureaucratic, and academic circles in Washington that in the wake of the Pollard affair, attitudes toward American Jews employed by the federal government, especially by the Pentagon and the State Department, have been adversely affected. Nevertheless, for obvious reasons there is no documentation or analysis of that development, and it is not surprising that officials refuse to discuss the matter. Similarly, there are rumors that because of doubts about their loyalty, U.S. government officials of Cuban origin are mistrusted, but again no discussion or analysis of that. Moreover, other than some occasional references to how the loyalty issue affects diasporas' relations with host countries, as in the United States immediately prior to and during World War II, there is almost no literature on the issue.

Not only practically but also conceptually, dealing with the loyalty issue is not an easy task. For reasons that have to do with the perceptions that prevail in host countries regarding sovereignty, the security concerns of host-country leaders, and the interactions of host countries with the homelands of the diasporans residing within their boundaries, politicians have neither encouraged examination of the tangled issues of diasporas' loyalties nor provided the information that would be needed for such an examination. As part of that prudent attitude, host governments are inclined to silence regarding any security risks arising from the partial or conflicting loyalties of diasporas, censoring any communication about real and potential subversive acts by members of diasporas, such as espionage and sabotage. An example of that pattern was the Egyptian government's behavior in the early 1950s regarding the trial of Egyptian Jews accused of spying for Israel, a case that became known as the Lavon affair and had far-reaching consequences for the Israeli elite and government (Teveth 1996). A more recent example is the July 2000 trial of thirteen Iranian Jews who were accused of spying for Israel and were sentenced to various periods of imprisonment.

For understandable reasons, host governments withhold the details of diasporas' support for guerrilla and terrorist groups acting on behalf of or in cooperation with their homelands. Thus, for example, it is extremely difficult to obtain from British, American, and Russian authorities information about the support Irish-Americans have extended and apparently still extend to the IRA, information about Palestinian-Americans' participation in terrorist activities in the United States and the aid that that community provides to the PLO and other Palestinian organizations, or information about Chechens living in Moscow who allegedly have been involved in series of terrorist bombings that have caused casualties and panic in the Russian capital. Similarly, it is difficult to obtain information from the German government about the Kurdish PKK's activities in Germany (Angoustures and Pascal 1996). This applies also to information about bin Laden and his network.

Host governments suppress such information for a number of reasons. In some cases they hope to calm domestic fear and tension and avoid conflict with the diasporas' homelands, and thus reduce international instability. They want to guard the secrecy and details of the activities of their intelligence agencies – and sometimes conceal gaffes and inefficiencies in those intelligence and security agencies in dealing with terrorists. Governments try to avoid information leaks concerning threatening developments stemming from diasporas' conflicting loyalties that might further exacerbate explosive situations, and they also try to prevent harm to other domestic ethnic groups and those in other countries. Only when domestic or international circumstances compel host governments to disclose details about such events will they admit to problems in that arena. Yet, again for understandable reasons, in their public statements host governments try to minimize the significance of such problems. Such were the reactions of the Argentine, British, and

U.S. governments to acts of terrorism carried out by members of various diasporas within their territories. Also, such denials are intended to minimize the possibility of contagious influences on other groups and withhold any acknowledgment of success by the leaders and activists of militant ethnic groups that might inspire them to additional violent actions. Lastly in this context, host governments tend to downplay the political significance of those issues so as to avoid further damage to people's perceptions of their legitimacy and control.

Similarly, scholars have ignored this subject partly because they share the inherent tendency to want to downplay the problems involved in such sensitive matters, partly because of their own late awakening to the renewed growth of ethno-national diasporas, and partly because they have not yet fully realized the actual dimensions of diasporism and its political significance. However, because the issue of loyalty has recently resurfaced and has been receiving greater public and governmental attention, academic interest in such matters has increased. Thus, in the 1990s some authors dealt with the "tangled web of loyalty" (Worchel and Coutant 1995), referring to the intricate connections among racism, nationalism, ethnocentrism, and patriotism. It seems that political psychologists have been at the fore in this academic field (Bar-Tal 1993). The gist of their argument is that a diaspora's loyalty to a host state, on the one hand, or to its ethnic group and nation, on the other, is determined mainly by the psychological needs of members of the diaspora to forge and especially to maintain their particular identity. Those authors argue that, therefore, allegiance to an ethnic minority inevitably will come into conflict with loyalty to a host state that claims full sovereignty and control within its boundaries. Similar arguments have been advanced by what can be called the constructionist literature on ethnicity and ethno-nationalism (Anderson 1994). The main argument of the constructionists is that patriotism is an attitude that is artificially inculcated in citizens by the state, regardless of their ethnic origin. Proponents of that view add that by implication, and as part of the creation and operation of modern states, that sentiment is drummed into members of the dominant ethnic group as well as ethnic minorities, including ethno-national diasporas permanently residing there. Consequently, even members of indigenous ethnic groups face a situation that can lead to clashes with their governments. In the case of diasporas, that situation can also lead to clashes with their homelands. According to the constructionist view, in some cases that leads to "radically unaccountable" politics (Anderson 1994, p. 327).

Proponents of a third approach to this issue observe that even Western liberal democracies that pride themselves on their enlightened tolerance show great concern about the loyalty of "alien" groups. Those observers argue that, rather than introducing problems of ambiguous loyalties and creating unbridgeable rifts, diasporas challenge the democratic polities and push them to explore new forms of integration and multiculturalism and to work for global human rights. They believe that the renewal of activism in diaspora groups is part of a self-learning process which is necessary for becoming politically effective communities. Those scholars and other observers conclude that in the long run, hosts should not be apprehensive or suspicious, because the presence of diasporas in their midst is potentially an enriching force, particularly so because those states will eventually become post-national and multicultural polities (Werbner 1997).

In view of those conclusions from academic studies and observations in the news media regarding loyalties, what follows here is an exploratory and methodological discussion, and, like some discussions earlier in this book, it leads to a new approach to the issue of the loyalties of ethno-national diasporas.

A Theoretical Synthesis Approach to the Loyalty Issue

New theoretical and analytical constructs for the loyalty issue are needed in view of two seemingly contradictory trends that influence relationships within diaspora communities as well as the multiple relationships involving diasporas, their host countries, their homelands, other segments of the same diaspora, and regional and global parties.

The first trend is closely related to globalization and includes loss of control over porous regional and state borders and increasing liberalization of economic, political, and social systems. As noted, in Western democracies those two developments encourage greater tolerance toward ethno-national diasporas. Such tolerance facilitates diasporas' integration into host countries' politics, but not necessarily the degree of assimilation into their social and cultural systems that eventually would lead to disappearance of the diasporas. The second trend, which is partly a consequence of the first, is ethnic diasporas' new confident adherence to their traditional identities and their readiness to identify as such.

In line with the general views expressed earlier, the analysis that follows is anchored in what might be termed a synthesis approach or integrated approach to the study of recent ethnic revival and ascendance

(Kellas 1991; Smith 1994). There is no need to present this approach in full here or to compare it with other approaches to ethnicity and ethnic identity. Yet it is fair to comment that none of the other main approaches to the study of the reemergence of modern ethnicity is totally reductionist in the sense of claiming absolute exclusivity in explaining the phenomenon at hand. In fact, the proponents of all those approaches have maintained that aside from the elements each emphasizes, there are additional factors influencing the current ethnic revival. According to that logic, there is a place for an additional step: the formulation of a synthesis approach that can integrate certain features from each of the preceding approaches and reach a more comprehensive explanation of the issue that will better describe the real situation.

Thus, the synthesis approach attempts to put together the most salient components of the other approaches to form a more comprehensive, but still coherent, construct capable of dealing with the complexity of the phenomenon at hand (Kellas 1991, pp. 6, 159–70).

It is possible to integrate some of the elements suggested by primordialists, proponents of the psychological-symbolic view (who tend to accept also the perennialist position), and instrumentalists (who on the whole espouse the modernist view) when explaining the origins of ethnicity. Like the approaches of some of those scholars (Connor 1994; Smith 1998), essentially a synthesis approach suggests that biological factors, combined with notions about a common ancestry, shared traditions, joint historical experience, and a deep sense of communal solidarity, are consequential elements of any explanation for the durability – that is, the perennialism – of ethnic groups. Furthermore, along with some proponents of the instrumentalist/modernist approach, a synthesis approach argues that calculations about possible gains and losses affect decisions to become and remain active members of an ethnic entity and to act within its frameworks and organizations. Finally, like the constructionist/modernist approach, the synthesis approach maintains that a combination of primordial and instrumental factors determines affiliations to a given ethnie. Those affiliations facilitate the establishment of close-knit social and political organizations and can reshape and rekindle the identities of their members, and tenaciously maintaining an ethno-national identity can facilitate the establishment of such close-knit formations.

This synthesis approach better captures the intricate reasons for the current forms of loyalties of contemporary ethno-national diasporas. It facilitates a more comprehensive analysis of the roots, nature, and consequences of that sensitive issue. In addition, it provides a suitable framework for an inquiry into the reasons for the bounded rational choices made by members of those groups. It sheds light also on the collective and personal emotive reasons for the development of overlapping and ambiguous loyalties. Furthermore, it allows a better understanding of homelands' ability or inability to manipulate their diasporas and offers some reasons for difficulties of full integration and assimilation of those groups into their host societies.

Diasporas do not act in a vacuum, and their members are strongly influenced by their changing domestic and global environments. Therefore, certain demographic and social factors that have recently influenced and further complicated the loyalty issue should be briefly reiterated here. Most important among those factors is the increase in the number of ethno-national diasporas, along with their rapidly growing memberships and their wide dispersal in host countries. That has generated and exacerbated anxieties among nationalists, racists, and other conservative segments of host societies that diaspora groups may "contaminate" host cultures and weaken host economies by increasing unemployment, remitting money to foreign countries, absorbing local benefits, and so forth. The second factor is the aforementioned awakening of some dormant ethno-national diasporas, especially because of national upheavals in their homelands. The third is the general retreat from the melting-pot integrationist and assimilationist ideas once held by various governments. The reversal of that trend, which previously had contributed to the seeming possibility of imposing limitations on the scope of diaspora communities' autonomous activities, is now raising apprehensions about the behavior of diasporas vis-à-vis host countries. That is especially the case in view of the spreading inclination among diaspora members to rescind their previously held integrationist and assimilationist strategies.

As the old concepts of sovereignty and citizenship change and even erode, and as greater respect for "others" and for "otherness" emerges in some Western countries, members of incipient and dormant diasporas are becoming more open about their ethno-national origins and identities, publicly identifying with their nations and their homelands. Seeing the issue of diasporas' loyalties in that broad context should bring the matter into focus and highlight its significance and complexity.

Patterns of Diasporas' Loyalties

Generally, ethno-national diasporas demonstrate ambiguous, dual, or divided loyalties to their host countries and homelands. Of the three, the easiest to characterize are the dual loyalties, consisting in a collective state of mind such that diasporans feel they owe allegiance to both host country and homeland. In other words, they do not see a substantial contradiction between their two loyalties. Thus they accept the general social and political norms of their hosts and comply with the legal, political, and economic regulations of their host countries. At the same time, they feel affinity for and maintain contacts with their families and other groups in their homelands and are willing to promote their homelands' interests in host countries and elsewhere. Although in their host countries they may face disparagement, false accusations, discrimination, and persecution, core activists in such diaspora communities are prepared to cope with those attitudes provided they can maintain their contacts with their homelands and offer support to their kin there. As long as relations between their homelands and host countries are friendly, or at least cordial, most diasporans will not face major difficulties in determining the balance between their loyalties and maintaining the patterns of loyalties they have forged. That will not be the case, however, if disagreements arise between host countries and homelands.

Analytically and practically the pattern of divided loyalties is more complex and therefore more difficult to conceptualize. Essentially, the pattern of divided loyalties is one according to which members of diasporas demonstrate loyalty to their host countries in the domestic sphere and loyalty to their homelands in regard to homeland politics and transstate politics. Under those circumstances, most diasporans will show loyalty to their host countries and comply with the laws and the norms and principles prevailing in those countries. They will comply with regulations in the economic and financial spheres, and some will participate in the defense of their host countries during wars. In practicing democracies, they will campaign for election to parliaments and local legislative bodies and even compete for executive positions. That has been the pattern in the United States, where Latinos run for office at all levels of politics (*Economist* 2000). On the other hand, in other spheres, such as contributing money to worthy causes, gathering and passing on information, supporting political and diplomatic activities, and engaging in cultural exchanges, those same diasporans will show loyalty to their homelands. In such cases they will direct some of their activities to promoting their homelands' interests in host countries and in international organizations, and they may transfer substantial resources to their homelands. Clearly, such attitudes and actions offer fertile ground for germination of tension and disputes with their host societies and governments.

Whereas established diasporas usually adopt one of the two patterns of loyalties just discussed, members of incipient diasporas and members of groups that are in the process of reawakening and changing from dormant to active diasporas may have difficulty in clearly defining their identities, in making decisions about their identifications, and therefore also in determining their loyalties. As a way out, they may take a wait-and-see approach, preferring a dash of ambiguity amid their loyalties. Only after making their critical decisions about permanent settlement and integration or assimilation into their host societies, as well as the extent of their contacts with their homelands, will they be ready to clarify their positions on loyalties. Some diasporans will maintain an ambiguous stance for long periods. Such ambiguity can result from dissatisfaction with the cultural, social, and political situations prevailing in their homelands, unfavorable conditions in host countries, or simply confusion and indecision about how much contact they want with homelands and about their willingness to assimilate into host countries.

As with other aspects of diasporas' political behavior, the adoption of a particular form of loyalty is largely a matter of individual and collective choices. Entire diaspora communities, smaller groups within those communities, and individual members all must make their own decisions about loyalties after careful consideration of the conditions prevailing in host countries, the extent of the relations they want with their homelands, and the conditions in their homelands. Because older and richer diasporas have many political and economic interests at stake, as well as long traditions and established patterns of behavior, they can have greater difficulty in accurately calibrating and coordinating all the variables that go into determining their attitudes and loyalties toward host and homeland at any given time.

The adoption of one of those patterns of loyalties is not determined solely on the basis of which stage in its historical development a given diaspora is going through. That is, it does not depend only on whether a diaspora is historical, modern, or incipient. Additional factors go into determining a community's pattern of loyalties.

The first of those factors is the special mix of primordial, psychological-symbolic, instrumental, and situational ingredients that determines the identity and identification of each diaspora. When the instrumental or situational elements in a community's identity are stronger than the primordial and psychological-symbolic components, the chances are that the diaspora will adopt a pattern of either ambiguous loyalties or divided loyalties. Because, in addition to the primordial and psychological-symbolic factors, diasporas' identities and identification depend on instrumental factors, cost–benefit considerations in the widest meaning of that term are important in determining individual and collective communal decisions concerning the preferred pattern of loyalties. The main rationale for adopting one of those patterns of loyalties is connected to a diaspora's attempts to avoid the appearance of loyalty to its homeland so strong that it precludes any loyalty to its host countries. In other cases, diasporas that try to avoid confrontations with their host societies and political institutions, but at the same time maintain close relations with their homelands, tend to adopt a pattern of ambiguous or divided loyalties.

The second factor that influences a diaspora's stance on loyalty is the depth of its commitment to its ethno-national identity and its degree of identification with its homeland and with other communities of the same origin. The greater that commitment and the clearer its identification with its homeland, the more will a diaspora be ready to choose the pattern of dual loyalties. Adoption of that posture can lead to involvement in disputes, particularly with host societies and governments. Any lesser commitment to the ethno-national entity will diminish the propensity to identify with the homeland and the inclination to invest energy in trying to help it.

The third factor concerns the operative strategies that diaspora communities adopt vis-à-vis host societies regarding daily life (a reminder that those strategies form a spectrum: assimilation, integration, communalism, corporatism, autonomy, separation, secession, and irredentism). The closer diasporas position themselves to the assimilationist pole on the strategy spectrum, the greater the possibility that they will adopt a posture of ambiguous loyalties toward homelands and hosts. They will try to minimize evidence of their identification with homelands and conceal their commitment to the people there. When following the communal or corporatist strategy, diaspora communities tend to take a position of dual loyalties. And diasporas that follow the strategies of autonomism and separatism tend to adopt the pattern of divided loyalties.

The fourth factor influencing the loyalty choices of diaspora communities is their degree of organization. In most cases, the more comprehensive and efficient the organization and activities of their communal institutions, the greater the chances that diaspora communities will adopt a pattern of either divided or dual loyalties. The rationale of that argument is that, generally, members of the better-organized and more active diasporas maintain closer connections with their homelands, but they also feel more secure in their dealings with societal and political forces in their host countries, so they will also feel confident about either splitting or duplicating their loyalties.

The fifth factor pertains to the structure, scope, and intensity of the activities of the trans-state networks created and operated by ethnonational diasporas. Those networks are essential elements in diaspora life, maintaining their most vital connections with homelands and other co-ethnic communities and carrying resources from and to diaspora communities, and they tend to boost members' sense of security and self-confidence. When those networks are effective, the result is that entire diasporas, including their marginal members, begin to develop substantial degrees of loyalty to their homelands.

The sixth and last factor that influences the choice of one of the three patterns of loyalties concerns the social and political environments, both domestic (the situations in host countries) and international, and how they affect diasporas. Those sources of influence include the extent of host governments' authority and power and their grip on internal and external sovereignty, the meaning and applicability of the concept of citizenship, the presence of regional unions, and the political trends in the global system. Among those environmental factors, the social and political situations in host countries are the more potent influences. Thus, for example, increasing openness and porosity of borders, substantial tolerance toward "others" and "otherness," wider acceptance of multiculturalism and pluralism, and societal acquiescence to the establishment of diaspora communities and organizations, including diasporas' trans-state networks, are likely to prompt diasporas to choose dual loyalties. That pertains to the situation prevailing in liberal democracies; it is not generally applicable to authoritarian regimes. On the other hand, political and economic discrimination against diasporas, actions that force them into isolation, substantial degrees of intolerance in host societies and governments, especially in non-democratic countries, tensions with other minorities, and regional and world organizations' disregard and disrespect toward diasporas all are likely to lead to ambiguous loyalties.

Though probably less influential than domestic factors in their host countries, the attitudes toward ethnicity and diasporas that prevail in the international system will also have some impact on diasporas' loyalties. Thus, much like the situation on the domestic level, a general atmosphere of openness and tolerance in the international arena will encourage dual loyalties. However, that does not mean that under such circumstances diasporas will not comply with the legal norms prevailing in their host countries, nor will they under all circumstances and at any cost always support their homelands.

The patterns of loyalties shown by diasporas toward their host countries and homelands will depend on the interplay among all the factors mentioned in this section. Because the number of possible combinations of such interacting factors is large, each case must be considered separately, and a specific assessment of the loyalty pattern of each diaspora must take into consideration all of those factors.

In addition, it is important to take into consideration the fact that those patterns are neither static nor immutable, that they can change with the passage of time, and that they can vary among different diaspora communities of the same origin residing in different host countries. In other words, there is a realistic possibility that some diaspora communities will adopt different loyalty patterns during different periods of their development.

An Example: The Loyalties of the Jewish Diaspora

Because there have been few recent publications on this issue, specific detailed studies of the loyalties of various ethno-national diasporas are urgently needed. Such studies would allow comparative analyses, which will be essential for a better understanding of this sensitive and neglected aspect of diasporas' existence. Strictly as an example, the following is an attempt to apply the theoretical and analytical framework and observations presented earlier to the Jewish diaspora.

Two preliminary points concerning the general situation of the Jewish diaspora should be emphasized at this stage. First, the Jewish diaspora's strong and continuous primordial and psychological-symbolic attachment to Eretz Israel (the land of Israel) posed and still poses political dilemmas for many diaspora members in their various host countries, both democratic and non-democratic. In this connection, suffice it to recall two well-known historical events involving Jewish diaspora communities: first, the infamous Dreyfus affair in France toward the end of the nineteenth century and its multiple ramifications for Jewish diaspora communities and, in fact, for the development of Zionism (Marrus 1980; Lindemann 1993); second, the myths connected to the forged *Protocols of the Elders of Zion* and the ensuing allegations and accusations about Jewish loyalty to capitalism and to foreign states made since the early twentieth century by racists and ultranationalists in various countries, and especially by the Nazis, on the one hand, and extreme leftists and Soviets, on the other. Those myths still prevail and serve as a rallying point for neo-Nazi and extreme rightist groups in the United States and Europe. Other anti-Semites in Europe and leaders and rank and file in Arab countries made similar acerbic allegations against Jews, especially Zionists, on the eve of and following the establishment of Israel. A more recent case in point involves the allegations made by such groups in the United States regarding the Pollard affair (Bookbinder 1988; Blitzer 1988; Hunderson 1988; Kumaraswamy 1996). Those and similar incidents have affected diaspora Jews' attitudes and loyalties to their host countries and to Israel.

The second basic point is that past and current patterns of loyalty have not been identical among different Jewish diaspora communities residing in different host countries. Likewise, during the long history of the Jews, the intensity of the loyalty of different Jewish diaspora communities to their various host countries has never been constant. Rather, it has varied with time, even in a given host country. In some host countries, such as the Soviet Union, most of its former satellite states, and Arab countries, Jews were denied the right to freely express their national identification and to translate their personal and collective sentiments toward their ancient homeland into meaningful actions. That was enforced by extensive use of those regimes' coercive mechanisms (secret services, police forces, the courts, etc.). For example, in the Soviet Union, the Zionist movement was outlawed and its members persecuted. Jews in the Soviet Union and its empire were forbidden to maintain relationships with the Jewish community in Palestine before the establishment of the Jewish state in 1948, and with Israel for most of the time until the late 1980s (Baron 1964; Pinkus 1993, 1999). Under those circumstances, the issues of loyalty and support to the homeland became hypothetical matters, void of any practical meaning. That was augmented by the fact that some Jews in the Soviet Union expected support from their homeland, but that did not materialize.

In a sense, the fate of the Jewish communities in South Africa and Argentina during their apartheid and non-democratic periods was similar. It is true that in those two countries the freedom of the Jews to establish Zionist organizations, to express their affinity with the homeland, and to maintain contacts with Jewish communities in other host countries (especially Anglo-Saxon countries) was far greater than in the Soviet Union or in Arab countries. Nevertheless, the possibility of translating these contacts into full and open pro-Zionist and especially pro-Israel actions was restricted. In those and similar cases, the Jews were compelled to limit their connections, especially in the political, economic, and financial spheres, with Eretz Israel, Zionism, and Israel. The main argument for such limitations was that they would tend to undermine Jews' loyalties to their host countries and endanger some vital interests of the hosts, such as their relationships with Arab and Muslim states. Under such circumstances, most members of the Jewish communities in those countries had no other option but to develop and manifest ambiguous loyalties. That had a stifling effect on Russian Jews, as eventually well reflected in Jewish emigration patterns prior to and especially after the collapse of the Soviet Union. During those two periods, most of the Russian Jews who emigrated preferred the United States, Canada, and Australia over Israel (Elkins 1980; Elazar and Medding 1983; Sachar 1985; Sowell 1996).

The situation was different in democratic countries. In most of those host countries, Jews were able to maintain their contacts with the ancient homeland and their national movement and pursue their interests there. Yet at the same time, they were expected, and sometimes compelled by social pressures and governmental insistence, to show loyalty to their host countries. For example, during certain periods of the British mandate over Palestine (1917–1948), that was the case for the Jewish corporatist community in Great Britain. At the very least, British Jewry was frowned upon when some of its leaders, clearly not the majority, promoted the Zionist cause and rendered assistance to the Zionists and later to Israel. Yet in most of those host countries the Jews adopted and were able to pursue a cautious strategy of dual loyalties.

In liberal democratic regimes, most notably the United States, Canada, Australia, Denmark, Holland, and Norway, the Jews were able to maintain open and intensive relationships with the Jewish community in Palestine and later with Israel. In such host countries, where Jewish communities enjoyed the privilege of relatively freely and openly shaping their political positions toward the homeland, they were divided on the question of the desirable balance between their commitments to homeland and host countries and on the public posture that should be shown toward host countries and homeland. Certain segments in those communities, especially those who were inclined toward assimilation, demonstrated total loyalty to their host societies and governments. Those who preferred social and cultural integration in their host countries developed ambiguous loyalties toward hosts and homeland. And those who openly identified as supporters of the Zionist movement and of the

Jewish community in Palestine (the Yishuv) and later of Israel developed dual loyalties. The most resolute Zionists and other supporters of Israel adopted the divided-loyalties stance; that is, in certain respects they were loyal to their host countries, and in other respects to the homeland.

As the world is changing, along with our conceptions of borders, sovereignty, citizenship, and loyalty to the nation-state in general, and to host countries in particular, Jewish communities abroad are modifying their attitudes. Those modifications should be attributed mainly to new trends within the diaspora that are influencing its relations with Israel. As reactions to those trends, "entrenchment" and "revision" are the two most significant tendencies that have emerged in Jewish communities around the world. Actually, those are two sides of the same coin, resulting from a situation in which certain groups in the Jewish diaspora want to ensure both "continuity" (which is another central concept and catchword in contemporary world Jewry) and integration into their host societies. Consequently they are revising their views about the centrality of Israel and leaning toward limiting the homeland's involvement in the diaspora's affairs. The first tendency relates to a recent determination to try to prevent assimilation, which is rapidly reducing the number of members of diaspora communities globally. That determination is being translated into attempts to invest more resources in diaspora communities (and reduce the allocation of funds for Israel), intensify Jewish education, strengthen communal welfare organizations, fortify the local federations, and reorganize the community institutions in the host countries.

A second closely related trend is an effort to revise the diaspora's view of Israel, to reconsider Israel's role in the ethnic-religious nation, and to reassess diaspora–Israel relations. The most significant new development there is the increasing opposition to unquestioning acceptance of Israel's centrality in world Jewry. With certain exceptions, such as the Jewish communities in Australia and Argentina (on the Australian Jewish diaspora, see Rutland 1997), the challenge to Israel's predominance is coming from leftist and liberal segments as well as from rightist and ultra-orthodox religious segments in all kinds of Jewish communities: the richer and stronger (such as the American and Belgian), as well as the newer and weaker (such as the German and Russian).

Israel has contributed more than a fair share to the deterioration of its central position in the eyes of the diaspora, and thus it has also contributed to a considerable decrease in diaspora Jews' readiness to pledge their loyalty to Israel. Because it is difficult to assess the weight of each of the following inputs into that change, they are not ranked, but appear in a random manner (for detailed analyses and references, see Sheffer 1988, 1993b, 1996).

In the Jewish diaspora there has been a dramatic change in the widely held perception of the homeland's centrality. That can be attributed to the fact that whereas in the 1950s, the 1960s, and the first part of the 1970s Israel was perceived as a culturally and socially creative society, now large segments in the diaspora view it as a mediocre country that is far from fulfilling the goal of becoming a "light unto the nations." That change in perception has been accelerated because of the increasingly important social and political roles that both the Sephardic and Ashkenazi ultra-orthodox have been given in Israeli politics – a trend that is delpored by many secular groups and moderate religious groups in the diaspora.

A second source of diaspora disappointment with the Jewish state that has contributed to perceptions of its diminishing stature and evanescing centrality, and hence to a decrease in the diaspora's inclination to identify with it and pledge continuous loyalty, concerns laws and policies that alienate younger and more liberal groups in the diaspora. That includes Israeli laws and policies regarding personal rights, as well as matters such as education, conversion, marriage, divorce, and burial. The disappointment and criticisms are aimed directly at the inordinate influence of the officially appointed Rabbinate and Haredi (ultra-orthodox) rabbis on Israeli politics, particularly on legislation regarding the matters just listed. Some of the laws and policies that Israeli governments adopted in the 1990s or intend to adopt in the early years of the twenty-first century, designed to placate Orthodox and Haredi leaders, have been responsible for marked decreases in the numbers of Reform, Conservative, and secular western European and American Jews migrating to Israel. Such discontent is also reflected in reduced donations to Israel from those sources, in the rerouting of donations toward the diaspora's needs, and in a generally growing sense of alienation from Israel. The effect of that trend is further increased by the fact that most of the disenchanted belong to the more able elements in the diaspora communities.

A third factor contributing to dissatisfaction is the increasing resentment of Israel's blatant attempts to manipulate diaspora Jews, pushing them to try to intervene in host countries' politics and policy-making processes on behalf of Israel. Their reluctance to act as Israeli proxies or agents is reflected in the fact that they have had little to say as the U.S.

government has pursued its agenda in the Middle East and in the peace process, including its votes in the United Nations to support some of the positions of the Palestinian leadership. The Jewish diaspora has been particularly critical of Israeli attempts to manipulate diaspora leaders and to recruit diasporans for espionage work in friendly countries, such as Jonathan Pollard in the United States. That affair provoked extremely negative reactions not only in the American Jewish community but also in Jewish diaspora communities in other host countries. The recruitment of such agents is a clear breach of the Ben-Gurion–Blaustein agreement of 1951, which stipulated that Israel would not interfere in the internal affairs of diaspora Jewry and would take no action that might give the impression that diaspora Jews were acting in ways that were contrary to the interests of their host countries and were harboring conflicting loyalties to their host countries and the homeland (Liebman 1977).

A fourth development concerns the increasingly negative reactions to the traditional intimate ties between Israeli politicians and bureaucrats, on the one hand, and the diaspora's wealthy donors, lay leaders, and professionals, on the other. After the establishment of the Jewish state, such close ties made it tempting for Israeli officials to meddle in the internal politics of the diaspora. Since the mid-1970s the situation has changed considerably, so much so that the main current tendency in Jewish diaspora communities is to ensure autonomy in the conduct of their affairs. That is evident in a marked reduction in the allocation of funds and actual financial transfers to Israel and in the diversion of the "saved" monies to communal purposes. Furthermore, such changed attitudes have extended to the political sphere, where both rightist and leftist Israeli governments find it increasingly difficult to muster diaspora support for their policies.

Finally, diaspora Jews feel less committed to the Jewish state because of changing conditions in most host countries. In view of their increasing acceptance by larger sectors of host societies and the related decrease in anti-Semitism, the feeling in many Jewish communities abroad is that Israel's value as a potential refuge has been considerably diminished. That does not mean that diaspora Jews totally dismiss the possibility that they might need to use that option, and the return of many Russian and Argentinian Jews to Israel is a good illustration of that point. Yet to many in the West, such a need seems very remote. There is ample evidence that despite the traumatic memories of persecution during the troubled history of the Jewish diaspora, the vast majority of Jews in Western democracies and elsewhere feel fairly secure in their host countries. That is complemented by a growing sense that the homeland is not under any immediate threat to its existence.

The Implications

Following are some tentative theoretical conclusions based on our general observations of ethno-national diasporas' loyalty patterns and on our first empirical analytical look into the question of the loyalties of the Jewish diaspora. The following observations are not arranged in any particular order of importance.

The loyalty patterns that diasporas adopt will depend on, among other things, to what extent their host states have a firm grip on power, as well as on the extent to which increasing liberalization, democratization, and pluralism lead to changes in traditional concepts of sovereignty and citizenship. The weakening of the nation-state concept and the expanding processes of liberalization and democratization usually promote pluralism, encourage renewal in ethnic and ethno-national diasporas, strengthen existing communities and their organizations, and facilitate the emergence of new diaspora communities. Those developments lead to changes in diasporas' perceptions of the limitations on their activities and consequently lead them to reassess the allocations of their loyalties. Under such circumstances diasporans tend to feel more secure, and consequently their loyalty to and support for their homelands may increase. On the other hand, the same trends that lead to greater tolerance and acceptance of diasporas may encourage their assimilation and integration into host countries. Whenever that scenario develops, activist core members of diasporas will first entrench to defend the integrity of the diaspora community, but ultimately will develop increasing loyalties to their host countries, to the detriment of their loyalties to their homelands.

The increasing openness of attitudes and of borders in the international and regional systems, the communications revolution, and the greater ease of transportation all facilitate the organization, elaboration, and operation of diasporas' organizations and trans-state networks, which are necessary for maintaining their ongoing connections with homelands and which are essential components of diasporas' identities. More important, those networks are indispensable for reinforcing diasporans' loyalties to their homelands. The trans-state networks make it possible for ethno-national diasporas to transfer resources worldwide, particularly to homelands. They also are important for obtaining political and diplomatic support from homelands and from other ethnic groups. The ultimate result is division and diversification of diasporas' loyalties.

Contrary to some widely held views, the ethno-national identities of many diasporas are very firmly rooted, and their loyalty cannot be bought even by generous gifts of material resources. Hence, the fact that in many host countries there are very unequal distributions of economic resources is not a reliable predictor of the possibility that ethnic diasporas might revolt against their host societies and governments. On the other hand, the fact that in some host countries there is equal access to economic resources, or even affirmative-action programs, will not necessarily moderate ethnic diasporas' attitudes toward their hosts and actions detrimental to their hosts and ensure their unequivocal loyalty. In the same vein, host countries' abilities to interrupt the international ties of diaspora communities, and thus to try to influence their loyalties, have been considerably diminished.

Viewed from the homeland perspective, it turns out that when the conditions of their diasporas in host countries are good and diasporans can freely pursue their wishes and inclinations, homeland governments cannot rely on either automatic loyalty or total loyalty from their co-ethnics abroad. Diasporas' loyalties to their homelands depend on numerous factors in the global and regional environments and on the social, political, and economic situations in host countries, but no less important is the fact that to a considerable extent diasporas' loyalties to their homelands depend on the attitudes and actions of homeland societies and governments. Thus, when homelands disregard the needs and interests of their diasporas and governmental actions openly reveal that disrespect, diasporas' loyalties to their homelands can decline. Also, when the cultural, political, and economic conditions in homelands are seen as inferior to those prevailing in host countries or within diasporas themselves, diasporas may increase their allegiance to host countries.

When all such factors are taken into consideration and examined empirically, it seems that large segments of stateless diasporas residing in democratic host countries tend to develop dual loyalties. For different reasons, that is also true for the well-established state-linked historical diasporas. Large groups in younger diasporas tend to develop divided loyalties, and incipient diasporas show clear patterns of ambiguous loyalties.

As noted, the implementation of one of those patterns not only has analytical and theoretical significance but also entails practical implications, especially in regard to homeland–diaspora relationships of mutual reliance and cooperation. Thus, from the homeland point of view, as far as loyalty is concerned, the most reliable diasporas are state-linked historical diasporas, and the least reliable are incipient diasporas. Yet, as I have argued elsewhere (Sheffer 1994), it would be erroneous to assume that because of their tendency to adopt dual loyalties, historical diasporas pose major challenges to their host societies and governments. Similarly, it would be unwise to underestimate the potential for incipient diasporas to provoke confrontations and tension in host countries and homelands simply because of their precarious existence and lack of political organization and experience.

10

Diasporas at Home Abroad

The Main Conclusions

Not so long ago most politicians and academics, both those on the right and those on the left of the political and intellectual-academic spectra, dismissed ethno-national diasporism and diasporas as ephemeral social and political phenomena that did not merit specific attention or detailed study. It was also held that the numbers of members in those communities were negligible and that their ability to influence cultural, political, and economic developments was minimal.

Politicians and academics subscribing to rightist and nationalist philosophies hoped that nation-states, ruled by dominant ethnic nations or ethnic groups, would be able to cope with all of the other ethnic groups, including ethno-national diasporas, residing within their borders. On rather questionable theoretical and empirical grounds they were confident that such nations, nation-states, and dominant groups, which they portrayed as superior to all other social and political entities, would be able to impose their norms and eventually achieve assimilation, or at least full integration, of all other groups. Leftist observers argued that the continuing existence of diasporas was attributable mainly to economic factors. They believed that either improvements in economic conditions, through further expansion of the welfare state, or success of the anticipated class struggle would remove the incentive for migration and reduce the tensions between host societies and their ethnic minorities and resident diasporas. Above all, they hoped for eventual disappearance of those ethnic entities. Liberal analysts and politicians argued that further extension of civil liberties and rights, equal personal opportunities, and greater freedom of choice would lead to the integration of those groups and their gradual dissipation.

More involved observers were inclined to equate ethno-national diasporism with the Jewish diaspora and, in line with the traditional Jewish self-perception, to regard diasporas as "exiles." Within that conceptual framework they regarded the Jewish diaspora either as sui generis or as a marginal and disappearing entity. Few observers thought that it was an archetypal diaspora and model for all other diasporas. In any event, those observers, too, regarded ethno-national diasporism as a temporary phenomenon.

Those various views had become so common that they were reflected in the entries concerning "diaspora" in most important dictionaries, encyclopedias, and scholarly works in the field of ethnic politics. Consequently, until the mid-1980s, scant attention was given to the idea that dispersed ethno-national communities constituted an undeniable and enduring phenomenon.

The late 1980s and especially the early 1990s saw a marked change in those skeptical and unreceptive attitudes. Observers of the general ethnic situation and the related ethno-national diaspora phenomenon realized that, like other developments in those arenas, diasporism was not an evanescent phenomenon. Recently, more observers have noted that the number of those entities, the sizes of certain diaspora communities, and the scope of their activities are increasing, that they are becoming more involved in local, regional, and trans-state cultural, economic, and political affairs, and that their influence in those spheres is rising.

The changes in diasporas' status and in the attitudes toward them have occurred not only because of new impressions and perceptions but also because of some actual quantifiable developments, such as the striking growth in international migration that has resulted in the permanent settlement of more migrants in host countries. Furthermore, the changes in the general attitudes toward diasporism have been influenced by the emergence, mainly in Western societies, of favorable conditions for pluralism, by the inability of host governments and social and political movements to curb migration and the development of new diasporas, by the awakening of dormant diasporas, and by the evident endurance of historical diasporas. Indeed, it has become clear to all that ethno-national diasporas are alive and active almost everywhere in the world.

Yet the greater openness and tolerance of host societies and governments toward ethnic diversity and the almost worldwide ease of movement and communication – which are both the causes and the effects of ongoing globalization, liberalization, and democratization – have created some diametrically opposite results that are significant for particular diasporas and for the general diaspora phenomenon. First, there have been ideologically motivated voluntary returns to homelands (ingatherings): Some Pontic Greeks, ethnic Germans, Jews, Armenians, and, more recently, Irish-Americans have returned to their homelands. Second, there have been expulsions and repatriations of individuals, groups, and entire diaspora communities, such as the Egyptians from Iraq, Yemenites from Saudi Arabia, and Palestinians from Kuwait during the Persian Gulf War. Also, from a slightly different perspective, countries such as Greece, Armenia, Ireland, Israel, China, and India, hoping to solve problems caused by a brain drain or by domestic economic stagnation, have tried to encourage successful members of their diasporas to return "home," or at least to invest time and money in their homelands.

However, the net result of those contradictory migratory trends, even when assimilation is taken into account, has not been a massive dissipation of older and newer diasporas nor their total disappearance, but rather increasing numbers of diasporas and diasporans. In turn, those factors have led to a new dedication by diasporans to communal organization and reorganization, to pursuit of their collective interests, to intensification of their activities (mostly according to moderate strategies), to emergence of new forms of ties with their homelands, and to enhanced roles and greater influence in domestic, regional, and global politics.

Hence, if we examine all categories of diasporas – be they "stateless," like the Palestinian, Kurdish, Tamil, and Gypsy, or "state-linked," like most diasporas, "historical," like the Jewish, Chinese, Indian, and Armenian, "modern," like the African-American, black, Greek, Polish, and Turkish, "incipient," like the Korean, Filipino, Thai, and Russian, or "dormant," like the American in Europe and Asia, and whether they be territorially concentrated, like the Ukrainian in the United States and Canada, or vastly dispersed, like the Jewish and Palestinian in the United States – it can easily be seen that the phenomenon is growing everywhere.

The contradictory trends of globalization, localization, and individuation, accompanied by tremendous increases in cultural, social, and political diversity, have influenced the emergence of highly complex structures and behavioral patterns among all ethnic groups, and especially among ethno-national diasporas. Because such groups constitute trans-state (rather than trans-national) entities that have deep roots in both their host countries and their homelands, they must cope with highly complex and frequently hostile environments. Therefore, the analysis here has had to consider a large number of factors in order to shed light on the resultant emotionally, cognitively, and practically problematic existence of members of those groups who live in host countries but maintain ties with their homelands.

The conclusions that follow answer the questions posed in the Introduction and discussed further in Chapter 1.

Accordingly, examination of the history of diasporism shows that some diasporas began in antiquity and that some of them have survived the tribulations of war and conquests, as well as social, political, and economic transformations. As the analysis of the very long history of the Jewish diaspora shows, an essential precondition for the rise of diasporas in antiquity or during the Middle Ages was settlement of ethnic groups in territories they gradually came to regard as home and homeland. A further precondition was development of a communal identity and solidarity among those residing in such territories.

Because of a combination of emotional and practical considerations, members of those groups began to migrate voluntarily from their homelands. Eventually they settled permanently in host countries but maintained their ethnic identities and regular contacts with their homelands. Other groups were forced to migrate because of severe political and economic pressures or because of expulsions. Their determination to maintain their contacts with their homelands had significant cultural, social, political, and economic ramifications for all those involved.

Those processes continued through the early Middle Ages and the modern period, peaking in the mid-1800s and again around the turn of the twentieth century. New peaks have occurred since the late 1980s, and the trend has not changed in the first two years of this century. In view of persistent demands for immigrants in the aging polities of Europe and in the still-developing United States, and because of difficult economic and political conditions in many developing countries, it seems that migration and permanent settlement of migrants in many host countries will continue to increase.

The historical analysis presented here leads to two main conclusions. The first is that the diaspora phenomenon is ancient and enduring. That is, the underlying reasons for the emergence of diasporas and their main characteristics and behavioral patterns are not recent. Diasporas have existed since the earliest periods in the development of human societies. Hence, ethnic diasporism is a perennial phenomenon. The histories of such entities have been influenced by local, regional, and international politics during each period in which the various diasporas have emerged, become established, and disappeared. The second, related conclusion is that the survival of historical diasporas through two or even three millennia is proof of their impressive persistence and historical roles in almost all cultural, social, economic, and political developments.

Yet the relative and absolute numbers and sizes of modern and incipient diasporas are larger than those of the historical diasporas. The answer to the question whether or not the nature of ethno-national diasporas has undergone changes over the past century or so is quite clear: Although older and newer diasporas share basic characteristics, such as their motivations for migrating out of their homelands, their determination to maintain the identities that tie them to their homelands, their development of communal solidarity, and their need to organize and establish local and international networks, there are also some evident differences.

The first new characteristic of contemporary ethno-national diasporas is connected to the greater openness of today's global environment and to the ease of transportation and communication. Those developments allow more people to move away from their homelands voluntarily in search of hospitable host countries. In this context, most important is the fact that in comparison with the past, now such migrants find it easier to settle permanently in host countries. Although host governments may try to restrict their entrance, limit their visits, and discourage permanent settlement, most of those who are determined to stay in host countries eventually succeed in doing so. Thus, recent migration waves and permanent settlement in host countries have mostly been voluntary acts that are difficult to arrest.

The second new aspect is that voluntary migrants, like expellees, refugees, and guest workers, make decisions about their future plans only after rather prolonged periods of dwelling in their host countries. For many of those who decide to settle permanently in host countries, assimilation is less appealing today. That is true even in hospitable and tolerant host countries.

In any event, the third new aspect concerns diasporans' need to cope with the difficulties facing them in host countries. Thus their need to make consequential decisions concerning identity and contacts with their homelands motivates them to establish multiple organizations to deal with their particular interests and concerns. Hence, significant new features of all existing diasporas are the multiplicity and scope of those organizations and their dedicated pursuit of the strategies they adopt vis-à-vis their multiple protagonists: host societies and governments, other ethnic groups in host countries, homelands, regional organizations, and other segments of the same ethnic nation.

Another novel facet is connected to the emergence of the new media. The media both influence the nature of and facilitate the establishment of diasporas and their trans-state networks. Those networks help to maintain contacts with homelands and other relevant actors, but their actions can also lead to suspicion and animosity among members of the host societies. That raises a complex set of practical questions about their loyalties. Although a number of states, especially in the West, are weakening and traditional notions about sovereignty and citizenship are waning and changing, as long as nationalism and statism are alive, diasporas, their hosts, homelands, and other interested actors will continue to face the twin problems of authority and loyalty.

Those issues are of great concern to all ethno-national diasporas. Yet our analysis here indicates that today the most basic political differences between the various categories of diasporas are those between stateless and state-linked diasporas. Essentially, those differences stem from the distinctive principal strategies that the two kinds of diasporas adopt. Whereas stateless diasporas often choose separatist or irredentist strategies in regard to their homelands, most state-linked entities tend to opt for communalism in their host countries. Different choices from among those divergent strategies will dictate different patterns of loyalties, as well as differences in allocation of resources, organization, political behavior, and relationships with relevant social and political actors.

Because in most cases stateless diasporas pursue separatist and irredentist strategies in regard to their homelands, they develop organizations designed to serve those purposes. The functions of those bodies are to assemble political, diplomatic, human, and material/economic capital, that is, money, weapons, and equipment, and supply them to both homeland governments and local diaspora organizations. In such cases, and as long as the struggles in homelands continue, the needs of the homelands take priority, and those of the diaspora communities are secondary. Nevertheless, diaspora organizations also must marshal their communities to gather the resources needed to sustain them in their daily struggle for survival, or sometimes revival, in their host countries.

Both stateless and state-linked diasporas develop and maintain trans-state networks and organizations, and the differences between them lie mainly in the kinds of resources channeled through them. Generally, state-linked diasporas' networks transfer less sinister resources than those transferred by stateless diasporas.

All said, the numbers of diasporic entities and their members, the levels on which they operate, and their organization and assertiveness have turned them into important cultural, social, economic, and especially political actors in host countries and homelands alike. Against the backdrop of increasing globalization and regionalization, diasporas are also developing interests and involvements in politics on those two levels. The other side of the coin is that the numbers of bystanders who are showing interest in diasporas and are becoming involved in diasporas' affairs have increased quite substantially.

Nevertheless, diasporas' expanded involvement in all those political arenas and the complex patterns of loyalties that they exhibit do not mean that all diasporas pose substantial threats to hosts or homelands. Potentially, certain activities of stateless diasporas can become dangerous to both host countries and their homelands. However, diasporas usually are limited in their scope and in their potential to cause damage. There are no situations in which diasporas alone could fundamentally change basic patterns of development in their homelands. Similarly, state-linked diasporas have the potential to generate unpleasant conflictual situations in their relations with homelands and host countries, but when weighing such dangers against their positive contributions, the latter win out.

Hence it is important to emphasize that diasporas are not as dangerous as they are sometimes perceived and portrayed. Actually, diaspora communities serve as important facilitators of internal, inter-state, and worldwide political, cultural, and economic connections. Taking all those characteristics together, it seems that ethno-national diasporas are indeed the precursors of post-modern trans-state social and political systems.

Ethno-national diasporas are bona fide actual entities. They are as viable as all other ethnic minorities and states. In other words, though today diaspora members increasingly use the new media in their elaborate global trans-state networks, they do not live in the "virtual reality" of the computer, nor are they invented or imagined communities. They are real, and their cohesion and solidarity are based on deeply rooted ethno-national identities that sometimes are augmented by religious creeds. It is true that their identities can evolve and develop in response to changes in their homelands and influences in their host societies, but their basic tenets are stable. Those basic tenets provide the foundation for identification of the dispersed members of diasporas with their ethnic nations, the majority of whom usually reside in the homelands. Though diaspora communities are influenced by their social and political environments in homelands and host countries and develop certain degrees of hybridity, nonetheless throughout their lifetimes their core groups maintain substantial cohesion and conformity to national religious and cultural mores and rites.

The Future of Diasporism and Diasporas

Before the closing sections, let us consider the future of the diaspora phenomenon, that is, the chances that existing diasporas will persist. This is not merely an academic concern or an exercise in social and political forecasting. Today, many members of established state-linked diasporas, organized stateless diasporas, and emerging incipient diasporas are well aware of their changing positions vis-à-vis their homelands, host countries, and global factors and actors, and many are pondering the odds for their continuity. That awareness has generated passionate discussions and studies of diasporas' current situations and possible scenarios concerning their future.

An assessment of the future development of ethno-national diasporism and of particular diasporas indicates that such development will not be linear. Rather, from the philosophical and methodological viewpoints, the indications are that because of the immense complexity that characterizes most ethno-national diasporas and their relationships with their homelands, host countries, and other regional and global actors, the possible scenarios about their future should be based on the ideas of chaos theory, rather than on any theory of deterministic or logical continuity of current situations and trends.

Thus, because the 1990s saw major changes in the positions of many diasporas and changes in their relationships with their homelands and host countries, their current situations must be given considerable weight in estimating the future development of ethno-national diasporism, which means that the influences of many factors that were important in their past will be more limited. In the Jewish case, for example, the traumatic influence of the World War II Holocaust can be expected to diminish considerably. The same applies to the memories and influences of holocausts and other national catastrophes that were experienced by other stateless and state-linked diasporas, such as the Armenian, African-American, Palestinian, and Gypsy.

Furthermore, because of the new conditions that have emerged over the past decade – especially because of the influence of liberalization and individuation – the nature of the future triangular relationships involving diasporas, their homelands, and their host countries will be determined mainly by multifaceted exchanges between individuals and new, smaller political and social groups in the diasporas and homelands, as well as by the extent of the weakening of state institutions and organizations. More than ever before, individual members of homeland societies and individual members of ethno-national diasporas will be freer to make their own choices and determine their futures. Those decisions will make their collective relationships even more complicated.

Many leaders and activists who are involved in diasporas' affairs know and admit that the public agendas of most contemporary homelands, host countries, and diasporas are overloaded and also too divergent. All of the actors involved in diasporic affairs face different sets of questions and dilemmas. Moreover, those leaders and activists are aware that because of the current features of the global, regional, and national arenas, they must address some new issues, but also reconsider some old questions. The older issues are those pertaining to the dispersal of ethnic nations, their identities, their connections to homelands, and their sometimes unsettled relationships with host countries and other diaspora communities. The issues that have recently emerged pertain mainly to the various effects of globalization, regionalization, and individuation on diasporas' current status and future situation. The basic affinity between homelands and diasporas gives rise to some common interests, and the main reason for their divergent views on other issues is that all diasporans who want to feel at home abroad feel torn between their homelands and host countries.

The main new clusters of issues facing diasporas are those mentioned earlier, having to do with continuity and the implications of a homeland's claim to centrality in the entire nation. On the other side, the main issues facing homelands are those pertaining to internal and external security, internal political arrangements, and economic development. The role of religion as a significant factor in survival and continuity is an issue faced mainly by diasporas. On the other side, homelands must deal with social and political pluralism. In any event, there is little doubt that the ethnic elements in the identities of diasporas will become more prominent, and their survival and continuity in the twenty-first century will be influenced by their attitudes on that issue and on the future of ethnicity in general.

Diasporans hold a variety of views about the future development of the phenomenon, as well as of their own entities, ranging from pessimism about continuity (based on the growing ease of assimilation and full integration into their host countries) to confident optimism (based on the increasing acceptance of pluralism and multiculturalism in larger numbers of host countries). However, both pessimists and optimists agree on one aspect: Survival and continuity will depend mainly on the intentions and actions of diaspora members.

Among some diasporans there is a new confidence in diasporas' ability to survive, to manage their affairs, and to guide their future development. And indeed, whereas in the past many diasporas were characterized by various degrees of passivity, today some of those communities are becoming more assertive and active. That new spirit will result in self-empowerment, insistence on rights, and determination to achieve their goals. More than anything else, those attributes can ensure diaspora continuity.

Those developments suggest that in the future there will be clearer distinctions between the agendas, interests, and needs of diasporas and those of homelands. Though there is no doubt that many connections between those two segments of a given nation will continue, their mutual reliance will further decline. In the meantime, diasporas have learned to rely less on inputs from their homelands. Similarly, homelands are less often using their diasporas as mediators with host countries' economic and political systems. Cumulatively, it seems that the future development of homeland–diaspora relations will be toward a new form of politics on the trans-state level: a federation of autonomous entities.

Toward a Theory of Diasporism

Despite the recent increase in the study of diasporas, this subspecialty of ethnic studies is still in its infancy. However, in view of the dramatic increases in the scope and impact of diasporas functioning within the "new world disorder," which itself can in part be attributed to ethnic unrest and conflict, the subject deserves additional investigation. That should yield further data and information on the phenomenon and, eventually, a better explanation of its essence.

Because ethnic diasporas exist under complex social and political circumstances more difficult and hostile than those faced by any other category of ethnic minorities, theoretically diasporism represents an "extreme case" of the entire ethnic phenomenon. Hence, further systematic study should yield clearer answers to some vexing general questions, such as whether ethnicity is an "invented" or "authentic" phenomenon, whether ethnic identity is inherent or is conditional on environmental factors, whether or not it is a permanent feature of post-modern life, and whether or not we currently have strategies adequate to reduce the tensions and conflicts associated with such groups. It is suggested, therefore, that future research on the politics of diasporas should address the following areas:

First, we need further examinations of the explanatory power of the basic distinctions between the various categories of diasporas suggested here, that is, stateless and state-linked, and historical, modern, and incipient.

More important, because the number of diasporas is still growing and because they develop gradually, special attention should be given to the study of incipient diasporas. Systematically monitoring the emergence and development of such groups should lead to significant insights into ethnicity and ethnic identity in general, and diasporas in particular. The analytical profile proposed in Chapter 3 should help in that endeavor. The profile is comprehensive enough to account for most of the existing ethno-national diasporas as well as those currently being established.

That profile also contains a sufficient range of factors and elements that it could lead to new hypotheses that could serve as a basis for further comparative studies. As noted in connection with that profile, and in view of the published data, it appears that about 300 million people can be regarded as diasporans. That figure, however, should be reexamined and verified using more sophisticated demographic and statistical methods. At the same time, it should be remembered that ongoing processes of return movements to homelands, expulsions from host countries, and processes of assimilation and marginalization are at work. Therefore, the figures pertaining to those aspects of contemporary diasporism should also be further checked so as to provide an accurate picture of the number of people involved.

Second, the contradictory demographic trends characteristic of diasporas, that is, migration, assimilation, and return – especially when considered within the broader context of the growing importance of ethnicity in general, and the interest in developing a theory of ethnic existence and revival in particular – indicate a need for studies of specific ethnic diasporas and especially for comparative studies in this field, for those kinds of studies are still in their initial phases. As in other fields of academic studies, without the development of such a perspective and body of knowledge it would be difficult to construct a sound, comprehensive theory of diaspora existence.

At this stage, therefore, it seems obvious that ethnic diasporas constitute the most salient and enduring outcomes of both voluntary and forced international migrations and the prolonged sojourns of ethnic groups in host countries. Yet that needs further elaboration and proofs. One obstacle is that the definitional boundaries between, on the one hand, individuals and groups of tourists, international migrants, guest workers, asylum-seekers, and refugees who reside in host countries for long periods and, on the other, permanent diasporas, are still blurred. That ambiguity must be resolved before we can have meaningful comparative studies of diaspora formation. The findings resulting from such an effort should provide some of the main building blocks of an overarching theory of diasporism. Concomitantly, it should be remembered that for emotional, political, and legal reasons, the periods of time that transient individuals and groups are allowed to remain and wish to remain in host countries before they finally make choices about the future, or are allowed to settle, acquire citizenship, and be socially accepted, are flexible and depend on host governments and mainly on the migrants.

Third, there is no agreement among politicians and academics regarding the precise point at which migrants cross their Rubicon and form new diasporas or join existing ones. The main reason for that ambiguity is connected to other sensitive issues pertaining to the migration and settlement of such ethnic groups. Clarification of those issues will have not only major theoretical implications but also practical effects. As indicated earlier, to facilitate further systematic study of diasporas, the distinctions among the various groups must be clarified. Conceptual and empirical work in that direction will lead to a better understanding of individual and group motivations to undertake the heavy burdens of diaspora existence.

Such studies are also necessary to facilitate assessment of the potential for diasporas' further development. But rather than employing legal definitions, such as the date of application for citizenship or its conferral, or using psychological tests, we should use individual- and collective-choice models for assessing that crucial aspect in the life cycle of migrants and for evaluating the development and survival potential of diaspora communities. That is necessary because in the debate over the origins and nature of ethnicity in general and of ethno-national diasporas in particular, the element of choice by individuals and small groups has largely been overlooked. Hence, the working hypothesis here should be that whereas in certain pluralist societies it is relatively easy to defect from ethno-national diasporas and assimilate, it is almost impossible for outsiders to fully assimilate into such communities, especially when those communities still retain distinctive physical characteristics and behavioral patterns.

Fourth, the preceding observations lead to the main theoretical issue requiring further exploration. The question is why – despite individual and collective hardships, multiple crosscutting and frequently contradictory forces (such as culturally assimilationist versus pluralistically tolerant, socially absorptive versus xenophobic, politically conflictual versus accommodationist, economically equalizing versus discriminatory), and the effects of modernization, mass communications, demographic inferiority, and territorial concentration or dispersal, all of which are at work in the international arena as well as in host countries' domestic affairs – members of ethnic diasporas maintain their identities, their connections with their homelands, their patterns of organization, and their determination to maintain a certain degree of freedom of collective action.

Here the applicability of some available theoretical explanations concerning the elusive issues of ethno-genesis and revival of ethnic minorities, namely, the primordialist, constructionist, psychological-symbolic, and instrumentalist approaches, as well as theories about economic modernization, rational choice, conflict–migration–conflict cycles, migration orders and crises, and imagined communities, all should be reconsidered and reevaluated. As discussed earlier, none of those explanations by itself is sufficient to unravel the vexing riddles of the revival of classical diasporas, the reorganization of modern diasporas, the awakening of dormant diasporas, and the establishment of new diasporas.

It appears that the most promising avenue toward a theory of ethno-national politics is to combine the psychological-symbolic and personal- and collective-choice approaches with a focus on elite–grassroots interactive behavior.

Fifth, closely connected to the foregoing theoretical issues are questions pertaining to the fundamental reasons for the adoption of and changes in the main strategies that diaspora communities pursue in their host countries to ensure their continued autonomous existence. As has been shown here, those can be arranged on a spectrum that includes assimilation, integration, communalism, corporatism, autonomism, separation, and irredentism. A better understanding of the reasons for their adoption is needed because the type of strategy adopted by a diaspora community indicates how it perceives its environment and, in turn, its relationships with host societies and governments, homelands, and other dispersed segments of the same nation.

It has been argued here that the strategy of full assimilation into host societies has become less fashionable among both older and newer diasporas. That conclusion is based on studies showing that whereas it is true that, after initial periods of residence in host countries, today's international migrants are increasingly inclined to settle there, but today they are less inclined to apply for citizenship than, say, a decade ago. Furthermore, it seems that many migrants today are determined to maintain their ethno-national identities; they are confident and secure enough to identify as members of their ethnic communities and are reluctant to undertake meaningful steps toward assimilation or even full integration in their host societies. That highlights the need for further data on this issue. It also raises additional questions about the connections between the motivations and reasons for migrating out of homelands (especially regarding whether voluntary or imposed) and the establishment and organization of diasporas in the host countries.

The findings discussed here call for a further examination of Armstrong's distinction, which is still widely accepted, between proletarian and mobilized diasporas (Armstrong 1976). Basically, that distinction rests on the assumption that poorer migrants who are driven out of their homelands put together the poorer and less well organized diasporas, and that those who leave their homelands of their own free will, and are able to transfer their wealth, establish mobilized diasporas. However, our initial examination of the current situation shows that the poorer and richer incipient state-linked diasporas mobilize, organize, and function similarly.

Further examination of that conclusion should begin with the working hypothesis that the motivations and reasons for migrating out of homelands are not decisive in determining the nature of the entities that will later be established in host countries. It should also be further considered whether or not the tendencies to preserve ethno-national identities and to form organized entities to maintain close ties with homelands do indeed stem from a growing realization among migrants that ethnic pluralism has become the norm in many democracies, that there is increasing tolerance toward more moderate forms of ethnic existence and organization, and that the separation between host societies and diasporas is decreasing in non-democratic countries.

Another issue that should be probed further is whether or not a basic distinction still exists between the strategic choices made by stateless but territorially concentrated diasporas and those made by less concentrated state-linked diasporas. It seems that for reasons connected to the prevailing ethno-nationalist ethos, diasporas in the former category (such as Palestinians and Kurds) tend to choose as their main strategy one that ultimately will lead to the establishment of sovereign states in their homelands. And especially for historical reasons, it should be reconsidered why political autonomy has not been chosen as a more popular option for ensuring the continued existence of diasporas in host societies.

But the critical question in this respect is whether or not most diasporas choose as their preferred strategy either communalism or corporatism. The conclusion that should be reexamined is whether or not the choice of communalism as the main strategy has indeed become almost universal among state-linked diasporas. The predominant factors that seem to prevent diasporas from pursuing secessionist and separatist, or even autonomist, strategies are their small sizes relative to the dominant ethnic groups, their wide dispersion within host countries, and the simple fact that they rarely feel secure enough to warrant a choice of autonomism, irredentism, and separatism. It has been suggested here that two other significant factors contribute to the popularity of communalism among diasporas. First, although in some situations adopting that strategy can lead to disputes with homelands and host societies (both sides demanding diasporas' loyalties), it is nevertheless the strategy least objectionable to most hosts and homelands; it is also the best method for achieving diasporas' goals and securing their vital interests. That strategy appears less menacing to host countries because it does not involve actual or potential challenges to their sovereignty and territorial integrity, that is, to their most cherished ethos. Also, without admitting it, host governments show greater tolerance toward diasporas' communalism because it can provide means for monitoring and controlling the activities of those groups, which, notwithstanding the increasing tolerance, still are regarded with suspicion.

Sixth, an important question regarding diasporas' adoption of their strategies and changes in those strategies that has been almost totally ignored concerns the contagion factor, which arises from international trends among other ethnic minorities and ethno-national diasporas or from ideas originating in homelands. Also in play here are the intricate relationships among diasporas, host countries, homelands, and a host of other international actors. It is clear that as collective actors in the societal and political arenas, members of ethno-national diasporas have the essential task of maintaining contacts with their homelands and, whenever such exist, with other dispersed communities of the same ethnic origin. The natural inclination of most activists is to conduct those contacts through institutional counterparts, rather than with unorganized masses and groups, and because of the sweeping changes in communications and transportation and the emergence of the global village, diasporas are creating elaborate formal and informal trans-state networks to connect their overseas communities with one another and with their homelands, and occasionally with diasporas of different ethno-national origins.

As argued earlier, contrary to accepted notions about that aspect of diaspora existence, not only historical and modern state-linked diasporas but also incipient diasporas have created and maintained such networks. Those networks are essential aspects of diaspora activities. However, it has escaped the attention of most analysts that as a result of the increasing self-assertiveness and empowerment of various diasporas, the functions of those networks are not only to serve homelands' needs but also to transmit diasporas' criticisms of their homelands and their demands concerning changes in homelands' behavior. That conclusion raises some further profound theoretical and practical questions: Do those trilateral and sometimes four- and five-party networks tend to create trans-state political systems that will exist alongside of and will complement established trans-national organizations, such as regional trading blocs, international defense organizations, and so on? And even more important, what is the precise relationship between the gradual weakening of the nation-states and diasporas' increasing room for political maneuvering?

In any event, in that connection the working hypothesis should be that diasporas' trans-state cultural and political exchanges are particularly significant because they touch on major issues pertaining to the identities of those communities. Not less important, however, is further study of the sensitive and sometimes more secretive exchanges that are conducted through those networks. Because of the increasing importance of the state of health of the global political economy, the economic and financial resources exchanged between homelands and their diasporas should be the focus of further study by more students. Their task will be aided somewhat because those exchanges are relatively tangible and quantifiable. That category includes unilateral transfers: donations and remittances, capital investments in homelands, and resources connected to other joint ventures either in homelands or in other states. Although the volume of those transactions is tremendous, until now very few studies have been done in this field. The initial studies of the Jewish and Palestinian trans-state networks that were cited earlier show that some transactions made through those channels are quite labyrinthine, involving various active participants other than merely diasporas and homelands. By no means is that only a one-way process starting with diasporas: Money can also be transferred from homelands to diasporas to finance their defense, maintenance, and promotional activities, and from one diaspora community to another. That aspect, too, merits additional studies.

Although most state-linked diasporas usually are engaged in relatively innocuous exchanges, those networks sometimes are used by stateless diasporas to support irredentist, secessionist, or national liberation movements in their homelands by transfers of less innocent resources, such as combatants, weapons, military intelligence, and cash. Similarly, those networks are used for communications and for shipment of resources needed for international networks of ethnic terrorists and freedom fighters. It has been suggested here that the existence of such networks and the transactions carried out through them can cause considerable discord between diasporas and host states, and because today diasporas are less dependent on their homelands and can pose threats to those regimes, conflicts can also erupt between the two sides. As noted earlier, for obvious reasons, information about donations, investments in homelands, joint ventures, and support for diasporas' clandestine activities is difficult and sometimes impossible to come by, but scholars in this field are digging harder to uncover the actual situation.

Seventh, there are several topics in diaspora–homeland relations that are in need of further study. A general conclusion of this book is that whereas in the relationships between host countries and diasporas, tension and confrontations are more frequently caused by the attitudes and actions of the latter, in homeland–diaspora relationships the former usually are responsible for friction. Even though the basic mutual wish of homelands and their diasporas to maintain close ties is a given, the actual situation should be thoroughly reexamined, for it is often far from idyllic.

In fact, as has been shown here, considerable tension and disputes are common in those relationships, usually because most homeland leaders believe that the raison d'être of their diasporas is to maintain constant contact with the homelands, demonstrate unwavering loyalty, and serve the homelands' purposes in host countries, particularly regarding issues of defense. As long as the relationships between homelands and host countries are friendly, then, despite host-country apprehension about homeland manipulation of diasporas and the networks they create, usually a modus vivendi comfortable for both sides can be found and maintained for relatively long periods. However, amicable relations can be shattered when homelands alter their attitudes and policies toward host countries or toward issues that are important to host countries, and hence to the diasporas living within their borders. In such extreme situations, diasporas can become hostages in host countries or can be expelled.

Close examination of the behavior of homeland governments shows that they tend to develop a rather cynical attitude toward "their" diasporas. Probably no homeland would go so far as to openly sacrifice its diaspora in order to promote its own interests, but in most cases of conflict between the needs of homelands and the needs of diasporas, the choice is clear: Homeland security and economic interests come first. Only when such interests are secured will homeland leaders consider involvement in disputes on behalf of their diasporas, which in the interim can find themselves in no small distress. Thus, whereas homeland governments tend to have no qualms about exploiting their diasporas nor about trying to mobilize them for clandestine activities that can affect the security of host countries, they tend to be highly reluctant to engage in open international confrontations on behalf of their diasporas. When homelands have been dragged into situations in which they have had to protect their diasporas, even then they have shown great reluctance to do so and have tried to defuse situations that might escalate into serious conflict with host countries. Again, because of the existing rosy perceptions and lack of information about those aspects, these sensitive issues should be probed further.

Finally, there is a need for additional studies of the embryonic development of pan-ethnic trans-national (rather than trans-state) diasporas, such as the Asian-American, Latino, Arab-American, Muslim, and North

African. Although for the time being that is mainly an American and European Union phenomenon, it is likely to appear in other host countries and regional unions. Here are the main questions to be addressed: Can such groups be regarded as cohesive ethnic diasporas? Is a common agenda, directed mainly toward the host society and its government, augmented by common cultural traits like language and religious affiliation, sufficient for forming cohesive organized diasporas that are capable of functioning like the diasporas that have been discussed here? That could perhaps emerge as an important development, but because there have been almost no studies of that emerging aspect, there is an urgent need to monitor that process.

Final Notes

Following John Armstrong's observations about the functions that classical diasporas performed in the days of the Hapsburg, Russian, and Ottoman empires, and in view of the existence of their current transstate networks and connections, it is to be strongly emphasized that contemporary diasporas can serve as effective mediators between states, especially between their homelands and host countries. Under certain circumstances, such ethnic communities, which often are portrayed by rightist, racist, and ultranationalist politicians and laypeople as predisposed to disruption and conflict, rather can facilitate peaceful cultural, political, trade, and commercial exchanges that can accord with the conceptions underlying the hope for a new world order.

Scholarly work is in progress on the various issues that have been mentioned or discussed here. It is hoped that those who are studying or will study ethno-national diasporas will be challenged by the long and rich agenda of definitional, theoretical, analytical, and comparative issues discussed here, and especially by the main points of this book: that ethno-national diasporism is not a modern phenomenon, but rather an ancient and enduring phenomenon. Essential aspects of the phenomenon are the endless cultural, social, economic, and especially political struggles of those dispersed but organized ethno-national groups to maintain their distinctive identities and connections with their homelands and with other dispersed co-ethnics. Diasporas are neither "imagined" or "invented" communities. Their identities are combinations of primordial, psychological/symbolic, and instrumental elements. They struggle for survival and continuity even as they do their utmost to feel at home abroad, that is, at home in their host countries, which in many instances are quite hostile toward them. Moreover, they survive despite their home-lands' inherent ambiguity toward them.

Further serious explorations of the issues that have been discussed here will be needed for our further understanding of the role of ethno-national diasporas as precursors of globalized political systems that certainly will occupy center stage in the world of the twenty-first century.

References

Ages, A. 1973. *The Diaspora Dimension.* The Hague: Martinus Nijhoff.

Aguirre, A., and J. Turner. 1995. *American Ethnicity. The Dynamics and Consequences of Discrimination.* New York: McGraw-Hill.

Alba, R. 1995. Assimilation's Quiet Tide. *The Public Interest* 119(Spring):3–18.

Ali, N. 1999. Virtually Kashmiris: The Emergence Discourse of Kashmiriyat. Paper presented at the Conference on Nationalism, Identity and Minority Rights, University of Bristol, September 16–19.

Amjad, R., ed. 1989. *To the Gulf and Back: Studies on the Economic Impact of Asian Labor Migration.* New Delhi: UN Development Program.

Anand, D. 1999. (Re)imag(in)ing the "Nation": Tensions within Tibetan Nationalism. Paper presented at the Conference on Nationalism, Identity and Minority Rights, University of Bristol, September 16–19.

Anderson, B. 1991. *Imagined Communities: Reflections on the Origins and Spread of Nationalism.* London: Verso.

——— 1992. Long Distance Nationalism: World Capitalism and the Rise of Identity Politics. The Werthem Lecture 1992, University of Amsterdam, Center for South Asian Studies.

——— 1994. Exodus. *Critical Enquiry* 20(2):314–27.

Anderson, J. 2000. The Internet's Two Histories and Role of the Diaspora in Bringing Arabia Online. Paper presented at the Inaugural MEVIC Online Conference. August.

Angoustures, A., and V. Pascal. 1996. Diasporas et Financement des Conflits. In: J. Rufin and J. C. Rufin, eds., *Economie des Guerres Civiles,* pp. 495–8. Paris: Hachette.

Anthias, F. 1998. Evaluating "Diaspora": Beyond Ethnicity. *Sociology* 32(3): 557–80.

Armstrong, J. 1976. Mobilized and Proletarian Diasporas. *American Political Science Review* 70(2):393–408.

——— 1982. *Nations before Nationalism.* Chapel Hill: University of North Carolina Press.

1995. Toward a Theory of Nationalism: Consensus and Dissensus. In: S. Periwal, ed., *Nations and Nationalism*, pp. 34–43. Budapest: Central University Press.

Avi-Yonah, M. 1981. *Art in Ancient Palestine.* Jerusalem: Magnes Press.

Bakalian, A. 1993. *Armenian Americans: From Being to Being American.* New Brunswick, NJ: Transaction Publications.

Bandhauer, C. 1999. A Global Socio-historical Look at Anti-immigrant Sentiment in California. Paper presented at a conference on Nationalism, Identity and Minority Rights, University of Bristol, September 16–19.

Banton, M. 1994. Modeling Ethnic and National Relations. *Ethnic and Racial Studies* 17(1):1–19.

Barghouti, I. 1988. *Palestinian Americans: Socio-political Attitudes of Palestinian Americans towards the Arab–Israeli Conflict.* Occasional Papers, series 38, pp. 4–35. Center for Middle Eastern and Islamic Studies, University of Durham.

Baron, S. 1964. *The Russian Jew under the Tsars and Soviets.* New York: Macmillan.

Bar-Tal, D. 1993. Patriotism as Fundamental Beliefs of Group Members. *Politics and the Individual* 3:45–62.

Barth, F. 1969. *Ethnic Groups and Boundaries*, pp. 9–38. Boston: Little, Brown.

Basch, L., N. Glick Schiller, and C. Szanton Blanc. 1994. *Nations Unbound: Transnational Projects, Postcolonial Predicaments and Deterritorialized Nation-States.* Amsterdam: Gordon & Breach.

Baubock, R., A. Heller, and A. Zolberg, eds. 1996. *The Challenge of Diversity: Integration and Pluralism in Societies of Immigrants.* Aldershot, Hants.: Avebury.

Beilin, Y. 1999. *The Death of the American Uncle.* Tel Aviv: Yediot Ahronot (Hebrew).

Ben Sasson, H. 1969. Introduction. In: H. Ben Sasson, ed., *History of the Jewish People*, pp. xi–xxx. Tel Aviv: Dvir (Hebrew).

Bernstein, A. 1993. Ethnicity and Imperial Break-up: Ancient and Modern. *SAIS Review* 13(1):78–95.

Bertelsen, J. 1980. *Non-State Nations in International Politics.* New York: Praeger.

Bilsborrow, R. E., and H. Zlotnik. 1995. The Systems Approach and the Measurement of the Determinants of International Migration. In: R. Van der Erf and L. Heering, eds., *Causes of International Migration*, pp. 61–76. Luxembourg: Office for Official Publications of the European Communities.

Blaschke, J. 1995. New Racism in Germany. In: D. Jolly, ed., *Scapegoats and Social Actors*, pp. 55–86. London: Macmillan.

Blitzer, W. 1988. *Territory of Lies.* New York: Harper & Row.

Bodryte, D. 1999. Today's Politics and Yesterday's Embitterments: Ethnic Restructuring and Its Aftermath in the Baltic States. Paper presented at a conference on Diasporas and Ethnic Migrants in 20th Century Europe, Humboldt University, May 20–3.

Bookbinder, H. 1988. *American Jews and Israel after the Pollard Affair.* In: W. Frankel, ed., *Survey of Jewish Affairs*, pp. 120–37. Cranberry, NJ: Associated Universities Press.

Bournoutian, G. 1994. *A History of the Armenian People. Vol. 2: 1500 A.D. to the Present*. Costa Mesa, CA: Mazda.

Boyarin, J. 1995. Powers of Diaspora. Paper presented to a panel on diasporas at the International Congress of Historical Sciences, Montreal.

Brand, L. 1988. *Palestinians in the Arab World, Institution Building and the Search for State*. New York: Columbia University Press.

Brandt, B. 1999. Agents of Change: Young Berliners of Turkish Origin and the Politics of Citizenship. Paper presented at a conference on Nationalism, Identity and Minority Rights, University of Bristol, September 16–19.

Brass, P. 1991. *Ethnicity and Nationalism*. London: Sage.

Brown, M., ed. 1993. *Ethnic Conflict and International Security*. Princeton, NJ: Princeton University Press.

  ed. 1996. *The International Dimensions of Internal Conflict*, pp. 1–31. Cambridge, MA: MIT Press.

Brubaker, R. 1996. *Nationalism Reframed: Nationhood and the National Question in the New Europe*. Cambridge University Press.

  1999. Accidental Diasporas and External "Homelands" in Europe Past and Present. Paper presented at a conference on Diasporas and Ethnic Migrants in 20th Century Europe, Humboldt University, May 20–3.

Brubaker, W., ed. 1989. *Immigration and the Politics of Citizenship in Europe and North America*. Lanham, MD: Universities Press of America.

Bruneau, M., ed. 1998. *Les Grecs Pontiques, Diaspora, Identité, Territoires*. Paris: CNRS Editions.

Brunn, S. 1981. Geopolitics in a Shrinking World. In: A. Burnett and P. Taylor, eds., *Political Studies from Spatial Perspective: Anglo-American Essays in Political Geography*, pp. 131–56. New York: Wiley.

  1996.The Internationalization of Diasporas in a Shrinking World. In: G. Prevlakis, ed., *The Networks of Diasporas*, pp. 259–72. Nicosia: Cyprus Research Center.

Brunn, S., and J. Jones. 1994. Geopolitical Information and Communication in Shrinking and Expanding Worlds. In: G. Demko and W. Wood, eds., *Reordering the World: Geopolitical Perspectives on the 21st Century*. Boulder, CO: Westview Press.

Brunn, S., and T. Leinbach. 1991. *Collapsing Space and Information*. New York: Harper Collins.

Buzan, B. 1992. Introduction: The Changing Security Agenda in Europe. In: W. Olem, B. Buzan, M. Kelstrup, and P. Lemaiter, eds., *Identity, Migration and the Security Agenda in Europe*, pp. 1–14. New York: St. Martin's Press.

Caesarani, D., and M. Fulbrook, eds. 1996. Introduction. In: *Citizenship, Nationality and Migration in Europe*. London: Routledge.

Caglar, A. 1997. Hyphenated Identities and the Limits of Culture. In: T. Modood and P. Werbner, eds., *The Politics of Multiculturalism in New Europe: Racism, Identity and Community*, pp. 169–85. London: Zed Books.

Campani, J. 1992. L'exemple de la Diaspora Italienne. *Information sur les Sciences Sociales* 31(2):333–54.

  2000. Trafficking for Sexual Exploitation and the Sex Business in the New Context of International Migration: The Case of Italy. *South European Society and Politics* 230–61.

Cannistraro, P., and R. Gianfausto. 1979. Fascist Emigration Policy in the 1920s: An Interpretative Framework. *International Migration Review* 13(4): 673–92.

Cappai, G. 1999. Migration, Association and Communication. The Case of the Sardinian Diaspora. Paper presented at the Workshop on Virtual Diasporas. Heidelberg, October.

Castells, M. 1996. *The Rise of the Network Society.* Oxford: Blackwell.

Castles, S., and M. Miller, eds. 1993. *The Age of Migration: International Population Movements in the Modern World.* London: Macmillan.

Cavalli-Sforza, L., and F. Cavalli-Sforza. 1995. *The Great Human Diasporas. The History of Diversity and Evolution.* Reading, MA: Addison-Wesley.

Chaliand, G., and J. P. Rageau. 1995. *The Penguin Atlas of Diasporas.* New York: Viking.

Chapin, W. 1996. The Turkish Diaspora in Germany. *Diaspora* 5(2):275–302.

Chapman, M. 1993. Social and Biological Aspects of Ethnicity. In: M. Chapman, ed., *Social and Biological Aspects of Ethnicity*, pp. 1–46. Oxford University Press.

Chazan, N., ed. 1991. *Irredentism.* Boulder, CO: Lynne Rienner.

Chipman, J. 1993. Managing the Politics of Parochialism. *Survival* 35(1): 143–72.

Citrin, J. 1990. Language, Politics and American Identity. *The Public Interest* 99:96–109.

Citrin, J., E. Haas, C. Muste, and B. Reingold. 1994. Is American Nationalism Changing? Implications for Foreign Policy. *International Studies Quarterly* 38:1–31.

Clifford, J. 1992. Traveling Cultures. In: L. Grossberg, C. Nelson, and P. Treicher, eds., *Cultural Centers*, pp. 96–116. London: Routledge.

1994. Diasporas. *Cultural Anthropology* 9(3):302–38.

Cohen, A. 1969. *Custom and Politics in Urban Africa.* Berkeley: University of California Press.

Cohen, E. 1990. The Future of Force. *The National Interest* 21(Fall):3–15.

Cohen, R. 1989. Citizens, Denizens and Helots: The Politics of International Migration Flows in the Post-War World. *Journal of Social Studies* 21(1): 153–65.

1997. *Global Diasporas.* London: UCL Press.

Cohen, S. 1995. Jewish Continuity over Judaic Content: The Moderately Affiliated American Jew. In: R. Seltzer and N. Cohen, eds., *The Americanization of the Jews*, pp. 395–416. New York University Press.

1998. *Religious Stability and Ethnic Decline: Emerging Patterns of Jewish Identity in the United States.* New York: Florence G. Heller, JCC Association Research Center.

Cohen, Y. 1990. The Arab–Israeli Conflict and the Emigration from Israel. *Megamot* 32(4):35–52 (Hebrew).

Comparative Documentation Project. 2001. *Citizens Organize Networks against Discrimination in Birmingham, Paris, Milan and Berlin.* Berlin: Edition Parabolis.

Connor, W. 1973. The Politics of Ethnonationalism. *Journal of International Affairs* 27(January):1–21.

1978. A Nation Is a Nation, Is a State, Is an Ethnic Group. *Ethnic and Racial Studies* 1(4):378–400.

1986. The Impact of Homelands on Diasporas. In: G. Sheffer, ed., *Modern Diasporas in International Politics*, pp. 16–45. London: Croom Helm.

1990. When Is a Nation? *Ethnic and Racial Studies* 13(1):92–103.

1993a. Beyond Reason: The Nature of the Ethnonational Bond. *Ethnic and Racial Studies* 16(3):373–89.

1993b. Diasporas and the Formation of Foreign Policy: The US in Comparative Perspective. In: D. Constas and A. Platias, eds., *Diasporas in World Politics*, pp. 167–80. London: Macmillan.

1994. *Ethno-nationalism: The Quest for Understanding*. Princeton, NJ: Princeton University Press.

Constas, D., and A. Platias, eds. 1993. *Diasporas in World Politics: The Greeks in Comparative Perspective*. London: Macmillan.

Coulmas, F. 1999. Japan's Minorities, Old and New. Paper presented at a conference on Nationalism, Identity and Minority Rights, University of Bristol, September 16–19.

Crow, D., and J. Kolsti, eds. 1991. *The Gypsies of Eastern Europe*. Armonk, NY: M. E. Sharpe.

Curry, K. 1999. One Scattered Race: Roma Identity and Legal Status in Post–Cold War Eastern Europe. Paper presented at a conference on Nationalism, Identity and Minority Rights, University of Bristol, September 16–19.

Curtin, P. 1984. *Cross-Cultural Trade in World History*. Cambridge University Press.

Dahan, M., and G. Sheffer. 2001. Ethnic Groups and Distance Shrinking Communication Technologies. *Nationalism and Ethnic Politics* 7(1):85–107.

Damian, N. 1987. *Israelis' Public Attitudes Towards the Yerida Phenomenon, Israelis Abroad, and the Policy for Encouraging Them to Return*. Research report. Jerusalem: Ministry of Immigration Absorption.

Darby, J. 1998. Approaches to Cultural Diversity in Northern Ireland. In: M. Crozier and R. Froggat, eds., *Cultural Diversity in Contemporary Europe*, pp. 4–12. Belfast: Institute of Irish Studies.

DeConde, A. 1992. *Ethnicity, Race, and American Foreign Policy: A History*. Boston: Northeastern University Press.

Dekmejian, H., and T. Angelos. 1997. *Ethnic Lobbies in US Foreign Policy*. Occasional Research Paper 13. Athens: Panteion University.

DellaPergola, S. 1992. *New Data on Demographics and Identification among Jews in the US: Trends, Inconsistencies and Disagreements*. Jerusalem: Institute of Contemporary Jewish Studies, The Hebrew University.

Demetriou, M. 1999. Beyond the Nation State? Transnational Politics in the Age of Diaspora. *The ASEN Bulletin* 16:17–25.

Dershowitz, A. 1997. *The Vanishing American Jew*. Boston: Little, Brown.

Diehl, P., and G. Goertz. 1991. Enduring Rivalries: Theoretical Constructs and Empirical Patterns. Paper presented at the annual meeting of the International Studies Association, Vancouver, March 19–23.

Dixon, P. 1976. *Barbarian Europe.* Oxford: Elsevier Phaidon.

Doyle, M. 1986. Liberalism in World Politics. *American Political Science Review* 80(December):1151–69.

Economist. 1994. Irish Americans, The Second Coming. September 17.

Economist. 1999. A Gypsy Awakening. September 11.

Economist. 2000. The New Americans. March 11.

Economist. 2001. Europe's Spectral Nation. May 12, pp. 29–32.

Edmondson, L. 1986. Black America as a Mobilizing Diaspora. In: G. Sheffer, ed., *Modern Diasporas in International Politics*, pp. 164–211. London: Croom Helm.

Elazar, D. 1976. *Community and Polity: The Organizational Dynamics of American Jewry.* Philadelphia: Jewish Publications Society of America.

1986. People and Polity. The Organizational Dynamics of Post-Modern Jewry. In: G. Sheffer, ed., *Modern Diasporas in International Politics*, pp. 212–57. London: Croom Helm.

1995. *Community and Polity.* Philadelphia: Jewish Publications Society of America.

Elazar, D., and P. Medding. 1983. *Jewish Communities in Frontier Societies: Argentina, Australia and South Africa.* New York: Holmes & Meier.

Elazar, D., and S. Trigano. 1998. *How European Jewish Communities Can Choose and Plan Their Own Future.* Jerusalem: World Jewish Congress.

Elkin, J. 1980. *Jews of the Latin American Republics.* Chapel Hill: University of North Carolina Press.

Elkins, D. 1997. Globalization, Telecommunication and Virtual Ethnic Communities. *International Political Science Review* 18(2):139–51.

Eller, J., and R. Coughlan. 1993. The Poverty of Primordialism: The Demystification of Ethnic Attachments. *Ethnic and Racial Studies* 10(2):184–201.

Encyclopaedia Britannica, Book of the Year, 1990, 1991, 1992, 1993, 1994, 1995, 1996, 1997, 1998, 1999.

Enloe, C. 1980. Religion and Ethnicity. In: P. Sugar, ed., *Ethnic Diversity and Conflict in Eastern Europe*, pp. 350–60. Santa Barbara, CA: ABC Clio.

Enneli, P. 1999. Religious and Ethnic Identities of Turkish-Speaking Youth in London. Paper presented at a conference on Nationalism, Identity and Minority Rights, University of Bristol, September 16–19.

Eriksen, T. 1993. *Ethnicity and Nationalism.* London: Pluto Press.

Esman, M. 1986. The Chinese Diaspora in South East Asia. In: G. Sheffer, ed., *Modern Diasporas in International Politics*, pp. 130–63. London: Croom Helm.

1992. The Political Fallout of International Migration. *Diaspora* 2(1):3–41.

1994. *Ethnic Politics.* Ithaca: Cornell University Press.

Faist, T. 2000. *The Volume and Dynamics of International Immigration and Transnational Social Spaces.* Oxford: Clarendon Press.

Finley, M. 1986. *The Use and Abuse of Ancient History.* London: Hogarth Press.

Frankel, J., ed. 1993. *Survey of Jewish Affairs.* Cranberry, NJ: Associated University Press.

Fraser, A. 1992. *The Gypsies.* Oxford University Press.

Friedman, T. 1999. *The Lexus and the Olive Tree*. New York: Farrar, Straus & Giroux.

Fukuyama, F. 1991. The End of History? *The National Interest* 16(Summer): 3–18.

—— 1992. *The End of History and the Last Man*. Tel Aviv: Or Am Publishing House (Hebrew).

Gal, A. 1997. *Envisioning Israel*. Jerusalem: Magnes Press (Hebrew).

Geertz, C. 1963. The Integrative Revolution: Primordial Sentiments and Civil Politics in the New States. In: C. Geertz, ed., *The Interpretation of Culture*, pp. 255–310. London: Fontana.

—— ed. 1973. *Interpretation of Cultures*. London: Fontana.

Gerholm, T., and L. Yngve, eds. 1988. *The New Islamic Presence in Western Europe*. London: Mansell.

Gilroy, P. 1987. *There Ain't No Black in the Union Jack: The Cultural Politics of Race and Nation*. London: Hutchinson.

—— 1993. *The Black Atlantic: Modernity and Double Consciousness*. London: Verso.

—— 1994. Diaspora. *Paragraph* 17(1):207–12.

Glazer, N., and P. Moynihan, eds. 1975. *Ethnicity, Theory and Experience*, pp. 1–26. Cambridge, MA: Harvard University Press.

Glick Schiller, N., L. Basch, and C. Blanc-Szanton. 1992. Toward a Transnational Perspective on Migration. *Annals of the New York Academy of Sciences* 645:1–24.

—— 1995. From Immigrants to Transmigrants; Theorizing Transnational Migration. *Anthropological Quarterly* 68(1):47–62.

Gold, S. 1992. *Refugee Communities: A Comparative Field Study*. Newbery Park, CA: Sage Publications.

—— 1997. Transnationalism and Vocabularies of Motive in International Migration: The Case of Israelis in the United States. *Sociological Perspectives* 40(3):409–27.

Gold, S., and B. Phillips. 1996. Israelis in the United States. *The Jewish Yearbook 1996*, pp. 51–101. New York: American Jewish Committee.

Gorny, A. 2001. Ukrainian Migrants in Poland – Formation of Transnational Community. Paper presented at EURO Summer School 2001, Cecina, Tuscany, July 8–17.

Gottlieb, G. 1993. *Nation Against State: A New Approach to Ethnic Conflicts and the Decline of Sovereignty*. New York: Council on Foreign Relations Press.

Gottmann, J. 1973. *The Significance of Territory*. Charlottesville: University Press of Virginia.

—— 1996. La Généralisation des Diasporas et ses Consequences. In: G. Prevalakis, ed., *The Networks of Diasporas*, pp. 21–8. Nicosia: Cyprus Research Center.

Graham, A. 1983. *Colony and Mother City in Ancient Greece*. Chicago: Ares.

Grosby, S. 1994. The Verdict of History: The Inexpugnable Tie of Primordiality. *Ethnic and Racial Studies* 17(2):164–71.

1995. Territoriality, the Transcendental, Primordial Feature of Modern Societies. *Nations and Nationalism* 1(2):143–62.

1999. The Chosen People of Ancient Israel and the Occident: Why Does Nationality Exist and Survive? *Nations and Nationalism* 5(3):357–80.

Guarnizo, L., and M. Smith. 1998. The Location of Transnationalism. In: P. Smith and L. Guarnizo, eds., *Transnationalism from Below*, pp. 3–34. New Brunswick, NJ: Transaction Publications.

Gurr, T. 1993. *Minorities at Risk*. Washington, DC: United States Institute of Peace Press.

Gurr, T., and B. Harff. 1994. *Ethnic Conflict and World Politics*. Boulder, CO: Westview Press.

Hall, S. 1990. Cultural Identity and Diaspora. In: J. Rutherford, ed., *Identity, Community and Cultural Difference*, pp. 222–37. London: Lawrence & Wishart.

1991. Old and New Identities, Old and New Ethnicities. In: A. King, ed., *Culture, Globalization and the World-System*, pp. 41–68. New York: Macmillan.

Hammar, T. 1990. *Democracy and the Nation State: Aliens, Denizens and Citizens in a World of International Migration*. Aldershot, Hants.: Avebury.

Hammond, P., and W. Kee. 1993. Religion and Ethnicity in Late-Twentieth-Century America. *Annals of the AAPSS* 527(May):55–66.

Handelman, D. 1977. The Organization of Ethnicity. *Ethnic Groups* 1:187–200.

Hanf, T. 1999. Germany on the Threshold to Open Democracy. Paper presented at a conference on Multiculturalism and Democracy in Divided Societies, University of Haifa, March 17–18.

Harik, I. 1986. The Palestinians in the Diaspora. In: G. Sheffer, ed., *Modern Diasporas in International Politics*, pp. 315–32. London: Croom Helm.

Harris, J. 1982. *Global Dimensions of the African Diaspora*. Washington, DC: Howard University Press.

Hechter, M. 1987. *Principles of Group Solidarity*. Berkeley: University of California Press.

1988. Rational Choice Theory and the Study of Ethnic and Race Relations. In: J. Rex and D. Mason, eds., *Theories of Ethnic and State Relations*. Cambridge University Press.

Helmreich, S. 1992. Kinship, Nation, and Paul Gilroy's Concept of Diaspora. *Diaspora* 2(2):243–9.

Helton, A. 1999. What Is Forced Migration? Paper presented at a conference on Diasporas and Ethnic Migrants in 20th Century Europe, Humboldt University, May 20–23.

Helweg, A. 1986. The Indian Diaspora: Influence on International Relations. In: G. Sheffer, ed., *Modern Diasporas in International Politics*, pp. 103–29. London: Croom Helm.

Hjarno, J. 1994. *Preventing Racism at the Workplace in Denmark*. Dublin: European Foundation.

1996. *Racism, Community and Conflict*. Esberg: South Jutland University Press.

Hobsbawm, E. 1990. *Nations and Nationalism since 1780*. Cambridge University Press.

Hoch, M. 1993. *Turkische Politische Organisationen, Der Bundesrepublik Deutschland*, pp. 3–21. Sankt Augustin: Konrad Adenauer Stiftung.

Horak, S. 1985. *Eastern European National Minorities.* Littleton, CO: Libraries Unlimited.

Horowitz, D. 1985. *Ethnic Groups in Conflict.* Berkeley: University of California Press.

1986. Diasporas and Communal Conflicts in Divided Societies. In: G. Sheffer, ed., *Modern Diasporas in International Politics,* pp. 294–315. London: Croom Helm.

Hourani, A., and N. Shehadi, eds. 1992. *The Lebanese in the World: A Century of Emigration.* London: Tauris.

Hovannisian, R. 1993. The Armenian Diaspora and the Narrative of Power. In: D. Constas and A. Platias, eds., *Diasporas in World Politics,* pp. 183–202. London: Macmillan.

ed. 1997. *The Armenian People from Ancient Time to Modern Times.* New York: St. Martin's Press.

Hu-Dehart, E. 1993. Rethinking America: The Practice and Politics of Multiculturalism in Higher Education. In: B. Thompson and S. Tyagi, eds., *Beyond a Dream Differed,* pp. 3–17. Minneapolis: University of Minnesota Press.

Hunderson, B. 1988. *Pollard: The Spy's Story.* New York: Alpha.

Huntington, S. 1993. The Clash of Civilizations. *Foreign Affairs* 72(3):22–49.

1997. The Erosion of American National Interest. *Foreign Affairs* 76(5): 28–49.

Hyatt, J. ed. 1964. *The Bible in Modern Scholarship.* Nashville, TN: Abingdon Press.

Ifestos, P. 1993. Ethnic Lobbies and Foreign Policy: The American Experience. Paper presented at the 34th annual convention of the International Studies Association, March 23–27.

Iglesias, E. 2001. Sending a Lot of Money Home. *International Herald Tribune,* July 13.

Iwanska, A. 1981. *Exiled Governments: Spanish and Polish.* Cambridge, MA: Schenkman.

Jarkoa, L. 2000. Gypsies and the European Union. Paper presented at the EUROFOR Conference on Ethnic Radicalization, Jerusalem, January 15–17.

Jerusalem Post, Magazine, September 1, 2000.

Johnson, P. 1988. *A History of the Jews.* New York: Harper Perennial.

Kaufman, M. 1996. Envisioning Israel: The Case of the United Jewish Appeal. In: A. Gal, ed., *Envisioning Israel: The Changing Ideals of North American Jews,* pp. 219–53. Jerusalem: Magnes Press.

Kearney, M. 1995. The Local and the Global. *Annual Review of Anthropology* 24:547–65.

Keely, C., and B. Tran. 1985. Remittances from Labor Migration. *International Migration Review* 23:500–25.

Kellas, J. 1991. *The Politics of Nationalism and Ethnicity.* New York: St. Martin's Press.

Kettani, A. 1986. *Muslim Minorities in the World Today.* London: Mansell.

King, A. 1999. Rhodesians in Hyperspace: The Maintenance of a National and Cultural Identity. Paper presented at a conference on Nationalism, Identity and Minority Rights, University of Bristol, September 16–19.

Kolsto, P. 1993. The New Russian Diaspora: Minority Protection in the Soviet Successor States. *Journal of Peace Research* 30(2):197–217.

1996. The New Russian Diaspora – An Identity of Its Own. *Ethnic and Racial Studies* 19(3):609–39.

Kosmin, B., et al. 1991. *Highlights of the CJF Jewish Population Survey*. New York: Council of Jewish Federations.

1999. Old and New World Diasporas: Similar Problems, but Different Solutions? In: I. Troen, ed., *Jewish Centers and Peripheries*, pp. 337–54. New Brunswick, NJ: Transactions Publishers.

Kotkin, J. 1992. *Tribes: How Race, Religion, and Identity Determine Success in the New Global Economy*. New York: Random House.

Kotler-Berkowitz, L. 1997. Ethnic Cohesion and Division among American Jews: The Role of Mass-Level and Organizational Politics. Unpublished paper.

Krau, E. 1991. *The Contradictory Immigrant Problem: A Psychological Analysis*. New York: Peter Lang.

Kumaraswamy, P. 1996. The Politics of Pardon: Israel and Johnathan Pollard. *Administrative Science Quarterly* 18(3):17–35.

Landau, J. 1986. Diaspora and Language. In: G. Sheffer, ed., *Modern Diasporas in International Politics*, pp. 75–102. London: Croom Helm.

1995. *Pan-Turkism: From Irredentism to Cooperation*. London: C. Hurst & Co.

2001. Diaspora Nationalism. In: A. Leoussi, ed., *Encyclopedia of Nationalism*, pp. 46–50. New Brunswick, NJ: Transactions Publishers.

La Porte, T. 1975. *Organized Social Complexity: Challenge to Politics and Policy*. Princeton, NJ: Princeton University Press.

Lesch, A. 1994. Palestinians in Kuwait. *Journal of Palestine Studies* 20(4):42–54.

Levine, I., and A. Mazar. 2001. *The Debate over the Historical Truth in the Old Testament*. Jerusalem: Yad Ben Zvi (Hebrew).

Liebman, C. 1977. *Pressure without Sanctions*. Rutherford, NJ: Fairleigh Dickinson University Press.

Liegeois, J. 1994. *Roma, Gypsies, Travelers*. Strasbourg: Council of Europe.

Lindemann, A. 1993. *The Jew Accused: Three Anti-Semitic Affairs*. Cambridge University Press.

Lloyd-Jones, H. 1965. *The Greek World*. Harmondsworth: Penguin.

McLaren, J. 1999. Citizenship in the Former Soviet Union – Ethnic Minorities and Political Communities. Paper presented at a conference on Diasporas and Ethnic Migrants in 20th Century Europe, Berlin, Humboldt University.

Magnifico, L. 1988. *Contemporary American Immigrants: Patterns of Filipino, Korean and Chinese Settlement in the United States*. New York: Praeger.

Malamat, A. 1969. The Beginning of the Nation. In: H. Ben Sasson, ed., *History of the Jewish People*, vol. 1, pp. 9–90. Tel Aviv: Dvir (Hebrew).

Malone, D. 1997. Haiti and the International Community. *Survival* 39(2):126–46.

Maoz, Z., and N. Abdolali. 1989. Regime Type and International Conflict, 1816–1976. *Journal of Conflict Resolution* 29(1):3–35.

Maoz, Z., and B. Russet. 1992a. Alliances, Contiguity, Wealth, and Political Stability: Is the Lack of Conflict between Democracies a Statistical Artifact? *International Interactions* 17(4):245–67.

1992b. Normative and Structural Causes of Democratic Peace, 1946–1986. Paper presented at the 33rd annual meeting of the International Studies Association, Atlanta, GA, March 31–April 4.

Margalit, G. 1996. Antigypsyism in the Political Culture of the Federal Republic of Germany: A Parallel with Antisemitism? Jerusalem: The Vidal Sassoon International Center for the Study of Antisemitism, The Hebrew University of Jerusalem. *Acta* 9:1–29.

Marienstras, R. 1989. On the Notion of Diasporas. In: G. Chaliand, ed., *Minority People in the Age of Nation States.* London: Pluto Press.

Marrus, M. 1980. *The Politics of Assimilation: The French Jewish Community at the Time of the Dreyfus Affair.* Oxford University Press.

Meadwell, H. 1989. Cultural and Instrumental Approaches to Ethnic Nationalism. *Ethnic and Racial Studies* 12(3):309–28.

Mele, C. 2000. Cyberspace and Disadvantaged Communities: The Internet as a Tool of Collective Action. In: M. Smith and P. Kollock, eds., *Communities in Cyberspace*, pp. 290–310. London: Routledge.

Miles, W., and G. Sheffer. 1998. Francophonie and Zionism: A Comparative Study of Transnationalism and Trans-statism. *Diaspora* 7(2):119–48.

Miller, M. 1981. *Foreign Workers in Europe: An Emerging Political Force.* New York: Praeger.

Mirga, A., and N. Gheorghe. 1997. The Roma in the Twenty-first Century: A Policy Paper. Princeton University Project on Ethnic Relations.

Misztal, B. 1990. The Polish-American Lobby: Past and Present. Paper presented at a conference on The Greek Diaspora in Foreign Policy, Panthios University, Athens, May.

Mitchell, K. 1997. Transnational Discourse: Bringing Geography Back In. *Antipode* 29:101–14.

Moneni, J. 1984. *Demography of Racial and Ethnic Minorities in the United States.* New York: Greenwood Press.

Montville, J., ed. 1991. *Conflict and Peacemaking in Multi-ethnic Societies.* Lexington, MA: Lexington Books.

Moscati, S. 1957. *Ancient Semitic Civilizations*, ch. 8. London: Elks Book.

Motyl, A., ed. 1992. *Thinking Theoretically about Soviet Nationalism.* New York: Columbia University Press.

Nasreen, A. 1999. Virtually Kashmiris: The Emerging Discourse of "Kashmiriyat." Paper presented at the Nationalism, Identity and Minority Rights Conference, University of Bristol, September 16–19.

Newman, S. 1991. Does Modernization Breed Ethnic Political Conflict? *World Politics* 43(3):453–78.

New York Times. 1992. The Emigres Lend a Hand to Homeland. April 22.

Nye, J. 1993. The Self Determination Trap. *The Washington Post*, May 2.

Owen, R. 1985. *Migrant Workers in the Gulf.* London: Minority Rights Group.

Panossian, R. 1998. Between Ambivalence and Intrusion: Politics and Identity in Armenia-Diaspora Relations. *Diaspora* 7(2):149–96.

Papastriyadis, N. 1997. Tracing Hybridity Theory. In: P. Werbner and T. Modood, eds., *Debating Cultural Hybridity*, pp. 257–82. London: Zed.

Parfit, M. 1998. Human Migration. *National Geographic* 4:6–35.

Patterson, O. 1975. Context and Choice in Ethnic Allegiance. In: N. Glazer and D. P. Moynihan, eds., *Ethnicity: Theory and Experience*, pp. 305–49. Cambridge, MA: Harvard University Press.

Pattie, S. 1994. At Home in Diaspora: Armenians in America. *Diaspora* 3:185–98.

Pedraz-Bailey, S. 1985. *Political and Economic Migrants in America: Cubans and Mexicans.* Austin: University of Texas Press.

Pienkos, D. 1991. *For Your Freedom Through Ours. Efforts on Poland's Behalf.* Boulder, CO: East European Press.

Pinkus, B. 1993. *National Rebirth and Reestablishment: Zionism and the Zionist Movement in the Soviet Union.* Sede Boker: The Ben-Gurion Research Center (Hebrew).

    1999. *The End of an Era: Soviet Jews in Gorbachev's Years, 1985–1991.* Sede Boker: The Ben-Gurion Research Center (Hebrew).

Posen, B. 1993. The Security Dilemma and Ethnic Conflict. *Survival* 35(1):27–47.

Prevalakis, G. 1998. *Les Grandes Metropoles Comme Carrefour des Diasporas,* no. 8. Paris: Institut National de la Recherche Scientifique.

Prunier, G. 1995. *The Rwanda Crisis 1959–1994: A History of a Genocide.* London: Hurst.

    1997. The Great Lakes Crisis. *Current History* 96(610):193–9.

Raphael, M. 1982. *A History of the UJA, 1939–1982.* Providence, RI: Scholars Press.

Rex, J. 2000. Communities, Diasporas and Multiculturalism. Paper presented at a conference on Migration and Ethnic Relations, Athens, May 25–30.

Rodrigues, G. 1995. From New Comers to New Americans. Paper presented at a national immigration forum, New York.

Rogers, R. 1993. Western European Responses to Migration. In: M. Weiner, ed., *International Migration and Security*, pp. 107–48. Boulder, CO: Westview Press.

Rogowski, R. 1985. Causes and Varieties of Nationalism: A Rationalist Account. In: E. Tiryakin and R. Rogowski, eds., *New Nationalisms of the Developed West; Toward Explanation.* Boston: Allen & Unwin.

Rollins, B. 1995. Some Versions of US Internationalism. *Social Texts* (Winter): 97–123.

Rothstein, R. 1992. Democracy and Conflict. Paper presented at a conference on Democracy, War and Peace, Center for International Studies, University of Wisconsin–Milwaukee, April.

Rubchack, M. 1992. God Made Me Lithuanian: Nationalist Ideology and Construction of a North American Diaspora. *Diaspora* 2(1):117–30.

Ruggie, J. 1997. The Past as Prologue? Interests, Identity, and American Foreign Policy. *International Security* 21(4):89–125.

Russel, S., and M. Teitelbaum. 1992. *International Migration and International Trade*. World Bank discussion paper 160. Washington, DC: World Bank.

Rutland, S. 1997. *Edge of Diaspora. Two Centuries of Jewish Settlement in Australia*. Sydney: Brandt & Schlesinger.

Sachar, H. 1985. *Diaspora: An Inquiry into the Contemporary Jewish World*. New York: Harper & Row.

Sacks, J. 1994. *Will We Have Jewish Children?* Ilford, U.K.: Vallentine Mitchell.

Safran, W. 1991. Diasporas in Modern Societies. *Diaspora* 1(1):83–99.

——— 1999. Comparing Diasporas: A Review Essay. *Diaspora* 8(3):255–92.

Sassen-Koob, S. 1990. *The Global City*. Princeton, NJ: Princeton University Press.

Scheff, J., and D. Hernandez. 1993. Rethinking Migration: Having Roots in Two Worlds. Paper presented at a conference on Immigrant Absorption, Technion, Israel Institute of Technology, May 30–June 2.

Schmeltz, U., and S. DellaPergola. 1995. World Jewish Population, 1993. In: *American Jewish Yearbook*. New York: The American Jewish Committee.

Schnapper, D. 1999. From the Nation State to Transnational World: On the Meaning and Usefulness of Diaspora as a Concept. *Diaspora* 8(3):225–52.

Scholte, J. 1996. Globalization and Collective Identities. In: J. Krause and N. Renwickl, eds., *Identities in International Relations*, pp. 38–78. London: Macmillan.

Scott, G. 1990. A Resynthesis of the Primordial and Circumstantial Approaches to Ethnic Group Solidarity: Towards an Explanatory Model. *Ethnic and Racial Studies* 13(2):148–71.

Segal, A. 1993. *An Atlas of International Migration*, pp. 84–106. London: Hans Zell Publishers.

Seliger, M. 1970. Fundamental and Operative Ideology: The Two Principal Dimensions of Political Argumentation. *Policy Science* 1(3):325–38.

Sen, F. 1999. A Test for the German Democracy: Incorporation of Immigrants in the Society. Paper presented at a conference on Multiculturalism and Democracy in Divided Societies, Haifa University, March 17–18.

Seton-Watson, H. 1977. *Nations and States*. Boulder, CO: Westview Press.

Shain, Y., ed. 1989. *The Frontiers of Loyalty: Political Exiles in the Age of the Nation-State*. Middletown, CT: Wesleyan University Press.

——— 1999. *Marketing the American Dream Abroad. Diasporas in the U.S. and Their Homelands*. Cambridge University Press.

Sheffer, G., ed. 1986a. *Modern Diasporas in International Politics*. London: Croom Helm.

——— 1986b. A New Field of Study: Modern Diasporas in International Politics. In: G. Sheffer, ed., *Modern Diasporas in International Politics*, pp. 1–15. London: Croom Helm.

——— 1986c. Fund Raising for Israel. In: G. Sheffer, ed., *Modern Diasporas in International Politics*, pp. 258–93. London: Croom Helm.

——— 1988. The Elusive Question: Jews and Jewry in Israeli Foreign Policy. *Jerusalem Quarterly* 46:104–14.

1991. Ethnic Diasporas: A Threat to Their Hosts? Paper presented at a conference on the Impact of International Migration on the Security and Stability of States, MIT Center for International Studies, December 5–6.

1993a. Ethnic Diasporas: A Threat to Their Hosts? In: M. Weiner, ed., *International Migration and Security*, pp. 263–86. Boulder, CO: Westview Press.

1993b. Jewry, Jews and Israeli Foreign Policy: A Critical Perspective. In: D. Constas and A. Platias, eds., *Diasporas in World Politics: The Greeks in Comparative Perspective*, pp. 203–29. London: Macmillan.

1994. Ethno-national Diasporas and Security. *Survival* 36(1):60–79.

1996. Israel Diaspora Relations in Comparative Perspective. In: M. Barnett, ed., *Israel in Comparative Perspective*. Albany, NY: SUNY Press.

1998. The Israeli Diaspora. In: *The Jewish Yearbook*, pp. xix–xxxii. London: Vallentine Mitchell.

1999. From Israeli Hegemony to Diaspora Full Autonomy: The Current State of Ethno-national Diasporism and the Alternatives Facing World Jewry. In: I. Troen, ed., *Jewish Centers and Peripheries. European Jewry between America and Israel Fifty Years after World War II*, pp. 29–40. New Brunswick, NJ: Transactions Publishers.

Shepperson, G. 1993. African Diaspora: Concept and Text. In: J. Harris, ed., *Global Dimensions of the African Diaspora*, pp. 41–9. Washington, DC: Howard University Press.

Shuval, J. 2000. Diaspora Migration: Definitional Ambiguities and a Theoretical Paradigm. *International Migration* 38(5):41–57.

Sicron, M. 1998. Demography of a Wave of Immigration. In: M. Sicron and E. Leshem, eds., *Profile of an Immigration Wave*, pp. 13–40. Jerusalem: Magnes Press (Hebrew).

Singh, D. 1999. *The Sikh Diaspora*. London: UCL Press.

Skinner, E. 1993. The Dialectics between Diasporas and Homelands. In: J. Harris, ed., *Global Dimensions of the African Diaspora*, pp. 11–40. Washington, DC: Howard University Press.

Skribs, Z. 1999. *Long-Distance Nationalism. Diasporas, Homelands and Identities*. Aldershot, Hants.: Ashgate.

Slevin, J. 2000. *The Internet and Society*. Oxford: Polity Press.

Smith, A. 1973. Nationalism, a Trend Report and an Annotated Bibliography. *Current Sociology* 21(3):1–178.

1981. *The Ethnic Revival in the Modern World*. Cambridge University Press.

1983. *Theories of Nationalism*. London: Duckworth.

1986. *The Ethnic Origins of Nations*. London: Blackwell.

1989. The Origins of Nations. *Ethnic and Racial Studies* 12(3):340–67.

1992. Chosen Peoples: Why Ethnic Groups Survived. *Ethnic and Racial Studies* 15(3):436–56.

1993. The Ethnic Sources of Nationalism. *Survival* 35(1):48–62.

1994. The Problem of National Identity: Ancient, Medieval and Modern? *Ethnic and Racial Studies* 17(3):375–99.

1998. *Nationalism and Modernism*. London: Routledge.

1999. Ethnic Election and National Destiny: Some Religious Origins of Nationalist Ideals. *Nations and Nationalism* 5(3):331–56.

Smooha, S. 1998. Ethnic Democracy, Israel as an Archetype. *Israel Studies* 2(2):198–241.

Sobel, Z. 1990. *Migration from the Promised Land*. Tel Aviv: Am Oved (Hebrew).

Sowell, T. 1996. *Migrations and Cultures. A World View*. New York: Basic Books.

Soyer, J. 1997. *Jewish Immigrant Associations and American Identity in New York, 1880–1939*. Cambridge, MA: Harvard University Press.

Soysal, Y. 1996. Changing Citizenship in Europe: Remarks on Postnational Membership and the National State. In: D. Caesarani and M. Fulbrook, eds., *Citizenship, Nationality and Migration in Europe*. London: Routledge.

Stock, E. 1987. *Partners and Powerstrings*. Lanham, MD: University Press of America.

Stock, J. 1981. Ethnic Groups as Emerging Transnational Actors. In: J. Stock, ed., *Ethnic Identities in a Transnational World*, pp. 17–45. Westport, CT: Greenwood Press.

Tadmor, H. 1969. The Days of the First Temple and the Return. In: H. Ben Sasson, ed., *History of the Jewish People*, pp. 93–173. Tel Aviv: Dvir (Hebrew).

Teveth, S. 1996. *Ben Gurion's Spy*. New York: Columbia University Press.

Ther, P. 1999. A Century of Ethnic Cleansing: Forced Migration in Europe 1912–1995. Paper presented at a conference on Diasporas and Ethnic Migrants in 20th Century Europe, Berlin, Humboldt University, May 20–23.

Tinker, H. 1977. *The Banyan Tree: Overseas Emigrants from India, Pakistan and Bangladesh*. Oxford University Press.

Tololyan, K. 1991. Exile Governments in the American Polity. In: Y. Shain, ed., *Governments in Exile in Contemporary World Politics*, pp. 167–87. London: Routledge.

1994. The Impact of Diasporas on US Foreign Policy. In: R. Pfalzgraff and R. Shultz, eds., *Ethnic Conflict and Regional Instability: Implications for U.S. Policy and Army Roles and Missions*, pp. 147–60. Washington, DC: U.S. Army.

1995. National Self-determination and the Limits of Sovereignty: Armenia, Ajerbaijan and the Secession of Nagorno-Karabagh. *Nationalism and Ethnic Politics* 1(1):86–110.

1996. Rethinking Diaspora(s): Stateless Power in the Transnational Moment. *Diaspora* 5(2):3–36.

van Alstyne, M., and E. Brynjolfsson. 1996. Electronic Villages or Global Balkans. Paper presented at the International Conference on Information Systems. December. Available online at *www.si.umich.edu*.

van Amersfoort, H., and R. Penninx. 1994. Regulating Migration in Europe: The Dutch Experience 1962–92. *Annals of the American Academy of Political and Social Science* 534:133–46.

1996. Migration and the Limits of Governmental Control. *New Communities* 22(2):243–57.

Van den Berghe, P. 1988. Ethnicity and the Sociobiological Debate. In: J. Rex and D. Mason, eds., *Theories of Race and Ethnic Relations*, pp. 246–63. Cambridge University Press.

1999. Multicultural Democracy: Can It Work? Paper presented at a conference on Multiculturalism and Democracy in Divided Societies, Haifa University, March 17–18.

Van Evera, S. 1994. Hypotheses on Nationalism and War. *International Security* 18(4):5–39.

Van Hear, N. 1993. Mass Flight in the Middle East: Involuntary Immigration and the Gulf Conflict 1990–1991. In: R. Black and V. Rodinson, eds., *Geography and Refugees: Patterns and Processes of Change*, pp. 64–83. London: Belhaven.

1998. *New Diasporas*. London: UCL Press.

Vertovec, S. 1997. Three Meanings of Diaspora. *Diaspora* 6(3):277–97.

Vishnevsky, A. 1999. The Dissolution of the Soviet Union, Ethnic Migration and the Problem of Diasporas. Paper presented at a conference on Diasporas and Ethnic Migration in 20th Century Europe, Berlin, Humboldt University, May 20–23.

Vital, D. 1990. *The Future of the Jews*. Cambridge, MA: Harvard University Press.

United Nations. 1985. *Demographic Yearbook*. New York: United Nations.

Wahlbeck, O. 1998. *Kurdish Diasporas*. New York: St. Martin's Press.

Walzer, M., et al. 1982. *The Politics of Ethnicity*. Cambridge, MA: Harvard University Press.

Wasserstein, B. 1996. *Vanishing Diaspora: The Jewish Europe since 1945*. Cambridge, MA: Harvard University Press.

Watanabe, P. 1993. Ethnicity and Foreign Policy: Greek-American Activism and the Turkish Arms Ban. In: D. Constas and A. Platias, eds., *Diasporas in World Politics, The Greeks in Comparative Perspective*, pp. 31–50. London: Macmillan.

Weidacher, A. 1999. Greek, Italian and Turkish Young Adults in Germany. Political Orientations: Adjustment or Identity Claims. Paper presented at a conference on Nationalism, Identity and Minority Rights, Bristol University, September 16–19.

Weiner, M. 1986. Labor Migrations as Incipient Diasporas. In: G. Sheffer, ed., *Modern Diasporas in International Politics*, pp. 47–74. London: Croom Helm.

1990. *Security, Stability and International Migration*. Boston, MA: MIT Center for International Studies.

1991. *The Impact of Nationalism, Ethnicity and Religion on International Conflict*. Boston, MA: MIT Center for International Studies.

1993. The Politics of Immigrant Absorption: A Comparative Perspective. Paper presented at a conference on Immigrant Absorption, Technion, Israel Institute of Technology, May 30–June 2.

Werbner, P. 1997. The Dialectics of Cultural Hybridity. In: P. Werbner and T. Modod, eds., *Debating Cultural Hybridity*, pp. 1–26. London: Zed.

Widgren, J. 1995. Global Arrangements to Combat Trafficking in Migrants. *Migration World* 23(3):19–23.

Wilkins, R. 1974. What Africa Means to Blacks. *Foreign Policy* 15:130–41.

Winland, R. 1995. We Are Now an Actual Nation: The Impact of National Independence on the Croatian Diaspora in Canada. *Diaspora* 4(1):3–30.

Wistrich, R. 1994. Do the Jews Have a Future? *Commentary* 98(1):23–6.

Worchel, S., and D. Coutant. 1995. The Tangled Web of Loyalty: Nationalism, Patriotism and Ethnocentrism. Unpublished paper.

Yaar, E. 1998. Emigration as a Normal Phenomenon. *New Outlook* 31(1): 14–17.

Yadlin, R. 1998. The Muslim Diaspora in the West. Paper presented at a conference on Ethnic Minorities and Diasporas in the Middle East, Hebrew University of Jerusalem, November 13–15.

Young, C. 1986. Nationalism, Ethnicity and Class in Africa: A Retrospective. *Cahiers d'Etudes Africaines* 26(3):421–95.

Index